Baedeker's
ROME

Imprint

Cover picture: The Spanish Steps

79 colour photographs
9 plans, 1 large city map

Conception and editorial work:
Redaktionsburo Harenberg, Schwerte
English language: Alec Court

Text:
Dr Heinz-Joachim Fischer, Rome

General direction:
Dr Peter Baumgarten, Baedeker Stuttgart
English translation: James Hogarth

Cartography:
Ingenieurburo fur Kartographie Huber & Oberländer, Munich
Hallwag AG, Berne (city map)

Source of illustrations:
dpa (22), Italian State Tourist Office (5), Mauritius (1), Prenzel (1), Rogge (13), Uthoff (37)

Following the tradition established by Karl Baedeker in 1844, sights of particular interest and hotels of particular quality are distinguished by either one or two asterisks.

To make it easier to locate the various sights listed in the "A to Z" section of the Guide, their coordinates on the large map of Rome are shown in red at the head of each entry.

Only a selection of hotels and restaurants can be given: no reflection is implied, therefore, on establishments not included.

In a time of rapid change it is difficult to ensure that all the information given is entirely accurate and up to date, and the possibility of error can never be entirely eliminated. Although the publishers can accept no responsibility for inaccuracies and omissions they are always grateful for corrections and suggestions for improvement.

Licensed user:
Mairs Geographischer Verlag GmbH & Co., Ostfildern-Kemnat bei Stuttgart

Reproductions:
Gölz Repro-Service GmbH, Ludwigsburg

The name *Baedeker* is a registered trademark

Printed in Great Britain by Jarrold & Sons Ltd
Norwich

0-13-058074-0 US & Canada
3-87504-164-X Germany

Contents

Preface

This Pocket Guide to Rome is one of the new generation of Baedeker guides.

These pocket-size city guides, illustrated throughout in colour, are designed to meet the needs of the modern traveller. They are quick and easy to consult, with the principal sights described in alphabetical order and practical details about opening times, how to get there, etc., shown in the margin.

Each guide is divided into three parts. The first part gives a general account of the city, its history, prominent personalities and so on; in the second part the principal sights are described; and the third part contains a variety of practical information designed to help visitors to find their way about and make the most of their stay.

The new guides are abundantly illustrated and contain numbers of newly drawn plans. At the back of the book is a large city map, and each entry in the main part of the guide gives the coordinates of the square on the map in which the particular monument or site is situated. Users of this guide, therefore, will have no difficulty in finding what they want to see.

Facts and Figures

General

Rome is the capital of the Italian Republic, the seat of the President (official residence the Quirinal Palace), of the government and of the two houses of Parliament (the Senate in Palazzo Madama, the Chamber of Deputies in Palazzo Montecitorio). Within the territory of Rome is the state of Vatican City, the smallest state in the world (area 0·44 sq. km – 110 acres), ruled by the Pope, who is also head of the Roman Catholic Church.

Rome is situated in the region of Latium in central Italy, in lat. 41°52′ N and long. 12°30′ E, on the River Tiber.

Situation

The city of Rome (Comune di Roma), chief town of the province of the same name and of the region of Latium (Lazio), has an area of 1507 sq. km (582 sq. miles) and a population of 2,830,000.

Area and population

Traditionally, Rome was built on seven hills – the Capitol (Campidoglio), Palatine (Palatino), Aventine (Aventino), Quirinal (Quirinale), Viminal (Viminale), Esquiline (Esquilino) and Caelian (Celio); the Janiculum (Gianicolo) and Pincian (Pincio) are not included within the traditional seven. The historic centre of the "Eternal City" was bounded on the W by the Tiber and on the E by the Servian Walls (parts of which are still visible), built in the 4th c. B.C. Around this central core there grew up whole new districts, which the Emperor Aurelian surrounded with a protective ring of walls at the end of the 3rd c. A.D. In the course of centuries further districts developed, such as the Borgo Pio round the Vatican and Ostiense around the church of San Paolo fuori le Mura; and after Rome became capital of a united Italy in 1870 new quarters including Prati and Parioli developed. The suburbs of Greater Rome now extend into the Alban Hills to the E, to the sea (Ostia) in the W and far into the surrounding plain, the Roman Campagna, in the N and S.

Topography

The city is traditionally divided into 22 *rioni* or wards (the older parts of the town), 18 *quartieri* (the new districts), 11 *suburbi* (suburban districts) and the Agro Romano, by far the largest of the units in area. Following the recent administrative reform Rome is now divided into 20 *circoscrizioni* (districts).

Districts

The Comune di Roma is governed by a Mayor and Municipal Council the headquarters of which are on the Capitol. Local government elections are held every five years. The organisation of the new *circoscrizioni* is still at an early stage.

Administration

 View from the Pincio

Population and Religion

Population

The rise of Rome to become the capital of a world empire was accompanied by a steady increase in population, so that by the beginning of the Christian era the city had a population of about a million. After the fall of the Western Empire the population dropped to 25,000, recovered during the golden centuries of the medieval period and then fell even lower, before beginning to increase again slowly after the Pope's return from exile in Avignon (15th c.). In 1870 the city's population was 200,000, in 1921 some 700,000. In the last sixty years the total has risen to some 3 million as a result of the drift of the rural population from the surrounding provinces and of the flood of immigrants from southern Italy.

But the population which fills the streets of Rome is not made up solely of Italians. Apart from the hundreds of thousands of tourists there are large numbers of priests and nuns from all over the world; and in recent years there have been increasing numbers of Africans from former Italian colonies such as Somalia.

Religion

The overwhelming majority of the membership of the Catholic Church is, in the truest sense of the word, *Roman* Catholic. The Jewish synagogue, the churches of other Christian denominations and the mosque and Islamic cultural centre, now under construction on Monte Antenne, are a reminder of the fact that almost every religious confession is represented in Rome. Many countries have their own national churches in Rome,

Priests – an everyday sight in the streets of Rome

People in Rome

including the Anglican church in Via del Babuino, the Church of Scotland in Via XX Settembre and the American church in Via Napoli.

Transport

Rome lies on both banks of the Tiber, some 20–30 km (10–20 miles) above its mouth. In ancient times seagoing ships could sail right up the river to the city, but in the course of centuries

Port

11

Culture

The Tiber has silted up and is now used only by small boats and houseboats. Ostia, which was one of the largest ports in the Mediterranean in Roman times, is now suitable only for fishing boats and pleasure craft. The Mediterranean port for Rome is now Civitavecchia, 85 km (53 miles) to the north-west of the city.

Airports

Rome has two large international airports, the Leonardo da Vinci Airport at Fiumicino (scheduled services, both domestic and international), situated on the coast 25 km (15 miles) E of the city, and Ciampino Airport (mainly charter flights and military traffic), about 14 km (9 miles) from the city on the Via Appia Nuova. The Aeroporto dell'Urbe is used only by light aircraft (and sightseeing flights for tourists).

Railway and Underground

Rome is an important railway junction for traffic between northern and southern Italy and to the E side of the country, but rail services play little part in transport within the city. Altogether Rome has only ten railway stations; the Vatican has its own station. The main station is Stazione Termini, at which most long-distance trains arrive (though some services use the Tiburtina and Ostiense stations).
Most of the city's business and commuting traffic is carried by buses.
Rome has two underground railway lines in the Metropolitana system. The first (line B) runs from the Termini station to the EUR district and on to Ostia; the second (line A), completed in 1980, runs from Cinecittà (Film City), SE of the city, by way of Termini to the district just N of St Peter's.
Visitors who are not pressed for time can have a leisurely trip around central Rome on the "Circolare", one of the few surviving tram routes.

Motorways and trunk roads

In ancient Rome nine great consular highways started from the Golden Milestone in the Forum Romanum – the Aurélia, Cassia, Flaminia, Salaria, Tiburtina, Prenestina, Casilina, Tuscolana and Appia. These main roads – now all represented by modern roads on the same line – were supplemented by an excellent network of secondary and minor roads.
Modern traffic is served by a ring road of motorway standard round the city, the Grande Raccordo Anulare, and a number of motorways which replace or supplement the old trunk roads:
A1: N to Florence, Bologna, Milan and the Brenner pass.
A2: S to Naples, Bari, Réggio di Calabria and Sicily.
A12: NW to Civitavecchia.
A24: E to L'Aquila, the Gran Sasso and Pescara.
There is also an expressway to Latina.

Culture

General

Although Rome was capital of the Papal States for many centuries, it did not become capital of the whole of Italy until 1870, and accordingly its dominance in the fields of culture and scholarship is less firmly established than in other more centrally organised states, since the old capitals of the various republics, grand duchies and kingdoms into which Italy was formerly divided still retain something of their former importance in these fields. But with its universities and scientific institutes, its libraries, its opera house, theatres and orchestras Rome has a rich cultural and intellectual life, and one that by no means looks back solely to its past greatness.

Rome's University City, home of the State University of Rome, was built between 1932 and 1935. For many centuries higher education was in the hands of Papal academies and institutions run by religious orders, in particular the "Sapienza"; and in addition to the University of Rome with its 14 faculties and 130,000 students, an important part is still played by the Università Cattolica del Sacro Cuore (Catholic University of the Sacred Heart, a school of medicine), the Pro Deo International University of Social Studies and the Papal universities, chief among them the Gregoriana (a Jesuit institution), which train candidates from all over the world for the priesthood.
Numerous libraries (State-run, Papal and private), with their stocks of manuscripts and incunabula as well as later printed books down to the most recent literature, cater for the needs of scholarship.

Universities and libraries

With its wealth of ancient buildings, churches and museums Rome offers unique scope for artistic, historical, archaeological and religious studies. There are numerous State-sponsored and Papal academies and institutes concerned with the study of the Roman past and with the promotion of culture and scholarship, including the Accademia Nazionale dei Lincei (founded 1603) and the Accademia Nazionale San Luca (with its own gallery). Many foreign countries maintain learned institutions of high standing in Rome, including the British, American and Swedish Schools, the French Academy and the German Archaeological Institute.

Academies and learned societies

Rome has some 30 theatres, with a new one being established every now and then or an old one closing down. Music-lovers are catered for by a number of excellent orchestras and chamber orchestras, including those of the Accademia di Santa Cecilia, the Opera House and the RAI (the Italian radio and television corporation). During the summer concerts and recitals are given in churches and in some of the squares, and there are also excellent operatic performances in the Baths of Caracalla.

Theatres and orchestras

Commerce and Industry

As capital of the Roman Empire, Rome was also the leading economic and commercial centre in the Mediterranean: a role it has never recovered, either under the Popes, the kings of Italy or the present republic. In the industrial development of Europe and the commercial activity of modern times it has occupied a marginal position: Rome has established its international status in the fields of art and religion but has rarely played a comparable part in the economic and social fields.

International status

The main centres of industry and commerce in Italy have long been in the N, in Piedmont and Lombardy, Liguria and Veneto; but since much of the Italian economy has been nationalised in

National position

recent years, Rome has gained increased importance as the headquarters of various State-run industries. Its situation in central Italy also gives it an important economic role as a bridge between the N and S of the country.

Industrial tradition

Now as in the past Rome has little industry, and the majority of the working population is employed in administration and the service trades. This distortion of the employment pattern reflects the fact that Rome has never established an industrial tradition but has continued to acquire increased administrative functions as well as being one of the great Meccas for tourists. In recent years, however, the number of small industrial establishments in the area around Rome has increased. The city is now a fashion centre.

Prominent Figures in Roman History

Pope Alexander VI
(c. 1431–1503)

Posterity has branded Alexander VI (Pope 1492–1503) as a nepotist and libertine. Though he brought no credit to the Church, his reign is commemorated by a small coat of arms on the walls of the Vatican Palace (at the end of the right-hand colonnade, near the post office). His main object was the aggrandisement of the Borgia family to which he belonged: using the Papacy as an instrument, he sought to establish himself as the ruler of a hereditary monarchy and for this purpose to secularise the States of the Church.

A cardinal at the age of 26, he learned in the world of the Italian Renaissance to forget all scruple. Although a man of driving energy and a great patron of the arts, he dishonoured his position as the "vicar of Christ" and successor to St Peter by his addiction to sexual pleasures. Savonarola, falling foul of the Borgias, died at the stake: the Papacy survived.

Augustus
(63 B.C.–A.D. 14)

Augustus, originally Gaius Octavianus, Caesar's grand-nephew and adoptive son, became the first Emperor (Imperator) of the Roman Empire. In 43 B.C. he allied himself with Mark Antony and Lepidus as a member of the Triumvirate established to conduct the war against Caesar's murderers. The three triumvirs divided the territories held by Rome between them, Augustus taking the west, Mark Antony the east and Lepidus Africa. After defeating Antony and Cleopatra at Actium in 31 B.C. Augustus became sole ruler. In the Augustan age which followed he pacified the Empire, strengthened its frontier defences and was a generous patron of art and learning. The poets of the period included Virgil, Horace and Ovid. His most notable monuments in Rome are his Mausoleum, with the Ara Pacis (Altar of Peace), and his house on the Palatine. A bust and a marble statue in the Vatican Museums depict him in a magnificent – if idealised – aspect.

Gian Lorenzo Bernini
(1598–1680)

Baroque Rome would be unthinkable without Gian Lorenzo Bernini, son of the sculptor Pietro Bernini, who left his mark on the city both as architect and as sculptor. Popes and cardinals commissioned countless buildings and works of sculpture from him, and his patrons can often be identified by the heraldic devices which he incorporated into the decoration of a building. Under the 17th c. Popes, Urban VIII (1623–44: the three bees of the Barberini family), Innocent X Pamphili (1644–55: a dove holding a branch, surmounted by lilies) and Alexander VII Chigi (1655–67: a tree and a star over a hill) Bernini created a whole series of masterpieces, spurred on by his bitter rivalry with his great contemporary Boromini: the bronze baldacchino and the tomb of Urban VIII in St Peter's, the figure of St Teresa in ecstasy in Santa Maria della Vittoria, the Fountain of the Four Rivers in the Piazza Navona, St Peter's Square with its colonnades, the church of Sant'Andrea al Quirinale, the Scala Regia in the Vatican and the statues now to be seen in the Villa Borghese Museum, to name only a few.

Gaius Julius Caesar, a talented general, ambitious politician, generous victor and historian who prided himself on his literary skill, was the outstanding figure of the closing years of the republican period, of such commanding historical stature that his name was given to the holder of supreme political power, the Caesar (which later gave the German "Kaiser").

Julius Caesar (100–44 B.C.)

Originally destined for the priesthood, he began his military career in 81 B.C., studied in Rhodes from 76 to 73 and was elected to the post of Pontifex Maximus in 63. He allied himself with Pompey and later also with Crassus, and thereafter, as a member of the first Triumvirate, was able to put his political and social ideas into effect against the will of the Senate. From 58 to 51 he was engaged in the Gallic War, first dealing with the Helvetii and then subduing Gaul (53 B.C.); in 55 he crossed the Rhine into Germany, and in that and the following year launched two brief invasions of Britain. In 49 he crossed the River Rubicon in northern Italy, thus bringing his army, without permission, into territory under the authority of the Senate. After fighting in Spain and Greece, spending half a year in the Egyptian city of Alexandria (where the Egyptian queen Cleopatra bore him a son) and waging further wars with his opponents in Africa and Spain he was appointed Dictator in 48 B.C. and confirmed in that office, with a ten-year tenure in 46. As Dictator he ruled like an absolute monarch, lived in regal state and claimed quasi-divine veneration (in the Forum of Caesar which he built under the Capitol). All this increased the number of his enemies, and on the Ides of March he was murdered by a group of conspirators, including his "son" Brutus.

Constantine (Flavius Valerius Constantinus) lived as a young man at Diocletian's court, and thus gained at an early age some understanding of the conduct of public business, as well as witnessing the Diocletianic persecutions of Christians. In 306 he became joint Caesar along with Maxentius, whom he defeated at the Milvian Bridge (still standing) in 312. In 324 he defeated his other rival, Licinius. With the Edict of Milan (313), which allowed Christians freedom of worship, he prepared the way for Christianity to become the state religion. In 330 he transferred the imperial capital from Rome to the newly founded city of Constantinople (later Byzantium, and still later Istanbul). He was baptised shortly before his death in 337, and is venerated as a saint by the Greek, Armenian and Russian churches.

Constantine I, the Great (c. 285–337)

Remains in Rome dating from his reign include the Basilica of

Maxentius in the Forum (which he completed), Santa Costanza (built to house the tomb of his daughter), parts of a colossal statue of the Emperor in the Palazzo dei Conservatori on the Capitol and the early Christian basilicas which were begun during his reign.

Pope Gregory I, the Great
(*c.* 540–604)

Gregory was a scion of the Roman senatorial aristocracy. The judgements of his contemporaries and of ecclesiastical historians range from admiration to condemnation, for he was a man of contrasts, with good qualities and bad. He is perhaps best known nowadays for sending the first missionaries to England. Extremely wealthy, he himself founded the monasteries in which he lived as a Benedictine monk. He had voluntarily chosen a lowly manner of life; but there was no true humility in this, for he strove too hard and too blatantly to gain the favour of the Romans. In the style "servant of the servants of God" which he assumed for himself and his successors there is an element of the false modesty which counts itself as a merit. Gregory was a monk, a vocation which in him seemed to carry with it a certain narrowness and pettiness; but this nevertheless had the result of enhancing the religious dimension of the Papacy. When old and ailing, tortured by gout, he wrote edifying literature, including a "Pastoral Rule" which was diligently studied by the churchmen of the Middle Ages.

Pope Gregory VII
(*c.* 1019/1030–1085)

Gregory VII (Pope 1073–85), "a monk from his mother's womb" – fanatically devoted to the spiritual life and despising all things terrestrial, uncompromising to the point of self-forgetfulness – restored the standing of the Papacy after centuries of decadence. The "monk Hildebrand", feared and cursed by emperors and kings but canonised by the Church, sought to bring the Church back to purity. Small in stature and physically unimpressive but filled with inflexible determination, with a manner that was seldom winning and usually harsh and challenging, he had only one object – to raise the status of the Papacy and renew the spirit of the Church – and he was strengthened in his endeavours by the assurance of his transcendental mission. He employed a variety of means to help towards achieving his aims – the prohibition of simony (the sale of ecclesiastical offices) and of the marriage of priests, the excommunication of King Henry IV of Germany, crusades against the infidel. He did not scruple to enforce the Church's claims by the sword. Nor did he seek to conceal his urge to dominate and command: he demanded only one thing – obedience. Showing little love for any man and inspiring little love in return, a bitter hater and bitterly hated, he drove the course of history on, and the German king was compelled to do penance at Canossa. Gregory had no sense of moderation; but had he not set himself such far-reaching goals the Papacy would have sunk into mediocrity.

Hadrian
(76–138)

Hadrian (Publius Aelius Hadrianus), Trajan's successor and, like him, born in Spain, was Emperor from 117 to 138. One of the first concerns of his long reign was to strengthen the defences of the Empire, and he was responsible for the construction of two fortified frontier lines, Hadrian's Wall in Britain and the Limes in Germany, of which substantial remains survive. He liked to travel widely, and is said to have visited every province in the Empire: as far away as Luxor in Egypt there is an inscription in his name (on the Colossi of Memnon). This Emperor with the beard of a philosopher, whose favourite city was Athens, was a great admirer of Greek culture and promoted the diffusion of Hellenistic thought in the Roman world. He was a great builder, and there is much evidence of this still to be seen in Rome – the Mausoleum of Hadrian (Castel Sant'Angelo), the Pantheon and Hadrian's Villa at nearby Tivoli.

The desperate rising of the Jews under Bar Kochba in Judaea (132–135) took place during Hadrian's reign.

A member of the Lombard nobility who became Pope at the age of 37, Innocent III was a man of commanding personality. Imperious and a born ruler, he nevertheless sought conciliation. There were many sides to his nature: he could be haughty and commanding or mild and sympathetic, winning and humorous or majestic and unapproachable. He saw the kingdoms and peoples of the world as fit subjects for his rule. Innocent was a shrewd politician, but not wise enough to leave politics alone on occasion, and too much of a politician to be always wise. He was the most fully rounded man to occupy the Papal throne, and during his reign the Papacy was seen in its most powerful form.

Pope Innocent III
(c. 1160/1–1216)

Two Popes are generally granted the style of "the Great", Leo I and Gregory I. Leo (Pope 440–461), a Tuscan, was determined to assert his rule and to extend the powers of the Papacy and use them to the full. He was the first Pope to realise clearly the potentialities of his office, and the pride of the aristocrat whose secular power had been destroyed by the fall of the Western Empire was now projected into the spiritual field. The primacy of the Church in Rome was established and consolidated through Leo's skill in formulating its doctrines and his bold conception of the role of the Pope; it was reflected in the practical administration of the Church and given expression in the orthodox creed. Leo's courage was demonstrated during the troubled period of the great migrations. Raphael did him honour in the Stanze in the Vatican, Leo XII in a marble relief in St Peter's (far end of left-hand aisle).

Pope Leo I, the Great
(d. 461)

Marcus Aurelius Antoninus was Emperor from 161 to 180. Born in 121, he attracted the interest of Hadrian at an early age and by his desire was adopted by Hadrian's successor Antoninus Pius and initiated into the business of government. Marcus Aurelius was faced throughout his reign with ever increasing external dangers – the Chatti in Germany, the Caledonians in Britain – while in Syria the Parthians shook off the Roman yoke. The security of the Empire was threatened by risings of the Quadi and Marcomanni, the Jazyges, a people of herdsmen in the Nile delta, and the Moors in Spain. Marcus Aurelius died in Vindobona (Vienna) in 180. In spite of his numerous wars he is thought of as the philosopher on the Roman Imperial throne.

Marcus Aurelius
(121–180)

Michelangelo Buonarroti, a Renaissance genius who was sculptor, painter, architect and poet at the same time, and perhaps the greatest artist of all time, was born in Caprese (Casentino, Tuscany) and spent his youth and period of apprenticeship in Florence, to which he constantly returned

Michelangelo
(1475–1564)

after a year spent working in Bologna (1494–5) and several long stays in Rome. Florence was then ruled by the Medici, those great patrons of the arts, for whom Michelangelo produced numerous works.

His first stay in Rome, during which he created the "Pietà" in St Peter's, began in 1496. In 1505 Pope Julius II della Rovere summoned him back to the Vatican and invited him to design his tomb. (This commission was a burden to Michelangelo for most of his life: even after the Pope's death there were still disputes with his heirs.) Between 1508 and 1512 Michelangelo laboured on the frescoes of the Creation on the ceiling of the Sistine Chapel; in 1513–14 he carved two figures of slaves (now in the Louvre) for Julius' monument; and thereafter, until 1516, worked on his famous figure of Moses, now in San Pietro in Vincoli in Rome. The completion of the Pope's tomb continued to be delayed, with repeated alterations in the design.

In Florence (1520–34) Michelangelo was responsible for the building of the Medici chapel of San Lorenzo and the sculpture for the Medici tombs.

Between 1536 and 1541 Michelangelo created the famous fresco of the Last Judgment on the altar wall of the Sistine Chapel, perhaps the most magnificent painting in the world. In 1545 Julius II's tomb was finally set up in San Pietro in Vincoli. Michelangelo now occupied himself increasingly with architecture, working on the Palazzo Farnese, the Piazza del Campidoglio and St Peter's, whose gigantic dome is his greatest architectural achievement.

After a richly creative life, during which he had known difficulties but could look back on tremendous achievements, Michelangelo died in Rome in 1564. His tomb is in the church of Santa Croce in Florence.

Nero
(A.D. 37–68)

Claudius Drusus Germanicus Nero, who liked to see himself as a poet, musician and painter rather than a ruler required to take political decisions, was Emperor from A.D. 58 to 68. Coming to power as a mere youth, he was only 31 when he died. In his early years of rule he behaved with moderation, but later instituted a reign of terror, in the course of which he murdered both his mother (A.D. 59) and his wife Octavia (62). He was believed to have been responsible for the burning of Rome in 64, though he himself attributed the blame to the Christians, whom he accordingly persecuted. In the year 68 there was unrest in many provinces of the Empire, and Nero, outlawed by the Senate, committed suicide.

The name of the Colosseum comes from the colossal statue of Nero which stood there. His "Golden House", a gigantic palace on the Mons Oppius, provided a stimulus for Renaissance painters and sculptors.

Pope Paul V
(1552–1621)

This Pope of the Baroque period can fairly be mentioned in the same breath as the great figures of antiquity: indeed he himself invited the comparison by setting up a statue of himself on the façade of St Peter's, with the inscription "Paulus Burghesius Romanus" and a crowned eagle in his coat of arms. During his reign (1605–21) he incurred the charge of nepotism, though in other respects his life style was modest.

It was long since the world had revolved round Rome (indeed it was now known to revolve round the sun: Galileo's first trial was held in Paul's reign), and the States of the Church were now of only marginal importance in European affairs. Although this was apparent to others, Paul – a cultivated but stubbornly contentious lawyer – did not fully appreciate it and overestimated his influence on the great powers. All the efforts of his diplomats could not prevent the outbreak of the Thirty Years War, in which the whole of Europe was soon embroiled.

Raphael – Raffaello Santi or Sanzio – was born in 1483 in Urbino (Marche region) and died in 1520 in Rome. He was like Michelangelo – a painter, sculptor and architect – but it is mainly his paintings that have earned him his world renown. He began his career as an assistant to his father Giovanni Santi, who was also a painter, and thereafter became a pupil of Perugino. In 1504 he went to Florence and in 1508 to Rome, where seven years later, at the age of 32, he was put in charge of the building of St Peter's and made conservator of ancient monuments. The young painter gained the favour of Roman society and was given many commissions, while he appealed to ordinary people with the fervent piety of his Madonnas, works of incomparable beauty. His greatest achievement is to be seen in the Stanze di Raffaello in the Vatican – the magnificent frescoes which represent the high point of Renaissance painting.

Raphael
(1483–1520)

Whether Romulus and Remus ever existed may be questioned; but at any rate legend ascribes the foundation of Rome to Romulus, who is said to have established the first settlement on the Palatine, to have laid down military and civil regulations for the new town and to have formed the Romans on the Palatine and the Sabines on the Quirinal into a single community. His origins were also shrouded in legend. Romulus and Remus were said to have been the twin sons of the god Mars and Rhea Silvia, daughter of King Numitor of Alba Longa. Amulius, Numitor's brother, had driven him from the throne and made Rhea Silvia a vestal virgin (and accordingly subject to a vow of chastity), thus securing undisputed power to himself. He caused the twins, Romulus and Remus, to be exposed soon after their birth, but they were suckled by a she-wolf (which became the heraldic animal of Rome) and later found by a shepherd named Faustulus. They then killed their uncle, founded Rome and carried out the rape of the Sabine women to provide wives for the men of Rome. During the battle with the Sabines Romulus killed his brother Remus.
The death of Romulus was also the subject of numerous legends. He was said to have been murdered, to have disappeared into the earth, along with his horse, on the site of the Forum and to have ascended to join the gods. However this may be, he was worshipped in Rome as a god.

Romulus and Remus

Trajan (Marcus Ulpius Traianus) was the first native of Spain to become Emperor. Having been adopted by the Emperor Nerva in virtue of his outstanding military and political capacity, he came to the imperial throne in 98 and reigned until 117.
During Trajan's reign the Roman Empire reached its greatest extent. In the two Dacian wars he subdued Dacia, a country rich in gold (cf. the scenes on Trajan's Column), and in the Parthian war he advanced into Mesopotamia and Assyria. In 117, however, the oppressed Parthians and Jews rose against

Trajan
(A.D. 53–117)

Roman rule. Trajan's frequent campaigns earned him the name of the "soldier Emperor". He died in the town of Selinus in Asia Minor on his way back from the Persian Gulf.

He left his monument in the form of the Forum of Trajan, with the famous column, originally crowned by a statue of 'the Emperor.

History of Rome

Chronology

Many explanations have been put forward to show why a group of small Etruscan, Latin and Sabine settlements in the lower Tiber valley developed into the great city of Rome, the "Eternal City", *caput mundi* ("head of the world"), capital of the Roman Empire, focal point of western Christendom and the Roman Catholic Church and one of the great artistic centres of the world. It is one of the enigmas of history, however, how great centres of political power and culture come into being.

Origins to mastery of the Mediterranean

The Romans dated the foundation of Rome to 21 April 753 B.C. and surrounded the event with a web of lengend: the story of Romulus, who along with his twin brother Remus was exposed and left to die by a wicked king but was found and brought up by a she-wolf (or by a shepherd) and established the settlement on the Palatine to which he gave his name. However this may be, there is evidence of the existence of a settlement at the beginning of the first millennium B.C.; this increased in size, had its religious, political and military centre on the Capitol, was ruled for a period by kings probably stemming from northern Etruria and then, in 510 B.C., threw off the Etruscan yoke and became a republic. Religious and political leadership lay in the hands of the better class of citizens, the patricians, but their position was continually threatened by the ordinary people, the plebeians. In spite of these internal conflicts and of external threats from the neighbouring peoples and the Gauls (387) the city grew in size and in the 4th c. B.C. extended its authority into Latium. By the 3rd c. the republic was, militarily, economically and culturally, so strong – having gained control of the whole of central and southern Italy in 270 B.C. – that it was ready to aim at becoming the dominant power in the Mediterranean. After the defeat of Carthage in the three Punic Wars (between 264 and 146) there was no rival power to prevent Rome from conquering the countries bordering the Mediterranean.

Civil wars

The more powerful Rome became – a rise which was reflected in the erection of ever larger and more handsome buildings – the more acute became the city's internal tensions and conflicts. Peasants, soldiers and officials, nobles and plebeians were all at odds with one another, and Rome suffered a succession of civil wars, under Spartacus and the Gracchi (133–121), Marius and Sulla (120–70), Pompey and Caesar (70–44). Conspiracies and the ambitions of individuals (Catiline) brought constant unrest, and the climax came with the murder of Caesar by Brutus on the Ides of March in the year 44.

Although the Republic, under the rule of the consuls, had seen great constructional enterprises – aqueducts, roads, temples, public buildings – the Emperors set new standards of scale and magnificence. Augustus (31 B.C.–A.D. 14) found a city of brick and left one of marble. Nero (54–68), whether or not he ordered the burning of Rome which destroyed its slums, used the space thus made available for the erection of splendid buildings such as his Domus Aurea or "Golden House". Vespasian (69–79) began the construction of the Flavian Amphitheatre or Colosseum, which was inaugurated by his son Titus (79–81) with a series of splendid spectacles. In the reign of Trajan (98–117), a native of Spain, the Empire reached its greatest extent – from Scotland to Mesopotamia, from the Danube to Morocco.

The Empire

Each Emperor vied with his predecessors in altering and embellishing the city, each seeking to impose his indelible stamp on Rome, in the knowledge that his successors in turn would seek to outdo him. Temples and baths, victory columns and triumphal arches, theatres, palaces and mausoleums gave Rome imperial dignity and splendour, and many of them are still imposing landmarks in the modern city.

In the reign of Constantine (306–337) the power of Rome declined and took on a different aspect. The edict issued by the Emperor Galerius in 311, giving all religions equal rights, ended the persecutions of Christians and enabled the Christian community to erect public buildings for the purposes of worship. Constantine's victory over his co-Caesar Maxentius in the battle of the Milvian Bridge paved the way for Christianity to become the predominant religion of the Empire (Edict of Milan, 313).

Constantine and Christianity

Rome now became the spiritual centre of Christendom. Evidence of this new status is given by the large basilicas which were founded in the 4th and 5th c. and which still exist – St John Lateran (San Giovanni in Laterano) and St Peter's (San Pietro in Vaticano), St Paul without the Walls (San Paolo fuori le Mura) and St Lawrence without the Walls (San Lorenzo fuori le Mura), St Sebastian (San Sebastiano) and St Stephen (San Stefano Rotondo), SS. Cosmas and Damian (Santi Cosma e Damiano) and St Clement (San Clemente), Santa Maria Maggiore and Santa Croce in Gerusalemme. The Bishop of Rome, as successor to St Peter, now attained a position of predominance in the Western Empire and throughout western Europe.

This first flowering of Christian culture was blighted by the troubled period of the great migrations of barbarian peoples. Rome was captured and plundered by Alaric's Visigoths in 410, Genseric's Vandals in 455 (though without the destruction commonly associated with the name of the Vandals) and Totila's Ostrogoths in 546. The Western Empire came to an end

The great migrations

21

when Odoacer deposed the Emperor Romulus Augustulus in 476, and thereafter the Germanic peoples and the Byzantines contended for the succession. Popes Leo the Great (440–461) and Gregory the Great (590–604) sought to protect the city, but without lasting success, and the population of Rome shrank to no more than 25,000.

The city began to recover only when Pope Stephen II appealed to the Frankish king, Pippin or Pepin the Short, for help against the Lombards and in return for legitimising the Carolingian line was presented by Pippin with territories which became the nucleus of the States of the Church, and when this alliance between the German kings and the Papacy in the "Holy Roman Empire" was confirmed by Charlemagne's coronation as Emperor by Pope Leo III in St Peter's on Christmas Day in the year 800.

Rome's recovery was promoted by the support which the secular power of the Emperor was able to give to the spiritual authority of the Pope. But this help was not always available, and when it was not the great families of the city – the Frangipani, Pierleoni, Colonna and Orsini – and the nobles of the surrounding area became involved in bloody feuds with one another and with the Pope.

The history of the Papacy in the 9th and 10th c. is wrapped in obscurity, but about the year 1000 the Popes began to regain increased authority. Their new wealth was reflected in the building and embellishing of churches: the four churches dedicated to the Virgin, Santa Maria in Cosmedin, in Trastevere, in Aracoeli and sopra Minerva, are perhaps the most notable among many more. Innocent III (1198–1216), master of Emperors and kings, brought the Papacy to a peak of authority which it retained for a century.

Resistance to the Pope as a temporal ruler found expression in the risings led by Arnold of Brescia (executed 1155) and Cola di Rienzo (murdered in Rome in 1354).

Exile of the Popes in Avignon

Rome faced a further threat when, under pressure from the French king, the Popes were compelled to reside at Avignon in southern France. During this "Babylonian captivity" (1309–77) Rome declined once again. Churches and palaces fell into ruin, the streets and squares were deserted and the population sank to 20,000.

Things were no better when the Popes returned to Rome, for between 1378 and 1417 western Christendom was racked by the Great Schism, with rival candidates competing for the Papal throne.

Renaissance and Baroque

During the 15th c. a succession of shrewd and intelligent Popes, inspired by the ideas of humanism and the Renaissance which was just beginning, deployed the inherited resources of the Papacy and gradually restored Rome to its position as the centre of Christendom and of European art – though they must also bear their share of responsibility for the division of western Christendom into two by the Reformation. Over three centuries, from 1417 to the end of the 17th c., the Popes turned Rome into a stage for the display of their magnificence, creating the world's most splendid city, an enchanted garden of handsome streets and squares, churches and fountains which exploited to the full the artistic resources of the Renaissance and Baroque. The greatest artists of the day vied with one another in embellishing Rome. Without Bramante, Michelangelo, Raphael, Bernini and Borromini the Popes would not have enjoyed the stature they do; but without such princely patrons – the demanding Julius II della Rovere, the art-loving Leo X Medici, Paul III Farnese, Gregory XIII Boncompagni, Paul V Borghese – these artists could not have achieved what they did. The three bees from the Barberini coat of arms, the heraldic trademark of the great builder Urban VIII (1623–44), are found all over Rome – on the baldacchino over the high altar in St Peter's, on the Chapel of the Sacrament (also in St Peter's), on churches and fountains; but so, too, are the flowers and animals, the stars and hills which are the emblems of other Popes.

The sack of Rome by the Emperor Charles V's landsknechts in 1527 barely disturbed this great burst of building activity: indeed it rather provided a stimulus to fresh endeavour.

During these centuries the Popes devoted themselves almost entirely to the embellishment of their city; but their temporal power now began to decline, and with it the importance of Rome. While in earlier days they had set armies in motion in order to achieve their aims, they were now compelled to rely on the skill and the intrigues of their diplomats.

Decline of Papal power

The French Revolution and the Napoleonic whirlwind which upset the old order in Europe did not leave Rome unscathed. In 1798 it became the capital of the Roman Republic, and from 1809 to 1811 it was part of the French Republic and the residence of Napoleon's only son, who bore the title of Roi de Rome. In 1814 the Congress of Vienna restored the city's status as capital of the States of the Church, with the Pope as sovereign ruler; but in 1870 the position was changed again, when the French troops which supported Papal authority were withdrawn on account of the Franco-Prussian War and Italian forces moved into the city through the Porta Pia. In the same year Rome became capital of the new kingdom of Italy, and in protest against the loss of his territories the Pope withdrew behind the walls of the Vatican.

Rome's position as the capital of Italy was reflected in the construction of numbers of government offices and public buildings, mingling the styles of the 19th c. with the architecture of earlier periods. There was a further burst of building activity when Mussolini came to power in 1922, and Rome now grew to become the largest city in the Mediterranean area. The Lateran Treaties of 1929 re-established good relations between the Italian government and the Papacy, and the Pope became sovereign ruler of the Vatican State and its extraterritorial enclaves. 19th and 20th century Italian governments and successive Popes have fostered art and research.

Kingdom and Republic of Italy

Notable recent events in Papal Rome are the Second Vatican Council (1962–5), in which more than 3000 bishops from all over the world took part, and the election of Karol Wojtyla, Archbishop of Cracow, as Pope John Paul II in 1978 – the first non-Italian Pope for 453 years. 1981 attack on the Pope.

In 1984 the USA resumed full diplomatic relations with the Vatican after more than 100 years. A new concordat was signed between Italy and the Holy See (this guarantees religious freedom, but Roman Catholicism ceases to be the state religion in Italy and Rome is no longer the "Holy City").

Emperors and Popes

Not all usurpers and co-Caesars are listed.
The regnal dates for all Popes before Pontianus (230–235) are based on later reconstructions. All Popes from Peter to Gelasius (d. 496) are venerated as saints; later Popes who have been canonised are indicated by the prefixed "St".

Year	Emperors	Popes
B.C.		
44	Murder of Caesar	
27	Octavian becomes Augustus	
A.D		
14	Tiberius	
37	Caligula	
41	Claudius	
54	Nero	
63/67		Martyrdom of Peter
64/67		Linus
68	Galba	
69	Otho	
69	Vitellius	
69	Vespasian	
79	Titus	Anencletus (Anacletus I, c. 79)
81	Domitian	Clement I (90/92)
96	Nerva	
98	Trajan	Evaristus (99/101)
		Alexander I (c. 107)
117	Hadrian	Xystus (Sixtus I, c. 116)
		Telesphorus (c. 125)
138	Antoninus Pius	Hyginus (136/138)
		Pius I (140/142)
		Anicetus (154/155)
161	Marcus Aurelius, with Lucius Verus	
	(d. 169)	Soter (c. 166)
		Eleutherius (c. 174)
180	Commodus	Victor I (c. 189)
193	Pertinax	
193	Didius Julianus	
193	Septimius Severus	Zephrinus (198/199)
211	Caracalla, with Geta (d. 212)	
217	Macrinus	
218	Elagabalus	Calixtus I (c. 217)
222	Alexander Severus	Urban I (222)
230		Pontianus (230–235)
235	Maximinus I	Antherus (235–236)
236		Fabian (236–250)
238	Gordian I and II	
238	Pupienus	
238	Balbinus	
238	Gordian III	
244	Philip the Arab	
249	Decius	
251	Hostilianus	
253	Trebonianus Gallus	Cornelius (251–253)
253	Aemilianus	Lucius I (253–254)
254	Valerian	Stephen I (254–257)

Year	Emperors	Popes
257	Gallienus	Sixtus II (257–258)
268	Claudius II	Dionysius (*c.* 259–268)
270	Aurelian	Felix I (*c.* 269–274)
275	Tacitus	Eutychianus (*c.* 274–283)
276	Probus	
282	Carus	
283	Carinus and Numerian	Caius (*c.* 282–296)
284	Diocletian	
286	Maximian (co-Caesar until 305)	
296		Marcellinus (*c.* 296–304)
		Then a vacancy for three years
		during the Diocletianic persecutions
305	Constantius I (d. 306)	
	and Galerius (d. 311)	
306	Constantine I (sole ruler 324–337)	
306	Severus (d. 307)	
308	Licinius (to 324, d. 325)	Marcellus (307/308)
309	Maximinus II (d. 313)	Eusebius (308/310)
		Miltiades
		Sylvester I
		Marcus
337	Constantine II (d. 340)	Julius I
	Constantius II (sole ruler 350–360,	
	d. 361)	
	Constans (d. 350)	
352		Liberius (325–355, 358–366)
		Felix II (355–358)
361	Julian (the Apostate)	
363	Jovian	
364	Valentinian I (d. 375)	
	and Valens (d. 376)	
366		Damasus I
375	Gratian (d. 383)	
375	Valentinian II (d. 392)	
379	Theodosius I (sole ruler 392–395)	
383	Arcadius	
384		Siricius
	Western Empire	
395	Honorius (reigned in West	
	395–423)	
399		Anastasius I
401		Innocent I
417		Zosimus
418		Boniface I
422		Celestine I
425	Valentinian III	
432		Sixtus III
440		Leo I, the Great
455	Petronius Maximus	
455	Avitus	
457	Majorian	
461	Libius Severus	Hilary
467	Anthemius	
468		Simplicius
472	Olybrius	
473	Glycerius	

Emperors and Popes

Year	Emperors	Popes
474	Julius Nepos	
475	Romulus Augustulus	
476	*Fall of Western Empire*	
483		Felix III
492		Gelasius I
496		Anastasius II
498		Symmachus
514		Hormisdas
523		John I
526		Felix IV
530		Boniface II
533		John II
535		St Agapetus I
536		St Silverius
537		Vigilius
556		Pelagius I
561		John III
575		Benedict I
579		Pelagius II
590		St Gregory I, the Great
604		Sabinian
607		Boniface III
608		St Boniface IV
615		St Deusdedit (Adeodatus I)
619		Boniface V
625		Honorius I
640		Severinus
640		John IV
642		Theodore I
649		St Martin I
654		St Eugenius I
657		St Vitalian
672		Adeodatus II
676		Do(m)nus
678		St Agatho
682		St Leo II
684		St Benedict II
685		John V
686		Conon
687		St Sergius I
701		John VI
705		John VII
708		Sisinnius
708		Constantine I
715		St Gregory II
731		St Gregory III
741		St Zacharias
752		Stephen II
752		Stephen III
757		St Paul I
767		Constantine II
768		Philip
768		Stephen IV
772		Adrian I
795		St Leo III
	Revival of Western Empire	
800	Charlemagne	

26

Year	Emperors	Popes
814	Louis I, the Pious (813, d. 840)	
816		Stephen V
817		St Paschal I
824		Eugenius II
827		Valentine
827		Gregory IV
843	Lothair (823)	
844		Sergius II
847		St Leo IV
855	Louis II (852)	Benedict III
858		St Nicholas I
867		Adrian II
872		John VIII
875	Charles the Bald (d. 877)	
881	Charles the Fat (d. 888)	
882		Marinus I
884		Adrian III
885		Stephen VI
887	Arnulf (896, d. 899)	
891		Formosus
896		Stephen VII
897		Romanus
897		Theodore II
898		John IX
900	Ludwig the Child (German king)	Benedict IV
903		Leo V
903		Christopher
904		Sergius III
911	Conrad I (German king)	Anastasius III
913		Lando
914		John X
919	Henry I (German king)	
928		Leo VI
928		Stephen VIII
931		John XI
936	Otto I	Leo VII
	Holy Roman Empire (962)	
939		Stephen IX
942		Marinus II
946		Agapetus II
955		John XII
963		Leo VIII
964		Benedict V
965		John XIII
967	Otto II	
973		Benedict VI
974		Benedict VII
983	Otto III	John XIV
985		John XV
996		John XVI
999		Silvester II
1002	Henry II (1014)	
1003		John XVII
1003		John XVIII

Emperors and Popes

Year	Emperors	Popes
1009		Sergius IV
1012		Benedict VIII
1024	Conrad II (1027)	John XIX
1032		Benedict IX
1039	Henry III (1046)	
1045		Gregory VI
1046		Clement II
1048		Damasus II
1049		St Leo IX
1055		Victor II
1056	Henry IV (1084)	
1057		Stephen X
1059		Nicholas II
1061		Alexander II
1073–85		St Gregory VII (Hildebrand)
1086		Victor III
1088		Urban II
1099		Paschal II
1106	Henry V (1111)	
1118		Gelasius II
1119		Calixtus II
1124		Honorius II
1125	Lothair (1133)	
1130		Innocent II
1138	Conrad III of Hohenstaufen (German king)	
1143		Celestine II
1144		Lucius II
1145		Eugenius III
1152	Frederick I Barbarossa (1155)	
1153		Anastasius IV
1154		Adrian IV
1159		Alexander III
1181		Lucius III
1185		Urban III
1187		Gregory VIII
		Clement III
1190	Henry VI (1191)	
1191		Celestine III
1198	Philip of Swabia (German king) Otto IV (1209)	Innocent III
1212	Frederick II (1220)	
1216		Honorius III
1227		Gregory IX
1241		Celestine IV (d. 1241)
1243		Innocent IV
1250	Conrad IV (German king)	
1254	*Interregnum*	Alexander IV
1261–4		Urban IV
1265–8		Clement IV
1271		Gregory X
1273	Rudolf of Habsburg (German king)	
1276		Innocent V
		Adrian IV
		John XX or XXI
1277–80		Nicholas III
1281		Martin IV

Year	Emperors	Popes
1285–7		Honorius IV
1288–92		Nicholas IV
1292	Adolf of Nassau (German king)	
1294		St Celestine V
		Boniface VIII
1298	Albert I (German king)	
1303–4		Benedict XI
1305–14		Clement V (d. 1314)
1308	Henry VII of Luxembourg (1312)	
1314	Ludwig the Bavarian (1328) (Frederick of Austria)	
1316		John XXII
1334		Benedict XII
1342		Clement VI
1346	Charles IV of Luxembourg (1355)	
1352		Innocent VI
1362		Urban V
1370		Gregory XI
1378	Wenceslas (German king)	Urban VI
1389		Boniface IX
1400	Rupert of the Palatinate (German king)	
1404		Innocent VII
1406		Gregory XII (abdicated 1415, d. 1417)
1409		Alexander V
1410	Sigismund (1433)	John XXIII (deposed 1415, d. 1419)
1417		Martin V
1431		Eugenius IV
1438	Albert II (German king)	
1440	Frederick III (1452)	
1447		Nicholas V
1455		Calixtus III
1458		Pius II (Aeneas Sylvius Piccolomini)
1464		Paul II (Pietro Barbo)
1471		Sixtus IV (Francesco della Rovere)
1484		Innocent VIII (Giovanni Battista Cybo)
1492		Alexander VI (Rodrigo Borgia)
1493	Maximilian I (1508: not crowned)	
1503		Pius III (Francesco Todeschini Piccolomini)
		Julius II (Giuliano della Rovere)
1513		Leo X (Giovanni de' Medici, d. 1521)
1519	Charles V (1530)	
	Last Emperor crowned in Italy	
1522		Adrian VI (Dedel of Utrecht)
1523		Clement VII (Giulio de' Medici)
1534		Paul III (Alessandro Farnese, d. 1549)
1550		Julius III (Giovanni Maria del Monte)
1555		Marcellus II (Marcello Cervino)

Emperors and Popes

Year	Emperors	Popes
		Paul IV (Giovanni Pietro Caraffa)
1556	Ferdinand I	
1559		Pius IV (Giovanni Angelo de' Medici, d. 1565)
1564	Maximilian II	
1566		St Pius V (Michele Ghislieri)
1572		Gregory XIII (Ugo Boncompagni)
1576	Rudolf II	
1586		Sixtus V (Felice Peretti)
1590		Urban VII (Giovanni Battista Castagna)
		Gregory XIV (Niccolò Sfondrati)
1591		Innocent IX (Giovanni Antonio Facchinetti)
1592		Clement VIII (Ippolito Aldobrandini)
1605		Leo XI (Alessandro de' Medici)
		Paul V (Camillo Borghese)
1612	Matthias	
1619	Ferdinand II	
1621		Gregory XV (Alessandro Ludovisi)
1623		Urban VIII (Maffeo Barberini)
1637	Ferdinand III	
1644		Innocent X (Giovanni Battista Pamphili)
1655		Alexander VII (Fabio Chigi)
1658	Leopold I	
1667		Clement IX (Giulio Rospigliosi, d. 1669)
1670		Clement X (Emilio Altieri)
1676		Innocent XI (Benedetto Odescalchi)
1689		Alexander VIII (Pietro Ottoboni)
1691		Innocent XII (Antonio Pignatelli)
1700		Clement XI (Giovanni Francesco Albani)
1705	Joseph I	
1711	Charles VI	
1721		Innocent XIII (Michelangelo Conti)
1724		Benedict XIII (Vincenzo Maria Orsini)
1730		Clement XII (Lorenzo Corsini)
1740		Benedict XIV (Prospero Lambertini)
1742	Charles VII	
1745	Francis I	
1758		Clement XIII (Carlo Rezzonico)
1765	Joseph II	
1769		Clement XIV (Giovanni Antonio Ganganelli, d. 1774)
1775		Pius VI (Giovanni Angelo Braschi, d. 1799)
1790	Leopold II	
1792	Francis II	
1800		Pius VII (Gregorio Chiaramonti)
1806	*Francis II gives up the Imperial crown: end of the Holy Roman Empire*	
1823		Leo XII (Annibale della Genga)

Year	Emperors	Popes
1829		Pius VIII (Francesco Saverio Castiglioni, d. 1830)
1831		Gregory XVI (Mauro Capellari)
1846		Pius IX (Giovanni Maria Mastai-Feretti)
	Kingdom of Italy	
1861	Victor Emmanuel II (King of Italy)	
1878	Umberto I	Leo XIII (Gioacchino Pecci)
1900	Victor Emmanuel III	
1903		Pius X (Giuseppe Sarto)
1914		Benedict XV (Giacomo della Chiesa)
1922		Pius XI (Achille Ratti)
1939		Pius XII (Eugenio Pacelli)
1946	Umberto II (leaves Italy on 13 June 1946)	
1958		John XXIII (Angelo Giuseppe Roncalli)
1963		Paul VI (Giovanni Battista Montini)
1978		John Paul I (Albino Luciani, d. 28 September 1978)
1978		John Paul II (Karol Wojtyla)

Quotations

(The Emperor Constantius visits Rome in the 4th c.)
"As the Emperor reviewed the vast city and its environs, spreading along the slopes, in the valleys and between the summits of the Seven Hills, he declared that the spectacle which first met his eyes surpassed everything he had yet beheld. Now his gaze rested on the Temple of Tarpeian Jupiter, now on baths so magnificent as to resemble entire provinces, now on the massive pile of the amphitheatre, massively compact, or Tivoli stone, the summit of which seems scarcely accessible to the human eye; now on the Pantheon, rising like a fairy dome, and its sublime columns, with their gently inclined staircases, adorned with statues of departed emperors; not to enumerate the Temple of the City, the Forum of Peace, the Theatre of Pompey, the Odeum, the Stadium and all the other architectural wonders of eternal Rome. When, however, he came to the Forum of Trajan, a structure unequalled by any other of its kind throughout the world, so exquisite, indeed, that the gods themselves would find it hard to refuse their admiration, he stood as if in a trance, surveying with a dazed air the stupendous fabric which neither words can picture nor mortal ever again attempt to rear."

Ammianus Marcellinus (b. about A.D. 330)

"Whoever has nothing else left in life should come to live in Rome: there he will find for society a land which will nourish his reflections, walks which will always tell him something

François-René de Chateaubriand (1768–1848)

Quotations

new. The stone which crumbles under his feet will speak to him, and even the dust which the wind raises under his footsteps will seem to bear with it something of human grandeur."

Charles Dickens
(1812–70)

"We entered on the Campagna Romana; an undulating flat . . . where few people can live; and where, for miles and miles, there is nothing to relieve the terrible monotony and gloom. . . . We had to traverse thirty miles of this Campagna; and for two-and-twenty we went on and on, seeing nothing but now and then a lonely house, or a villainous-looking shepherd . . . tending his sheep. At the end of that distance, we stopped to refresh the horses, and to get some lunch, in a common malaria-shaken, despondent little public-house. . . . When we were fairly going off again, we began, in a perfect fever, to strain our eyes for Rome; and when, after another mile or two, the Eternal city appeared, at length, in the distance, it looked like – I am half afraid to write the word – like LONDON!!! There it lay, under a thick cloud, with innumerable towers, and steeples, and roofs of houses, rising up into the sky, and high above them all, one Dome. I swear, that keenly as I felt the seeming absurdity of the comparison, it was so like London, at that distance, that if you could have shown it me in a glass, I should have taken it for nothing else."

Edward Gibbon
(1737–94)

"It was at Rome, on the 15th of October, 1764, as I sat musing amidst the ruins of the Capitol, while the barefooted friars were singing vespers in the Temple of Jupiter, that the idea of writing the decline and fall of the city first started to my mind."

Johann Wolfgang von Goethe
(1749–1832)

"I have now been here for seven days, and am gradually getting some general idea of the city. We walk about Rome most diligently, and I familiarise myself with the layout of the ancient and the modern city, look at the ruins and the buildings, and visit this villa or that. I take the principal sights very slowly, look at them attentively, go away and come back again; for only in Rome can one prepare oneself for Rome.
"I must confess, however, that it is a bitter and sorry business disentangling the old Rome from the new; but one has to do it, and must hope that one's efforts will be rewarded. One encounters traces of inconceivable magnificence and inconceivable destruction: what the barbarians left standing the builders of modern Rome have devastated."

Ovid
(43 B.C.–A.D.17)

"Rome will give you so many pretty girls that you will say, 'This city has everything that the world can offer.' As many fields of corn as has Gargara, as many grapes Methymna, as many fish the sea, as many birds the trees, as many stars the sky, so many girls has this Rome of yours."

John Raymond
(17th c.)

"I found that (Rome) flourisheth beyond all expectation, this new even emulous to exceed the old, the remnants of the old adding to the splendour of the new. . . . A man may spend many months at Rome and yet have something of note to see every day."
("Il Mercurio Italico: an Itinerary contayning a Voyage made through Italy in the yeare 1646 & 1647", 1648)

"The society of Rome is excellent; and the circumstance of every man, whether foreigner or native, being permitted to live as he pleases, without exciting wonder, contributes essentially to general comfort. At Rome, too, every person may find amusement: for whether it be our wish to dive deep into classical knowledge, whether arts and sciences by our pursuit, or whether we merely seek for new ideas and new objects, the end cannot fail to be obtained in this most interesting of Cities, where every stone is an historian."
("Traveller's Guide", 8th edition, 1832)

Mariana Starke

"The head and crown of all churches is without any doubt St Peter's; and if the ancients held it a misfortune not to have seen the Temple of Olympian Jupiter, this could be said even more aptly of St Peter's. For this building is larger than the temples of the Greeks and Romans and surpasses them all in architectural quality and magnificence. I never go there without praising God for granting me the happiness of seeing this wonder, of seeing it and learning to know it over many years."

Johann Joachim Winckelmann (1717–68)

"All roads lead to Rome."

Proverb

Rome from A to Z

*Ara Pacis (Altar of Peace)   B3

Situation
Via di Ripetta/Piazza
Augusto Imperatore

Buses
2, 26, 81, 90, 90b, 115, 911

Opening times
Tues.–Sat. 9 a.m.–2 p.m.,
Tues. and Thurs. also
4–7 p.m.
Sun. 9 a.m.–1 p.m.

Closed
Mon.

Between the Mausoleo di Augusto (see entry) and the Tiber stands the Ara Pacis Augustae, Augustus' Altar of Peace. After the troubled period of civil war and his defeat of his opponents Augustus brought peace to the Roman Empire and made possible the glories of the Augustan age. Accordingly, we are told in the *Res Gestae*, the inscription recording Augustus' career which is reproduced on the outside of the building housing the Altar of Peace, "the Senate resolved to erect the Altar of the Augustan Peace as a votive offering on the Field of Mars." The Altar, constructed between 13 and 9 B.C., was brought to light again in the 16th and 19th c. It gives consummate expression to the Imperium Romanum of Augustus, the Roman world empire with its assertion of Roman power, its religious ceremonies, its Imperial house and the institutions on which it was based.

The lower part of the screen enclosing the altar, of Carrara marble, is richly decorated with reliefs of foliage ornament (acanthus, ivy, laurel, vines), with birds and reptiles interspersed among the leaves. The upper part is occupied by a

The Ara Pacis (Altar of Peace)

sculptured frieze, running round all four sides – mythological scenes on the ends, historical scenes on the long sides. A flight of ten steps leads up to the platform (11·62 by 10·60 m – 38 by 35 ft), in the centre of which stands the altar.

The altar itself, guarded by lion-sphinxes, was decorated with reliefs (only about a third of which have survived) representing sacrificial ceremonies.

*Arco di Costantino (Arch of Constantine)   C4

The triumphal arch erected by the Senate in honour of the Emperor Constantine, "liberator of the city and bringer of peace", after his victory over Maxentius in the battle of the Milvian Bridge (A.D. 312) is the largest (21 m (69 ft) high, 25·70 m (84 ft) wide, 7·40 m (24 ft) deep) and best preserved of Roman triumphal arches, in spite of the fact that it, like the Colosseum (see Colosseo), was incorporated in the castle of the Frangipane family and was not disengaged until the 16th (partly) and 19th c. (completely). The arch, with three openings, is decorated with reliefs taken from earlier structures, which the sculptors of the early 4th c. were unable to equal. Some of the scenes, therefore, have little to do with Constantine and his military achievements – a boar-hunt and a sacrifice to Apollo, taken from a monument of the time of Hadrian, scenes from the reigns of Trajan and Marcus Aurelius.

Situation
Piazza del Colosseo/Via di San Gregorio

Underground station
Colosseo (line B)

Buses
11, 15, 27, 81, 85, 87, 88, 118, 673

Trams
13, 30, 30b

Arch of Constantine

*Arco di Giano (Arch of Janus Quadrifrons)   C3

Situation
Via del Velabro

Buses
15, 90, 90b, 94

This marble structure in the Via del Velabro, in front of the church of San Giorgio in Velabro (see entry), was long thought to be part of a temple of Janus. In fact it was a covered passage (*janus*) with openings on four sides (*quadrifrons*) at a busy street intersection in the commercial quarter of Rome.

The arch was built in the Constantinian period, incorporating material from earlier buildings. During the Middle Ages it became a strong point of the Frangipane family.

*Basilica di Massenzio (Basilica of Maxentius)   C3

Situation
Via dei Fori Imperiali

Underground station
Colosseo (line B)

Buses
11, 27, 81, 85, 87, 88

The ruins of the Basilica of Maxentius or of Constantine (begun in A.D. 306–312 by Maxentius and completed by Constantine), between the Via dei Fori Imperiali and the Forum (see Foro Romano), still give an imposing impression of this great building, which, like other Roman basilicas, served both as a law court and a place for doing business. The central aisle, with a vaulted roof, measured 60 by 25 m (200 by 80 ft), and rose to a height of 35 m (115 ft); the lateral aisles were 24·50 m (80 ft) high. The basilica was modelled on the gigantic Baths erected by Caracalla and Diocletian. The main piers were fronted by massive Corinthian columns, one of which, bearing a statue of the Virgin, now stands in front of the church of Santa Maria Maggiore (see entry). This last great building of the Roman Imperial period – inaugurated in the year in which the capital was moved to Constantinople – provided the inspiration for later European architecture, including St Peter's (see San Pietro). The ruin of the basilica was hastened when Pope Honorius I removed the bronze roof-tiles and used them to roof Old St Peter's. – Concerts in summer.

Basilica di Porta Maggiore   C5

Situation
Via Prenestina 17

Buses
152, 153, 154, 155, 156, 157

Trams
13, 14, 19, 19b, 516, 517

This underground sanctuary (probably of the 1st c. A.D.), although well preserved, is still something of a puzzle to archaeologists. Discovered 13 m (40 ft) below ground level in 1917, it has the form of a basilica measuring 19 by 12 m (62 by 39 ft), with a porch and a semicircular apse. With its mosaic pavement, stucco decoration on the ceiling and cycles of mythological scenes, it seems to have been the shrine of some mystical cult (perhaps the Neo-Pythagoreans). It has been suggested that this building, of a type which was evidently widely distributed throughout the Empire, influenced the development of the Christian basilica.

Basilica di San Marco   C3

Situation
Piazza Venezia

This church, now partly incorporated in the Palazzo Venezia, is traditionally believed to have been founded by Pope Marcus (Mark) in honour of the Evangelist in 336. Its present form results from restoration and rebuilding about 800 and in the 15th and 18th c. Appropriately, since St Mark is the patron saint of Venice, the Palazzo Venezia was from 1564 to 1797 the residence of the Venetian ambassador to the Holy See.

Notable features of the church are the two-storey portico, the campanile adjoining the tower of the Palazzo Venezia and the mosaic in the apse of Christ transmitting the Law. Dating from the time of Pope Gregory IV (827–844), this shows Christ on a dais surrounded by Apostles and saints (Gregory, being still alive, is depicted with a square nimbus, above a frieze with symbolic representations of the Lamb of the Apocalypse, amid twelve other lambs, and of two cities.

Buses
46, 56, 60, 62, 64, 65, 70,
75, 85, 87, 88, 90, 95, 170

*Borsa (Exchange)   C3

The Exchange occupies part of the site of a large ancient temple, eleven Corinthian columns from which are preserved along one side. Long thought to have been a temple of Neptune, it is now identified as the Hadrianeum, a temple erected in honour of the deified Hadrian. The floor of the temple now lies below street level.

Situation
Piazza di Pietra

Buses
26, 87, 94

Camera dei Deputati (Parliament)   B3

The Palazzo Montecitorio, begun by Bernini in 1650 for Pope Innocent X Pamphili and completed in 1694 by Carlo Fontana, has been occupied since 1871 by the Chamber of Deputies, the lower house of the Italian Parliament. At the beginning of this century the palace was enlarged to meet Parliamentary needs. In the Piazza di Montecitorio is an ancient Egyptian obelisk (594–589 B.C.). Here German archaeologists are at present excavating what is claimed to be the largest sundial in the world, dating from the 2nd c. A.D., of which the obelisk was the gnomon. The great bronze base of the sundial, 60 m (200 ft) in diameter, has been brought to light behind the Chamber of Deputies at a depth of 6·5 m (20 ft) below the present street level. Below it is the still more famous sundial of Augustus.

Situation
Palazzo Montecitorio,
Piazza di Montecitorio

Buses
52, 53, 56, 58, 58b, 60, 61,
62, 71, 81, 85, 88, 90, 90b,
95, 115

Campidoglio (Capitol)   C3

The Capitol, the smallest of Rome's seven hills, was the political and religious centre of the ancient city. On its two summits stood the city's two principal temples, dedicated to Jupiter Optimus Maximus Capitolinus and Juno Moneta, on the sites now occupied by the Palazzo dei Conservatori and the church of Santa Maria in Aracoeli (see entries). The lower area between them is now occupied by the Piazza del Campidoglio. The square, flanked by palaces and approached by Michelangelo's ceremonial ramp and staircase, still conveys a feeling of the grandeur and dignity which the city has preserved down the centuries. Here victorious Roman generals came to celebrate their triumphs, making their way to the Capitol along the Sacred Way (Via Sacra); here in the Middle

Underground station
Colosseo (line B)

Buses
57, 85, 87, 88, 90, 90b, 92,
94, 95, 716, 718, 719

Ages poets were crowned and tribunes of the people were acclaimed; here in 1955 the Treaty of Rome, establishing the European Economic Community, was signed; and here, in the Palazzo Senatorio (see entry), the Mayor of Rome has his residence and receives distinguished visitors to the city. This has been since time immemorial the political centre of Rome, the counterpart of the city's spiritual and religious centre in the Vatican.

* Piazza del Campidoglio   C3

Buses
57, 85, 87, 88, 90, 90b, 92, 94, 95, 716, 718, 719

The Piazza del Campidoglio is reached from Via del Teatro di Marcello by way of the ceremonial ramp and staircase designed by Michelangelo, passing a monument (on left) to Cola di Rienzo, the 14th c. tribune of the people, and statues of the Dioscuri (Castor and Pollux), the Emperor Constantine and his son Constantine II.

The square, also designed by Michelangelo, is bounded by the façades of three palaces, the Palazzo dei Senatori (to rear), the Palazzo dei Conservatori (on right) (see entries) and the Palazzo Nuovo (see Museo Capitolino, on left). It is not, however, totally enclosed, since there are openings between the buildings which allow passage to streets leading down to the Forum. The palaces are not set at right angles to one another but form a trapezoid, within which Michelangelo laid out an oval (marked by steps) and a star formation (marked by lighter-coloured paving). This gives emphasis to the centre of

The statue of Marcus Aurelius in the Piazza del Campidoglio

the square, in which an equestrian statue of Marcus Aurelius (at present removed for restoration) was set up. The statue, of bronze which was originally gilded, had previously stood in front of the church of St John Lateran (see San Giovanni in Laterano). It was thought to represent the Emperor Constantine, who favoured Christianity, and was accordingly preserved from destruction. In 1538 Pope Paul III had it transferred to its present site. The calm and contemplative figure of the Emperor, a Stoic philosopher on the throne, and the vigour of his horse make this statue one of the finest surviving examples of ancient sculpture.

The restoration of the statue, badly damaged by air pollution, will take several years. When it is finished the statue will not be erected in the open but will be accommodated in a palace or a museum.

Campo Verano   B/C5/6

The Campo Verano, Rome's largest cemetery, lies – in accordance with ancient Roman practice – outside the city walls on the Via Tiburtina (the road to Tivoli). The tall marble and travertine structures in which the sarcophagi are housed and the tomb monuments give this cemetery its characteristic aspect.

The Campo Verano is particularly busy on All Saints Day (1 November), when the people of Rome visit their dead and decorate the graves.

Situation
Via Tiburtina

Buses
9, 11, 63, 65, 71, 109, 111, 163, 309, 311, 411, 415, 490, 492, 495

Trams
19, 19b, 30, 30b

Cappella di Sant'Ivo, in the Palazzo della Sapienza   C3

One of the most distinctive landmarks of Rome is the dome, with its airy lantern and spiral finial, of the church of St Ivo in the Palazzo della Sapienza. The "Sapienza" was the home of the University of Rome from its foundation by Pope Boniface VIII in 1303 until it was able to remove to more spacious accommodation in the University City in 1935. The three-storey palace, now housing the State Archives, was built by Giacomo della Porta for Pope Sixtus V in 1587.

Crossing the inner courtyard between the two massive wings of the palace, we come to the church of Sant'Ivo, a Baroque chapel with a lively façade mingling concave and convex forms. The interior with its semicircular and trapezoid elements was designed by Borromini in the form of a bee, the heraldic emblem of Pope Urban VIII, a member of the noble Barberini family.

The church as a whole is a masterly example of the work of Borromini, domestic architect of the Barberini family.

Situation
Corso del Rinascimento

Buses
26, 46, 62, 64, 70, 81, 88, 90

Carcere Mamertino (Mamertine Prison)   C3

From the 4th c. B.C. onwards the state prison of Rome stood at the foot of the Capitol hill (see Campidoglio), on the side nearest the Foro Romano (see entry). It consisted of two

Situation
Via dei Falegnami, adjoining the Forum

Castel Gandolfo

Underground station
Colosseo (line B)

Buses
85, 87, 88

Opening times
Winter 9 a.m.–4 p.m.,
summer 9 a.m.–5 p.m.

vaulted chambers, one on top of the other. In the lower chamber, also known as the Tullianum (after a water cistern), we are told by the Roman historians that the Numidian king Jugurtha (140 B.C.), the Gallic chieftain Vercingetorix (46 B.C.) and Catiline's fellow conspirators were confined. According to Christian tradition the Apostles Peter and Paul were also imprisoned here, and during his confinement Peter is said to have baptised the other prisoners with water from the Tullianum spring. Accordingly the chapel which was later constructed in the prison was named San Pietro in Carcere (St Peter in Prison). The church above it is dedicated to St Joseph the Carpenter (San Giuseppe dei Falegnami).

Castel Gandolfo

Underground station
Piazza Cinecittà (line A)

Buses
Regular services from Via
Tito Labieno

Rail
Ferrovia Roma–Albano

In Castel Gandolfo is the Pope's summer residence, the construction of which was begun by Urban VIII in 1624. The property enjoys extraterritorial status as part of Vatican City.
From the little town, which according to legend was founded by Aeneas' son Ascanius and which, as Alba Longa, was later destroyed by Rome, there are wide-ranging views over the Roman Campagna, extending as far as the dome of St Peter's (see San Pietro), and down to the Alban Lake (see Colli Albani).
In the main square, opposite the Papal palace, is the church of San Tommaso di Villanova, by Bernini.

*Castel Sant'Angelo   B2

Situation
Lungotevere Vaticano/
Lungotevere Castello

Buses
23, 28, 28b, 34, 64

Opening times
Tues.–Sat. 9 a.m.–1 p.m.,
Sun. 9 a.m.–noon

Closed
Mon.

The Castel Sant'Angelo (now a museum) is one of the most imposing buildings to survive from antiquity. It was originally a mausoleum, begun by Hadrian (A.D. 117–138) in the closing years of his reign to provide a last resting-place for himself and his successors, and completed by Septimius Severus (A.D. 193). When Rome was endangered by Germanic raiders from the N and was surrounded by Aurelian with a new circuit of walls (see Mura Aureliane) the mausoleum, strategically situated, was incorporated in the defences and became the strongest fortress in Rome. The original name of the structure (Hadrianeum) was changed to Castel Sant'Angelo, after a vision vouchsafed to Pope Gregory the Great in 590, when he saw an angel hovering over the mausoleum and sheathing his sword, heralding the end of the plague which was then raging in Rome. Hence the figure of an angel which now crowns the monument.
In 1277 Pope Nicholas III linked the castle with the Vatican Palace (see Palazzi Vaticani) by building a wall along which ran a covered passage known as the *passetto*. Pope Alexander VI, the Borgia Pope whose adventurous policy of conquest made adequate protection against attack very necessary, fortified the passage and strengthened the castle by building four corner bastions. In times of danger the Popes were able to take refuge in the Castel Sant'Angelo, as did Gregory VII (1084) when threatened by the German king Henry IV, Clement VII during the attack on Rome by the Emperor Charles

Castel Sant'Angelo

V (1527, sack of Rome) and Pius VII when in danger of capture by Napoleon's forces. Celebrated prisoners were confined in the castle, and executions took place on its walls. For a time it housed the Papal treasury and secret archives.

The Mausoleum of Hadrian consisted of a circular structure 64 m (210 ft) in diameter and 20 m (65 ft) high standing on a square base (84 m (275 ft) each way, 15 m (50 ft) high). Around the top of the walls, built of dressed travertine and tufa, were set a series of statues, and on the highest point was a bronze quadriga (four-horse chariot). This cylindrical structure with its simple geometrical forms and massive walls, within which were the tomb chambers of the Imperial family, formed the core of the Papal stronghold. In the course of 1500 years the building was altered by successive Popes according to their particular needs (whether for defence against attack or for purposes of display, with sumptuous decoration). The original structure, its different levels linked by a spiral ramp which is still used by visitors to reach the viewing platform, is now overlaid with an intricate complex of additions and alterations – halls and chambers of various kinds, courtyards, store-rooms, niches, staircases and passages going in all directions. From the upper platform there are magnificent views of Rome.

Castro Pretorio (Praetorian Barracks)   B5

The barracks of the Praetorian Guard, the Emperor's personal bodyguard, were built by Tiberius' minister Sejanus in A.D. 23 on a site measuring 460 by 300 m (500 by 330 yd). The

Situation
Viale Castro Pretorio

Buses
9, 163, 310, 415, 492

barracks, with their fortifications, were later incorporated by Aurelian in the city walls (see Mura Aureliane).

Catacombe di Domitilla (Catacombs of Domitilla)   D4

Situation
Via Ardeatina/
Via delle Sette Chiese 282

Buses
93, 671 or 118 and change
into 94 or 218

Opening times
8.30 a.m.–noon, 2.30–5 or
5.30 p.m.

Closed
Tues.

The Catacombs of Domitilla are among the most impressive of the Roman catacombs, the underground burial-places which were used by pagans as well as Christians (though the more famous and wealthier Romans might prefer to be buried beside one of the great trunk roads leading out of Rome). The Christians met in the catacombs to celebrate the commemorative day of notable members of their community: there is no real historical foundation for the belief that they frequently sought refuge in the catacombs to escape persecution.
In the Catacombs of Domitilla is the basilica of SS. Nereus and Achilleus, an underground church of highly impressive effect with its columns and marble fragments. From the basilica visitors enter the catacomb passages with their tomb chambers and wall recesses. There are well-preserved wall paintings on Christian themes.

Catacombe di Priscilla (Catacombs of Priscilla)   A5

Situation
Via Salaria 430

Buses
56, 57, 319

Opening times
8.30 a.m.–noon, 2.30–5 or
6 p.m.

Closed
Mon.

These catacombs are believed to be named after Priscilla, a member of the gens Acilia who became a Christian and was killed on the orders of Domitian. They contain a number of wall paintings of saints and early Christian symbols. Particularly notable is the "Greek Chapel", a square chamber with an arch which contains 2nd c. frescoes of Old and New Testament scenes. Above the apse is a Last Judgment. – Near this are figures of the Virgin and Child and the Prophet Isaiah, also dating from the 2nd c.

*Catacombe di San Callisto (Catacombs of St Calixtus)

Situation
Via Appia Antica 102

Buses
118, 218

Opening times
8.30 a.m.–noon, 2.30–5 or
6 p.m.

Closed
Wed.

The Catacombs of St Calixtus were called by Pope John XXIII "the sublimest and most famous in Rome". They extend over an area of 300 by 400 m (330 by 440 yd), with an intricate network of passages and chambers hewn from the soft Roman tufa on four levels. Some 20 km (12½ miles) of passages have so far been explored, and the total number of burials is estimated at around 170,000.
In six sacramental chapels, constructed between A.D. 290 and 310, are both pagan and early Christian wall paintings. In the "Papal Crypt", to which visitors descend by a flight of 35 steps, are the tombs of most of the martyred Popes of the 3rd c., identified by Greek inscriptions (Urban I, Pontius, Antherus, Fabian, Lucius, Eutychianus). To the left of the Papal Crypt is the tomb of St Cecilia, with wall paintings; the saint's remains are now in the church of Santa Cecilia in Trastevere (see entry). Other notable tombs are those of Pope Eusebius (309–311) and Pope Cornelius (251–253).

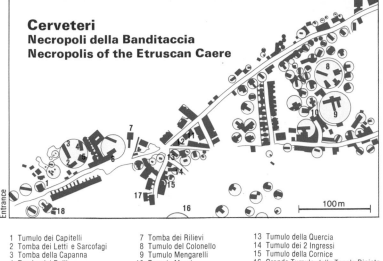

Cerveteri
Necropoli della Banditaccia
Necropolis of the Etruscan Caere

1 Tumulo dei Capitelli
2 Tomba dei Letti e Sarcofagi
3 Tomba della Capanna
4 Tomba dei Dolii
5 Tomba dei Vasi Greci
6 Tomba dei 13 Cadaveri

7 Tomba dei Rilievi
8 Tumulo del Colonello
9 Tumulo Mengarelli
10 Tumulo Maroi
11 Tomba di Marce Ursus
12 Tomba della Casetta

13 Tumulo della Quercia
14 Tumulo dei 2 Ingressi
15 Tumulo della Cornice
16 Grande Tumulo della Tegola Dipinta
17 Tomba dei 6 Loculi
18 Tombe della Spianata

Cerveteri

Cerveteri (a corruption of Caere Vetus) occupies the site of the Etruscan city of Caere, which was an important commercial and political centre from the 8th to the 4th c. B.C. The necropolis of Cerveteri, to the N of the present town, introduces the visitor to the life and the funerary cult of this people, who occupied large areas of central Italy before the rise of Rome and developed a high degree of artistic achievement in architecture, painting, sculpture and metalwork.

Gold and bronze objects, vases and paintings produced by the Etruscans can be seen in the museums of Rome as well as in the British Museum and the Louvre.

There are numerous impressive tombs, among the most notable being the Tomba dei Capitelli, dei Dolii, dei Vasi Greci, dei 13 Cadaveri, dei Rilievi, della Cassetta, and dei Letti e Sarcofagi and the tumuli (burial mounds) of the Cornice and of Ophelia Maroi.

Distance
51 km (32 miles) NW, just off the Via Aurelia

* Chiesa Nuova (the "New Church": officially Santa Maria in Vallicella)   C2

The church of Santa Maria in Vallicella was begun in 1575 on the initiative of St Philip Neri, founder of the Congregation of the Oratory. It was built on the site of an earlier (12th c.) church dedicated to St John, and is still popularly known as the "New

Situation
Piazza della Chiesa Nuova
(Corso Vittorio Emanuele II)

43

Cimitero Acattolico

Buses
46, 62, 64

Church". A number of different donors and architects were involved in its construction.

The exterior of the church is of imposing effect, with its massive façade and central dome rearing high above the close-packed houses in the older part of the city. The sumptuously decorated interior of this high cruciform three-aisled basilica is notable particularly for the frescoes by Pietro da Cortona and the paintings on the high altar (early works by Rubens).

On the left of the choir is the Chapel of San Filippo Neri, containing his tomb.

Cimitero Acattolico (Protestant Cemetery)   D3

Situation
Via Caio Cestio

Buses
11, 23, 57, 92, 95, 318, 673, 716

The Protestant Cemetery lies within the Aurelian Walls (see Mura Aureliane) near the Pyramid of Cestius (see Piramide di Caio Cestio). Among famous foreigners buried here are Keats, who died in Rome on 24 February 1821, and Shelley, drowned in the Gulf of La Spezia in 1822.

Città Universitaria (University City)   B5

Situation
Viale delle Scienze

Buses
11, 71, 109, 111, 309, 310, 311, 411, 415, 492

When the Papal University, the "Sapienza" (see Cappella di Sant'Ivo), became too small, plans were considered from 1870 onwards for replacing it with new university buildings. This large new complex was built by Mussolini in 1932–5, but it too soon became inadequate for the number of students. In the University City are a number of small museums.

Colli Albani, Lago di Albano (Alban Hills, Alban Lake)

Distance
20–30 km (12–18 miles) SE

Rail
Ferrovia Roma–Albano

In the past many Roman noble families and Popes built castles in these hills, and the region is therefore also known as the Castelli Romani ("Roman Castles"). In our own day many Roman citizens have made their homes here, attracted by the purer air and quieter surroundings of an area which lies considerably higher than Rome.

These volcanic hills rise to a height of 949 m (3114 ft) in Monte Cavo. The craters of the volcanoes have formed two lakes, the Lago di Albano (Alban Lake) and the Lago di Nemi (Lake Nemi). An excellent wine known as Castelli Romani is produced from grapes grown on the slopes of the hills. Around the old castles a series of little towns have grown up, like Frascati, Grottaferrata, Marino, Castel Gandolfo (see entry), Albano, Ariccia, Genzano, Nemi and Rocca di Papa.

Lago di Albano

This crater lake (about 3·5 km/2 miles long, 2 km/1¼ miles wide; alt. 293 m/960 feet; greatest depth 170 m/560 feet) is of extraordinary beauty from whatever viewpoint it is seen. The level of the lake is maintained at a constant height by an emissary or tunnel 2500 m (2700 yd) long, 1·20 m (4 ft) wide and 1·60 m (5 ft) high which drains surplus water into the Tiber. The emissary was originally constructed by Roman engineers in 397 B.C., following a prophecy that Rome could not conquer the Etruscan city of Veii until the water of the lake had been drained.

Colombario di Pomponio Hylas (Columbarium of Pomponius Hylas) D4

A columbarium was a communal burial chamber with niches in the walls for cinerary urns. The name comes from the resemblance of this type of structure to a dovecote (*columba*=pigeon).

A particularly well-preserved example is the columbarium built for Pomponius Hylas and his wife Vitalinis, which is situated near the Sepolcro degli Scipioni (see entry), between the Via Appia Antica and the Via Latina. Pomponius Hylas was a freed slave who seems to have risen to prosperity in the reigns of Augustus and Tiberius.

Situation
Via di Porta San Sebastiano

Bus
118

Opening times
10 a.m.–5 or 6 p.m.
Sun. 9 a.m.–noon

Closed
Mon.

*Colonna di Marco Aurelio (Column of Marcus Aurelius) C3

The Piazza Colonna, with the Palazzo Chigi (now housing the Prime Minister's office), is dominated by the Column of Marcus Aurelius. After Marcus Aurelius' defeat of the Marcomanni, Quadi and Sarmatae the column was erected by the Senate in the centre of a square flanked by temples dedicated to Hadrian and Marcus Aurelius and by other public buildings. The inscription at the foot of the column wrongly ascribes it to Antoninus Pius, and it is sometimes also known by the name of that Emperor.

The column, standing 29·60 m (97 ft) high (42 m (138 ft) if the base and capital are included) and 3·70 m (12 ft) in diameter, is constructed of 27 drums of Carrara marble. A spiral relief runs up the column, with scenes from the wars with the Germanic tribes (171–173) and the Sarmatians (174–175). The figures of soldiers and horses stand out more strongly from the background than on Trajan's Column, and like the reliefs on that column have yielded a wealth of information about the weapons and uniforms, the military techniques and the life of the period.

A staircase (190 steps) inside the column gives access to the platform on the top, once occupied by a figure of Marcus Aurelius. The monument is now crowned by a bronze statue of the Apostle Paul (by Domenico Fontana) set up in 1589.

Situation
Piazza Colonna

Buses
52, 53, 56, 58, 58b, 60, 61,
62, 71, 81, 85, 88, 90, 90b,
95, 115

**Colosseo (Colosseum) C4

The Colosseum, or Flavian Amphitheatre, is the largest structure left to us by Roman antiquity, and has provided the model for sports arenas right down to modern times: the football stadia of the present day have basically the same form as this monument created by the architects of the Flavian

Situation
Piazza del Colosseo

Underground station
Colosseo (line B)

Colosseo

Column of Marcus Aurelius

In the Colosseum

View of the Colosseum

Emperors, Vespasian and Titus. The object of the Emperors in raising the Colosseum was to satisfy the appetite of the Roman populace for *circenses* (games), and there is no doubt that they achieved their aim.

A bronze cross in the arena commemorates the Christian martyrs who were believed to have died here during the Roman Imperial period. There is some doubt, however, whether large numbers of Christians in fact met their death in the Colosseum. The structure of the Colosseum is so well preserved that it still creates a powerful impression of its original form, but it bears very evident marks of the damage and destruction it has suffered down the centuries – by fire, earthquake, neglect and dilapidation under the Christian Empire (when the games were abandoned), its conversion into a fortress of the Frangipane family, the pillaging of its marble, travertine and brick for the construction of palaces (see Palazzo Venezia, Cancelleria, Palazzo Farnese) and the constant thunder of modern traffic.

The building of the Colosseum was begun by Vespasian in A.D. 72 on the site of a colossal statue of Nero (hence the name Colosseum) which stood within the precincts of Nero's Domus Aurea (see entry). Vespasian's son Titus enlarged the structure by adding the fourth storey, and it was inaugurated in the year 80 with a series of splendid games.

The Colosseum was oval in form (though it appears to be almost circular), 186 m (610 ft) long by 156 m (510 ft) across, with an arena 78 by 46 m (260 by 150 ft) which could be used for theatrical performances, festivals, circus shows or games. It stood 57 m (190 ft) high and could accommodate some 50,000 spectators – the Imperial court and high officials on the lowest level, the aristocratic families of Rome on the second level, the populace on the third and fourth. Around the exterior, built of travertine, are pilasters – of the Doric order on the ground floor, Ionic on the next tier and Corinthian on the third. The interior structure was contrived with immense skill, the rows of seating and the internal passages and staircases being arranged so as to allow the 50,000 spectators to get to their places or leave the theatre within a few minutes. On the top storey there were originally 240 masts set round the walls to support an awning over the audience. Unfortunately the sumptuous decoration of the interior has been totally destroyed.

Underneath the arena were changing rooms and training rooms for gladiators, cages for wild beasts and store-rooms, the walls of which are now visible since the collapse of the arena floor. (Photographs of the Colosseum, p. 46.)

Buses
11, 15, 27, 81, 85, 87, 88, 118, 673

Trams
13, 30, 30b

Opening times
9 a.m.–3.30 or 7 p.m.

Domine Quo Vadis Church

This church takes its name from the legend that the Apostle Peter, fleeing from Rome to escape martyrdom, met Christ here and, not recognising him, asked, "Sir, whither goest thou?" ("Domine, quo vadis?"); whereupon Christ replied, "I come to be crucified a second time." Then Peter, realising who it was, was stricken with shame and returned to Rome.

On the basis of this legend the little church of Santa Maria in Palmis was built in the 9th c. and became known as the Domine Quo Vadis church; it was rebuilt in the 17th c. Within the church is a reproduction of the footprint of Christ.

Situation
Via Appia Antica, km 0·8

Buses
118, 218

Domus Aurea (Nero's Golden House) C4

Situation
Viale Monte Oppio

Underground station
Colosseo (line B)

Buses
15, 81, 85, 87, 88

Trams
13, 30, 30b

Opening times
in winter 9 a.m.–1 p.m.

Closed
Mon.

The burning of Rome in A.D. 64 happened very conveniently for Nero's purposes. In the huge area thus cleared of buildings he planned to erect a huge and sumptuously appointed new palace, and although the vast project, covering an area greater than that of the present-day Vatican City, was never completed, the site was used by Nero's successors for the erection of other buildings, including the Colosseum (see entry), approximately occupying the position of Nero's artificial lake.

Excavations which began at the Renaissance in the area between the Forum (see Foro Romano) and the Esquiline brought to light large numbers of works of art, frescoes and marble statues, including the famous Laocoön group, now in the Vatican Museum (see Città del Vaticano, Musei Vaticani).

*EUR (Esposizione Universale di Roma)

Underground station
EUR-Fermi (line B)

Buses
93, 97, 123, 197, 223, 293,
393, 493, 593, 671, 703,
707, 708, 762, 765, 775

The Italian Fascist government planned to hold a great international exhibition in Rome in 1942, but work on the project, which began in 1938, was suspended on the outbreak of war. Mussolini's plan was to create, between Rome and the sea, a satellite town the modern buildings of which should outshine the old palaces of Papal Rome, and new streets were laid out and vast buildings (Palace of Congresses, Palace of Labour, museums) erected in the monumental style of the Fascist period. After the war the development of the area continued, with some buildings of considerable architectural quality.

Fontana dell'Acqua Felice B4

Situation
Via Orlando
(corner of Piazza San
Bernardo)

Buses
16, 37, 60, 61, 63, 415

This fountain, with a figure of Moses as its central feature, was commissioned by Pope Sixtus V in 1585. The Pope, Felice Peretti (hence the name of the fountain), to whom Rome owes so many magnificent buildings, was unfortunate in his choice of a sculptor. Prospero di Brescia, who carved the figure of Moses, is said to have died of grief, or even to have committed suicide, on comparing his work with Michelangelo's Moses in San Pietro in Vincoli (see entry).

* Fontana delle Tartarughe (Tortoise Fountain) C3

Situation
Piazza Mattei

Buses
26, 44, 58, 60, 65, 75, 170,
710, 718, 719

This fountain was created by the Florentine sculptor Taddeo Landini in 1581–4 to the design of Giacomo della Porta. From the marble basin rises a base decorated with four shells, and four slender youths with outstretched arms support the upper basin. The tortoises from which the fountain takes its name were added in the 17th c.

*Fontana di Trevi (Trevi Fountain) C3

Rome's largest fountain, the Fontana di Trevi, stands in a small square closely hemmed in by buildings. It is supplied by an aqueduct originally constructed by Agrippa, the great art patron of the 1st c. B.C., to bring water to his baths, and later restored by the Popes. The fountain was created for Pope Clement XII between 1732 and 1751 by Nicolò Salvi, whose masterpiece it is.

The fountain, 20 m (65 ft) wide and 26 m (85 ft) high, is built against the rear wall of the palace of the Dukes of Poli. It depicts the "kingdom of Ocean" – the sea god Oceanus (Neptune), with horses (one wild, the other quiet), tritons and shells. The water swirls round the figures and the artificial rocks and collects in a large basin. In the basin can be seen the coins thrown into it by visitors, in virtue of the old tradition that if you throw a coin into the Trevi Fountain you will one day return to Rome. There are those who hold that the coin must be thrown backwards over your head.

Underground station
Barberini (line A)

Buses
52, 53, 56, 58, 58b, 60, 61, 62, 71, 81, 85, 88, 90, 90b, 95, 115, 415

*Fontana del Tritone (Triton Fountain) B3/4

In Piazza Barberini stands the Triton Fountain, a masterpiece created by Bernini in 1632–7 for Pope Urban VIII, a member of the Barberini family. Four dolphins support the Barberini coat of arms with its three bees, and on a large scallop shell sits a triton blowing a conch shell.

Opposite, at the end of Via Veneto (see entry), is the Bee Fountain (1644), also created by Bernini for Urban VIII.

Situation
Piazza Barberini

Underground station
Barberini (line A)

Buses
52, 53, 56, 58, 60, 61, 62, 71, 80, 415

Foro di Augusto (Forum of Augustus) C3

Little is left of the Forum of Augustus but three columns from the temple of Mars Ultor (Vengeful Mars), built by Augustus in 2 B.C. to commemorate the battle of Philippi in 42 B.C. (which avenged the murder of Julius Caesar). About 1200 the Knights of St John (later of Rhodes and Malta) used the ruins of the forum to build their palaces. In an exedra and in the Antiquarium are remains of the Priory of the Knights of Malta. (Plan, see Foro Romano.)

Situation
Via dei Fori Imperiali

Underground station
Colosseo (line B)

Opening times
Summer 9 a.m.–2 p.m., Sun. 9 a.m.–1 p.m., closed Mon. Winter Tues., Thurs., Sat. 4–7 p.m.

Foro di Cesare (Forum of Caesar) C3

The Forum of Caesar or Forum Julium lies at the foot of the Capitol hill (see Campidoglio), part of its area being now occupied by the gardens and car parks of the Via dei Fori Imperiali. It was built between 54 and 46 B.C. by Julius Caesar at his personal expense, with the object both of enhancing his own fame and meeting the needs of the citizens, for which the old Forum Romanum was no longer adequate. The scanty

Situation
Via dei Fori Imperiali

Underground station
Colosseo (line B)

Buses
85, 87, 88

Foro di Nerva

Opening times
Information: tel. 67 10 30 69
9 a.m.–2 p.m., Sun. 9 a.m.–
1 p.m.; closed Mon.

remains give little impression of the original structure, which covered an area 170 by 75 m (550 by 250 ft). Around the forum were shops, the Basilica Argentaria (occupied by money-changers' offices and the exchange) and the temple of Venus Genetrix. Nothing has survived of the sculptural decoration of the forum, including an equestrian statue of Caesar which is described by ancient writers. (Plan, see Foro Romano.)

Foro di Nerva (Forum of Nerva)   C3/4

Situation
Via dei Fori Imperiali

Underground station
Colosseo (line B)

Opening times
Information: tel. 67 10 30 69

Closed
Mon.

In the centre of the Forum of Nerva (Emperor A.D. 96–98), which adjoins the Forum of Augustus (see Foro di Augusto) on the E, stood a temple of Minerva which was pulled down by Pope Paul V to provide stone for the construction of an aqueduct. The remains consist of two Corinthian columns from the right-hand colonnade, pieces of the frieze from the entablature (upper part of the buildings, above the column) and fragments of a figural relief. (Plan, see Foro Romano.)

Foro Romano   .   C3/4

Underground station
Colosseo (line B)

Buses
11, 27, 81, 85, 87, 88

Opening times
Summer 9 a.m.–3.30 p.m.,
winter 9 a.m.–3 p.m.
Sun. 9 a.m.–1 p.m.

Closed
Tues.

No other site in Europe is so pregnant with history as the Roman Forum. Although the surviving remains give only a very inadequate impression of the splendour of the Forum in ancient times, this area at the foot of the Capitol (see Campidoglio) and the Palatine (see Palatino), with its columns still standing erect or lying tumbled on the ground, its triumphal arches and its remains of walls, still has the power to impress, for it was here during many centuries that the fate of Europe was decided. For more than a thousand years the might of Rome, the magnificence of Roman art, Roman law and Roman religion found imposing and enduring expression here.

The history of the Forum was, over this long period, the history of Rome and of the western world. Originally a marshy area between the hills of Rome, it was later drained. The first buildings erected here were temples, soon followed by various public buildings, and the area became the political centre of the city, the meeting-place of the Roman courts and the assemblies which took decisions on the internal and external affairs of the republic. This in turn led to the building of market halls in which the citizens of Rome could go about their business. The Forum thus developed into a complex of buildings serving the purposes of Rome's religious, political and commercial life, increasing in splendour as the city grew in power. Consuls and senators, Caesar and later the Emperors vied with one another in developing and embellishing this focal point of the Roman world which became the meeting-place of the peoples of Europe and the Empire. By the end of the Imperial period the Forum was a densely built-up complex in which "modern" buildings rubbed shoulders with ancient ones, carefully planned structures with casually sited later buildings. Not surprisingly, it is sometimes difficult to identify individual buildings in the huddle of the surviving remains.

The last monument erected in ancient times was the

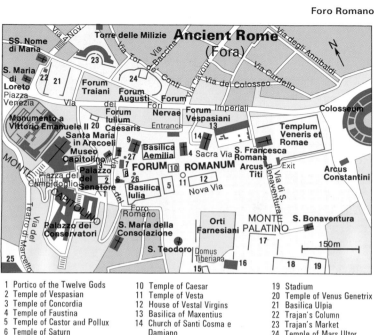

1 Portico of the Twelve Gods
2 Temple of Vespasian
3 Temple of Concordia
4 Temple of Faustina
5 Temple of Castor and Pollux
6 Temple of Saturn
7 Arch of Septimius Severus
8 Rostra
9 Curia Iulia (church of
   Sant'Adriano)
10 Temple of Caesar
11 Temple of Vesta
12 House of Vestal Virgins
13 Basilica of Maxentius
14 Church of Santi Cosma e
   Damiano
15 Temple of Cybele
16 House of Livia
17 Palace of Flavians
18 Palace of Augustus
19 Stadium
20 Temple of Venus Genetrix
21 Basilica Ulpia
22 Trajan's Column
23 Trajan's Market
24 Temple of Mars Ultor
25 Theatre of Marcellus
26 Column of Phocas
27 Lapis Niger

undecorated column set up in A.D. 608 for the Byzantine
Emperor Phocas. Thereafter the buildings fell into ruin, and the
Forum began to be used for other purposes. Churches and
fortresses were built amid the ancient remains, and the area
served as a quarry of building stone and a pasturage for cows,
becoming known as the Campo Vaccino. It was not until the
18th and 19th c. that systematic excavations brought the
ancient buildings to light under a layer of earth and rubble
between 10 and 15 m (30 and 50 ft) deep. It needs a good deal
of imagination (and small-scale plaster models) to summon up
a picture of the Forum in Imperial times; but the site, even in its
state of ruin, still retains a powerful evocative force. – The entire
area, however, suffers from heavy traffic surging around it. The
following features are especially notable.

**Tempio di Antonino e Faustina
(Temple of Antoninus and Faustina)

From the Via Sacra (Sacred Way) a broad flight of steps leads
up to the temple of Antoninus Pius and his wife Faustina. The
temple was built by resolution of the Senate in A.D. 141 in

Temples of Faustina and Vesta

Temple of Castor and Pollux

honour of the deified Empress, and was also dedicated to Antoninus after his death. This is recorded in the inscription, "Divo Antonino et Divae Faustinae ex S(enatus) C(onsulto)". Of the temple there survive six columns with Corinthian capitals along the front and a number of columns along the side.

In the 12th c. the temple was converted into the church of San Lorenzo in Miranda. On the occasion of the Emperor Charles V's visit to Rome in 1536 the columns were disengaged from the medieval masonry.

**Tempio di Castore e Polluce (Temple of Castor and Pollux)

The Dioscuri – Castor and Pollux – are the subject of numerous myths, partly of Greek and partly of Etruscan origin, featuring healings (in association with the god Aesculapius), beautiful women (including Helen of Troy) and horsemen with their horses. The first temple of Castor and Pollux was built in 484 B.C. by the son of the dictator Aulus Postumius in thanksgiving for the defeat of the Tarquins, which was attributed to the help of the Dioscuri. According to legend, after the victory Castor and Pollux rode to Rome and watered their horses at a spring in the Forum, the Lacus Juturnae (the position of which has been located).

The temple was rebuilt in the reign of Tiberius (1st c. A.D.), and of this temple there survive three Corinthian columns 12 m (40 ft) high, popularly known as the "Three Sisters".

The Forum Romanum

Tempio di Saturno (Temple of Saturn)

The first temple in the Forum was dedicated to Saturn, a god who was probably of Etruscan origin but was adopted by the Romans and worshipped as the supreme god. Built about 497 B.C., soon after the expulsion of the Tarquins, the temple was one of the most important and most venerated of republican Rome.

It was several times destroyed by fire (the last occasion being in the 4th c. A.D.) but was repeatedly rebuilt. It is represented by eight columns with Ionic capitals, now much weathered. Under the Republic the state treasury was kept in this temple. The celebration of the Saturnalia, observed annually on 17 December, started from the temple of Saturn.

Adjoining the temple is a fragment of the Miliarium Aureum, the "Golden Milestone" which was the starting point of the Via Sacra and all the Roman consular roads. On the stone, in golden figures, were inscribed the distance from Rome to the various provinces of the Empire.

**Arco di Settimio Severo (Arch of Septimius Severus)

It was a regular practice for the Senate and people of Rome to set up triumphal arches in honour of victorious Emperors and generals, and in A.D. 203 this arch, opposite the church of Santi Martina e Luca, was erected in honour of Septimius Severus and his sons Caracalla and Geta after their victories over the Parthians and various desert tribes.

Curia

Arch of Septimius Severus

On the arch, 23 m (75 ft) high and 25 m (80 ft) wide, are four
marble reliefs with vigorous representations of episodes from
these wars, the figures standing out prominently from the
background. Goddesses of victory with trophies and a large
inscription proclaim the glory of the Emperor and his sons
(though the name of Geta was later erased).
Other features of interest adjoining the arch are:
The base of a column commemorating the tenth anniversary of
Diocletian's accession.
The remains of the Rostra, the ancient orators' platform, which
was originally decorated with the prows (*rostra*) of captured
enemy ships.
The position of the Umbilicus Urbis, the "navel" or symbolic
centre of Rome.

Curia

The Curia, meeting-place of the Roman Senate, is one of the
best preserved ancient buildings in the Forum. The first such
building was erected in the time of the kings, and thereafter
rebuilding was frequently necessary, as a result of fires and
other forms of destruction in the time of Sulla, Caesar,
Augustus, Diocletian, Julian the Apostate, etc. Finally in the
7th c. the Curia was converted into a church and was thus
preserved from further destruction. Borromini adapted its
bronze doors to serve as the main doorway of St John Lateran
(see San Giovanni in Laterano).
The Curia, a plain and unornamented building both externally
and internally, was stripped of later accretions between 1931
and 1937. It is now sometimes used for special exhibitions.
The building measures 27 by 18 m (90 by 60 ft) internally, and
could seat some 300 senators. It preserves fragments of a
coloured marble floor. Here, too, are displayed the Anaglyphs
of Trajan, two travertine slabs with reliefs depicting the
Emperor and the people of Rome.

Tempio di Vesta (Temple of Vesta)

In ancient times the Temple of Vesta in the Forum – there is
another temple of Vesta in the Forum Boarium – contained the
"Sacred Fire" which was guarded by the Vestals (virgins
selected from the best families in Rome). The six priestesses
served in the temple between the ages of 10 and 14. The
Romans attached great importance to this "eternal fire": on the
first day of the new year (1 March) they put out the fires in their
houses and lit new ones from the flame in the temple of Vesta.
The present remains, dating from the time of Septimius Severus
(A.D. 193–211), indicate that the temple was circular, with 20
slender columns supporting the roof. Archaeological investigation has established that there was an opening in the
centre of the roof to let out the smoke from the sacred flame.

Atrium Vestae (House of the Vestals)

Adjoining the Temple of Vesta was the house of the Vestal
virgins, also built by Septimius Severus. It consisted of a large

atrium, the lodgings of the priestesses and various offices. The plan of the building, with remains of the foundations and numerous statue bases, can be readily identified. It is known from the works of Latin writers that the sacred Palladium (an image of Pallas Athene), which Aeneas was said to have brought from Troy to Latium, was preserved in the House of the Vestals.

Colonna di Foca (Column of Phocas)

In front of the Rostra (see above) is a Corinthian column 13·80 m (45 ft) high, erected in A.D. 608 in honour of the Byzantine Emperor Phocas and in recognition of his presentation of the Pantheon to Pope Boniface IV for conversion into a church.

Lapis Niger (Black Stone)

Outside the Curia, protected by a low roof, is a block of black marble, under which, according to Roman legend, is the tomb of Romulus founder of Rome. Close by is a stele, excavated in 1899, with the oldest known Latin inscription.

**Arco di Tito (Arch of Titus)

At the end of the Forum farthest from the Capitol is the Arch of Titus, the oldest of the Roman triumphal arches, erected after Titus' death by his successor Domitian.

Fresco in Santa Maria Antiqua

Titus, son of the Emperor Vespasian, was the Roman general who captured Jerusalem in the year 70 and thus put the final seal on the defeat of the Jewish people in Palestine. The reliefs on the arch, which has a single passageway, depict this event, and also the victorious general's triumphal procession to the Capitol. Titus (who became Emperor only in the year 79) is shown in his chariot accompanied by the goddess of Victory with a laurel wreath and by the booty brought back from the Jewish War – the seven-branched candlestick, the table with the shewbread and trumpets from the treasury of the Temple.

Santa Maria Antiqua Church

As its name indicates, the church of Santa Maria Antiqua (badly damaged and rarely open to the public) is the oldest and the most important Christian building in the Forum. Converted from a building of the Roman Imperial period in the 6th c. and richly furnished by various 8th c. Popes (John VII, Zacharias and Paul I), the church thereafter fell into a state of dilapidation, before being restored in the 13th c.
This extensive complex at the foot of the Palatine hill is of interest for its architecture and for its wall paintings, ranging in date between the 6th and 8th c.

---

*Foro di Traiano (Forum of Trajan)   C3

The Forum of the Emperor Trajan (A.D. 98–117), the last, largest and best preserved on the Imperial fora, comprised a considerable complex of buildings, including a temple and basilica as well as three monuments erected in honour of the Emperor himself – a triumphal arch, an equestrian statue and a victory column. The markets extended NE up the Quirinal hill. The forum, designed by Apollodorus of Damascus, was begun in A.D. 107 and completed in 143. During the Middle Ages new buildings were erected in the area of the forum by the Colonna and Caetani families, among them the Torre delle Milizie (see entry) still to be seen in Via Quattro Novembre, and later the twin churches of Santa Maria di Loreto and the Santissimo Nome di Maria were also built here. In the first half of the present century a wide motor road and a number of smaller streets were laid out in the area. A pedestrian precinct is now planned.

Excavations carried out since 1928 have revealed the layout of the forum. A triumphal arch erected in A.D. 116 gave access to an open rectangular area, in the centre of which stood an equestrian statue of the Emperor. At the far end was the Basilica Ulpia, a hall measuring 130 by 125 m (430 by 410 ft). In the present state of the site it is difficult to imagine a building of these dimensions; and indeed it was no easy matter at the time it was built to find space for it in this crowded part of central Rome. Built on to the rear of the basilica were two libraries, one for Latin and the other for Greek literature, and between the two reared up Trajan's victory column (see below). Beyond this, at the end of the forum (between the two churches dedicated to the Virgin), was a temple of the deified Trajan. Only Trajan's Column is left to represent this whole

Situation
Via dei Fori Imperiali

Underground station
Colosseo (line B)

Buses
85, 87, 88

Opening times
Tues.–Sat. 9 a.m.–1 p.m.,
3–6 p.m.
Sun. 9 a.m.–1 p.m.

Closed
Mon.

complex, much admired in ancient times, dedicated to honouring the Emperor under whom the Roman Empire reached its greatest extent. (Plan, see Foro Romano.)

* Colonna di Traiano (Trajan's Column)

This victory column, now suffering increasing damage from the elements and the polluted air of Rome, is a magnificent monument to Roman Imperial power and the skill of Roman sculptors. The column, 38 m (125 ft) high and constructed of marble from the Greek island of Paros, is covered with a spiral frieze 200 m (655 ft) long, with over 2500 figures, depicting Trajan's wars with the Dacians in 101–102 and 105–106. This whole frieze, with its fighting soldiers, prancing horses and the whole panoply of Roman military equipment, is worth studying in detail – though this is more difficult for the modern visitor than for the ancients, who could examine the reliefs from the windows of the two libraries. A spiral staircase of 185 steps runs up inside the column, lit by 43 narrow slits in the wall of the column. In the base of the column was a golden urn containing the Emperor's ashes, and on its summit was a golden statue of Trajan. The statue was lost during the Middle Ages, and in 1588 Pope Sixtus V replaced it with a figure of the Apostle Peter with his key. (Plan, see Foro Romano.)

* Mercati di Traiano (Trajan's Markets)

To the N of Trajan's Forum was a semicircular range of market halls in three tiers, the ruins of which, with their red-brick walls and high vaulted roofs, form an impressive termination to the group of Imperial fora, rising up the slopes of the Quirinal hill to Via Quattro Novembre. The difference in level was skilfully exploited by the architect, Apollodorus of Damascus (early 2nd c.). In establishing his markets Trajan was concerned to ease the financial burdens of the population by maintaining prices at a reasonable level and to reduce social tensions by the distribution of Imperial subsidies. (Plan, see Foro Romano.)

Foro di Vespasiano · C3/4

Situation
Corner of Via Cavour and Via dei Fori Imperiali

Underground station
Colosseo (line B)

Buses
11, 27, 81, 85, 87, 88

Adjoining the Forum of Nerva, at the point where Via Cavour now joins the Via dei Fori Imperiali, was the Forum of the Emperor Vespasian (A.D. 69–79), in the centre of which was the Temple of Peace (after which it was also known as the Forum of Peace). The forum, of which only a few fragments remain, was built by Vespasian and paid for from the booty won in the Jewish War. (Plan, see Foro Romano.)

Galleria Colonna (in Palazzo Colonna) · C3

Situation
Via della Pilotta 17,
Piazza SS. Apostoli

The huge palace of the Colonnas, one of Rome's leading noble families, which produced Pope Martin V (1417–31) and many other notable figures, was begun in the 15th c. and completed,

Forum of Trajan

Galleria Nazionale d'Arte Antica

Galleria Nazionale d'Arte Moderna (National Gallery of Modern Art)

Buses
56, 57, 60, 62, 64, 65, 70, 71, 75, 81, 85, 88, 90, 95, 170

Opening times
Sat. 9 a.m.–1 p.m.

Closed
Aug.

after successive extensions, in 1730. Within the precincts of the palace are the church of the Santi Apostoli (see entry) and the Galleria Colonna.

The gallery contains a famous collection of pictures originally founded by Cardinal Girolamo Colonna. This consists mainly of works by 17th and 18th c. masters (including Veronese, Tintoretto and Poussin), together with pictures recording the achievements of the Colonna family: e.g. the victory won by Marcantonio Colonna as commander of the European fleet at the battle of Lepanto (1571) against the Turks.

Galleria Nazionale d'Arte Antica

See Palazzo Barberini

*Galleria Nazionale d'Arte Moderna (National Gallery of Modern Art) B3

Situation
Viale delle Belle Arti

Bus
26

Trams
19, 19b, 30, 30b

The National Gallery of Modern Art, founded in 1883, has the largest collection of works by Italian painters and sculptors of the 19th and 20th c. The 35 rooms of the massive building in which it is housed present a survey of Italian and foreign painting and sculpture since 1800 – though some leading figures are missing and others are represented only by minor works. Notable among the non-Italian artists are Degas,

Gesù Church

Cézanne, Moore, Kandinsky and Vernet. Other items of particular interest are pictures by the Macchiaioli, a group of open-air painters from Tuscany comparable in style with the Impressionists, sculpture by Marino Marini and Giacomo Manzù and paintings by Giorgio de Chirico. (Photograph, p. 60.)

Opening times
Tues.–Sat. 9 a.m.–2 p.m.,
Wed. and Fri. also 3–6 p.m.;
Sun. 9 a.m.–1 p.m.

Closed
Mon.

*Gesù Church   C3

The Gesù is the principal church of the Jesuits. The initiative for its construction came from Ignatius Loyola, founder in 1540 of the Society of Jesus, an order which spread quickly throughout the Roman Catholic countries of Europe and organised the Counter-Reformation. Adjoining the church is a house (now a Jesuit college) in which Ignatius was living at the time of the church's foundation. Cardinal Alessandro Farnese, whose heraldic lilies recur frequently in the decoration of the interior, commissioned Vignola to design and build the church, which was completed by members of the Society. The basic innovation of the design was to set a dome over the crossing of the nave and transepts of a basilican church, a type familiar in Roman, early Christian and medieval models. The Gesù was much imitated by later churches, not only in the general plan but also in details and the form of the façade.

Situation
Piazza del Gesù

Buses
46, 56, 60, 62, 64, 65, 70,
75, 81, 88, 90, 170

The façade, completed in 1575, shows both Renaissance and Baroque features.

Façade

Interior

The interior is notable for its unified effect. Flanking the nave are lateral chapels, which seem almost cut off from the body of the church, and beyond the spacious transepts is the choir, terminating in an apse.

The decoration of the interior is of great richness, with variegated marble, sculpture, bronze statues, stucco ornament, gilding and frescoes. In the barrel vaulting of the nave is a painting of the "Triumph of the Name of Jesus", which glorifies the great missionary achievements of the Jesuits.

Particularly notable are the altars and tombs of Jesuit saints:
In the S transept the altar of St Francis Xavier, by Pietro da Cortona (1674–8).
To. the right of the high altar the monument of Cardinal Bellarmine, with a bust by Bernini (1622).
In the N transept the altar and tomb of St Ignatius (1491–1556), founder of the Jesuit order, by Andrea Pozzo (1696–1700).
The present statue of the saint is a copy of the original silver statue by Pierre Legros, which Pope Pius VII was obliged to melt down to meet reparations payable to Napoleon under the treaty of Tolentino.

Grottaferrata

Underground station
Cinecittà (line A)
and bus from there
(regular service)

Distance
21 km (13 miles)

No tour of the Castelli Romani area (see Colli Albani) would be complete without a visit to the old abbey of the Basilians (an order of the Greek Catholic Church) at Grottaferrata, described by Pope Leo XIII at the end of the 19th c. as "a jewel from the East in the Papal tiara". The abbey, situated at an altitude of 329 m (1080 ft), is not only a venerable old religious house with some notable works of art but an example of Renaissance defensive architecture.

Ianiculcum

See Passeggiata del Gianicolo

Isola Tiberina (Tiber Island)   C3

Buses
15, 23, 26, 44, 56, 60, 65,
75, 170, 710, 718, 719, 774

A Roman legend has it that the Tiber Island was formed when, at some time in the distant past, a heavily laden ship sank in mid stream; and indeed the island has something of the air of a huge vessel stranded in the Tiber. The obelisk which once stood on the island must, in its day, have looked like a mast. Another explanation, based on historical grounds, is that the island was formed by an accumulation of silt produced by waste from cargoes of corn after the expulsion of the Tarquins. About 200 B.C. there was a sanctuary of the healing god Aesculapius and his sacred snakes on the island, where, according to another legend, the god's boat had once called in.

The existence of the island made this a convenient place for bridging the Tiber. In 62 B.C. the consul L. Fabricius built the Ponte Fabricio, Rome's oldest surviving bridge, which links the island with the left bank of the river and the Capitol. It is popularly known as the Ponte dei Quattro Capi ("Bridge of the Four Heads") after two four-headed herms on the balustrades. On the island are the Fatebenefratelli Hospital – maintaining the tradition of healing associated with Aesculapius – and the

Ponte Rotto and Tiber Island

church of San Bartolomeo, built at the end of the 10th c. by the Emperor Otto III on the ruins of the temple of Aesculapius and restored in the Baroque period. Notable features of the church are the beautiful Romanesque campanile and a marble well-head at the entrance to the chancel (probably over the spring belonging to the ancient sanctuary) carved with figures of Christ, St Adalbert of Bohemia, an Apostle (probably Bartholomew) and Otto III.

The island is linked with the right bank of the Tiber (Trastevere) by the Ponte Cestio, built by Lucius Cestius in 46 B.C. and renewed on a number of occasions under the Empire.

To the S of the Isola Tiberina, in the river, is the Ponte Rotto ("Broken Bridge"), all that remains of the Pons Aemilius, which was begun in timber by the censors Aemilius Lepidus and Fulvus Nobilior in 179 B.C. and completed in stone in 142 (the first arched stone bridge in Rome).

Largo di Torre Argentina   C3

In the centre of the Largo di Torre Argentina, a few feet below the level of this busy square with its swirling traffic, is the Largo Argentina temple precinct. The name Torre Argentina is derived from the tower of a house (at Via del Sudario 44) occupied by a prelate named Burckhardt from Strasbourg (Argentoratum) who was Papal master of ceremonies at the beginning of the 16th c. An alternative explanation is that the square is named after the shops of the silversmiths (*argentarii*) who worked in this area.

Buses
26, 44, 46, 56, 60, 62, 64, 65, 70, 75, 87, 94, 170, 710, 718, 719

The temples which were excavated here in 1926–30 are one of the few such complexes dating from the republican period. There are four temples:

The rectangular Temple A (near the bus stops), with 15 columns still standing, within which was built the medieval church of San Nicola dei Cesarini (now destroyed).

The adjoining Temple, circular in plan, with six columns, which once housed a seated effigy of the goddess Juno.

The rectangular Temple C, the smallest and oldest (4th or 3rd c. B.C.) of the temples, on a lower level than the others.

Temple D, part of which is under the roadway.

It is not known with certainty which gods were worshipped in these temples.

Lido di Ostia

Railway
Rome–Ostia Lido branch of
Underground line B

Distance
24 km (15 miles) SW

The once beautiful beach of Ostia is still one of the weekend and holiday resorts most favoured by the people of Rome, and accordingly is one of the busiest and liveliest stretches of sand and promenades in the whole of Italy. In recent years, however, Lido di Ostia has grown into a town of considerable size (pop. 55,000); and since most of its sewage goes into the sea, where it is joined by the sewage carried down by the Tiber from Rome, bathing in the sea here is not to be recommended: indeed at times it is prohibited by the public health authorities.

Mausoleo di Augusto   B3

Situation
Piazza Augusto Imperatore

Buses
1, 2, 90, 95, 911, 913

At present closed

The present appearance of the Piazza Augusto Imperatore gives little hint of the importance this area once enjoyed. Here, some years before his death, the Emperor Augustus constructed a mausoleum for himself and his family (the Julio-Claudian dynasty). This took the form of a gigantic earthen mound 89 m (290 ft) in diameter, of the kind used for the burial of kings and princes in the Mediterranean area since prehistoric times.

Outside the entrance to the mound stood two Egyptian obelisks, now to be seen behind the church of Santa Maria Maggiore (see entry) and in the Piazza del Quirinale. By the entrance were the "Res Gestae", two bronze tablets on which Augustus recorded the achievements of his reign. (The original tablets are lost, but their text has been preserved in inscriptions.) During the Middle Ages the mausoleum was used by the Colonna family as a fortress, which was pulled down by Pope Gregory IX in 1241. Thereafter the mausoleum became a vineyard, a garden, an amphitheatre and even a concert hall, before being restored to its original state in 1936.

Monte Testaccio   D3

Buses
27, 92

Between the Tiber and Porta San Paolo is a small hill, 35 m (115 ft) high and 850 m (930 yd) in circumference, which was formed during the republican period by the deposit of rubbish,

Mausoleum of Augustus

National Monument to Victor Emmanuel II

mainly broken pottery from the nearby warehouses, on the banks of the Tiber where the merchant vessels discharged their cargoes.

The site was occupied in ancient times by large trading establishments and the Porticus Aemilius (2nd c. B.C.), a street of shops 487 m (530 yd) long. The hill is now honeycombed with wine-cellars, some of which have tavernas attached.

*Monumento Nazionale a Vittorio Emanuele II   C3

(National Monument to Victor Emmanuel II)

Situation
Piazza Venezia

Buses
46, 57, 85, 87, 88, 90, 90b, 92, 94, 95, 716, 718, 719

The National Monument to Victor Emmanuel II – a memorial to which there are varying reactions, of approval or disapproval – was built between 1885 and 1911 to celebrate the winning of Italian unity in 1870 and to commemorate the first king of united Italy, Victor Emmanuel II (d. 1878). The monument is 135 m (440 ft) long by 130 m (425 ft) deep and rears up to a height of 70 m (230 ft). Half-way up are the "Altar of the Fatherland" (Altare della Patria) and the Tomb of the Unknown Soldier, which regularly feature in city sightseeing tours.

At the E end of the National Monument is the Museum of the Risorgimento (see Practical Information, Museums).

Mura Aureliane (Aurelian Walls)   C2

The Aurelian Walls were built by the Emperor Aurelian in A.D. 270–275 to protect Rome – which had by now far outgrown the old Servian Walls – against the fresh dangers which were threatening the city from the northern provinces of the Empire. The main threat came from the Goths, who in A.D. 268 had pushed forward from the plain of the Po into Umbria.

The Aurelian Walls had a total length of some 20 km (12½ miles). They were about 4 m (13 ft) thick and originally stood 7·20 m (24 ft) high, but were raised by Stilicho, the great general of the Emperor Honorius (A.D. 395–423), to 10·60 m (35 ft) and reinforced by 380 towers standing some 30 m (33 yd) apart. There were 16 gates in the circuit. The very length of the walls, however, meant that they rarely served their military function.

The walls were kept in repair until the 19th c. Although parts of the circuit have been used as a quarry of building material in the last 100 years or so, some sections have been preserved, and in places it is possible to walk along the top.

Museo Barracco   C2

Situation
Corso Vittorio Emanuele II 168

Buses
46, 62, 64

The Museo Barracco, presented to the city by Baron Giovanni Barracco in 1902, contains a small but very interesting collection of Assyrian, Babylonian, Egyptian, Greek, Etruscan and Roman sculpture, both originals and copies, illustrating the development of ancient art in the pre-Christian centuries. Particularly notable items are some Assyrian reliefs of the 7th c.

In the National Etruscan Museum, Villa Giulia

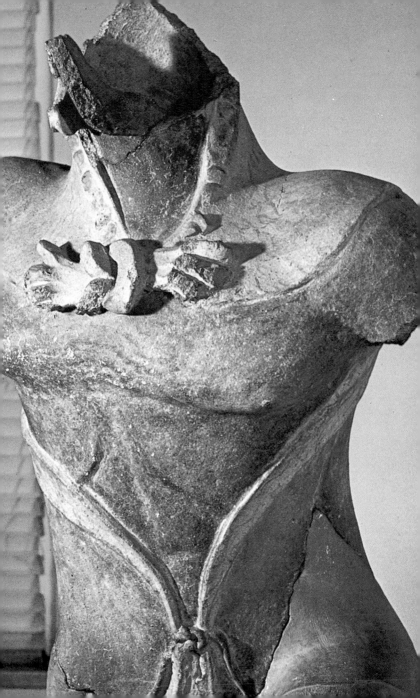

Museo Capitolino

Opening times
9 a.m.–2 p.m., Sun. 9 a.m.–
1 p.m., Tues. and Thurs. also
5–8 p.m.

Closed
Mon.

B.C., a sphinx with the head of Queen Hatshepsut (15th c. B.C.),
Greek statues of the early classical period and Etruscan cippi.
Also of interest are the head of the Diadumenos (second half pf
5th c. B.C.) by Polycletus, the head of an Apollo (mid 5th c. B.C.)
ascribed to Phidias, a bust of Epicurus (c. 270 B.C.), the head of
the Lycian Apollo, the "Wounded Bitch" (Lysippus) and a
head of Alexander Helios (late 4th c. B.C.).

---

*Museo Capitolino (Capitoline Museum)   C3

Situation
Campidoglio

Buses
57, 85, 87, 88, 90, 90b, 92,
94, 95, 716, 718, 719

Opening times
9 a.m.–2 p.m., Sun. 9 a.m.–
1 p.m., Tues. and Thurs. also
5–8 p.m., Sat. also
8.30–11 p.m.

Closed
Mon.

The Capitoline Museum, founded by Pope Sixtus IV in 1471, is
the oldest public art collection in Europe and has a rich stock of
classical sculpture.
In the Palazzo Nuovo of the Capitoline Museum, built about
1650 on the model of the Palazzo dei Conservatori (see entry)
on the opposite side of the square, the following pieces of
sculpture are outstanding: the "Dying Gaul", a Roman copy of
the figure of a dying warrior from the victory monument erected
by King Attalus of Pergamon in the 3rd c. B.C. after he had
defeated the Galatians; the "Wounded Amazon", a copy of a
work by Cresilas (5th c. B.C.); the "Capitoline Venus", a Roman
copy of the Cnidian Aphrodite of Praxiteles; and two
Hellenistic works, "Amor and Psyche" and the "Drunken Old
Woman". Also of the greatest interest are the collections of 64
portrait heads of Roman Emperors and members of their
families and 79 busts of Greek and Roman philosophers and
scholars.

---

*Museo della Civiltà Romana (Museum of Roman Culture)

Situation
EUR, Piazza Giovanni Agnelli

Underground stations
EUR-Marconi or EUR-Fermi
(line B)

The Museum of Roman Culture, housed in a building
presented to the city of Rome by the Fiat company, seeks to
illustrate the history of Rome with the help of models and
reconstructions. It offers an excellent survey of the development of the Roman world empire and of the changing
architecture of Rome under the Republic and the Empire.
Opening times: Tues. and Thurs. 9 a.m.– 5 p.m., Wed, Fri, and
Sat. 9 a.m.–2 p.m., Sun. 9 a.m.– 1 p.m.

Museo Nazionale d'Arte Orientale   C4
(National Museum of Oriental Art)

Situation
Via Merulana 248

Buses
11, 16, 93, 93b, 93c

Opening times
9 a.m.–2 p.m., Sun. 9 a.m.–
1 p.m.

The National Museum of Oriental Art displays in its 14 rooms
the art of Asia from Persia to Japan, over the period from
prehistoric times (5th c. B.C.) to the present day. Afghanistan
and China, Korea and India, Nepal and Tibet, Iraq and Pakistan
are all represented by a wide range of gold jewellery and
bronzes, ceramics and clothing, sculpture and paintings, busts
and vases.

The museum is closed on Mondays.

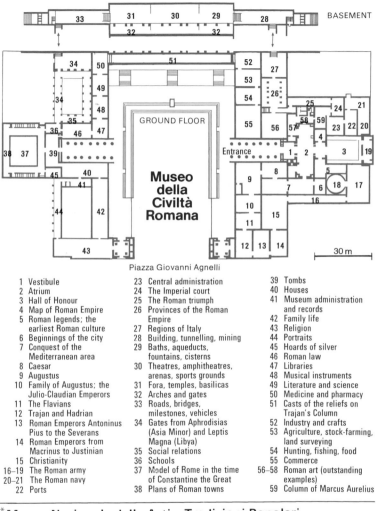

BASEMENT

GROUND FLOOR

Museo
della
Civiltà
Romana

Entrance

Museo Nazionale delle Arti e Tradizioni Popolari

30 m

Piazza Giovanni Agnelli

1 Vestibule	23 Central administration	39 Tombs
2 Atrium	24 The Imperial court	40 Houses
3 Hall of Honour	25 The Roman triumph	41 Museum administration
4 Map of Roman Empire	26 Provinces of the Roman	and records
5 Roman legends; the	Empire	42 Family life
earliest Roman culture	27 Regions of Italy	43 Religion
6 Beginnings of the city	28 Building, tunnelling, mining	44 Portraits
7 Conquest of the	29 Baths, aqueducts,	45 Hoards of silver
Mediterranean area	fountains, cisterns	46 Roman law
8 Caesar	30 Theatres, amphitheatres,	47 Libraries
9 Augustus	arenas, sports grounds	48 Musical instruments
10 Family of Augustus; the	31 Fora, temples, basilicas	49 Literature and science
Julio-Claudian Emperors	32 Arches and gates	50 Medicine and pharmacy
11 The Flavians	33 Roads, bridges,	51 Casts of the reliefs on
12 Trajan and Hadrian	milestones, vehicles	Trajan's Column
13 Roman Emperors Antoninus	34 Gates from Aphrodisias	52 Industry and crafts
Pius to the Severans	(Asia Minor) and Leptis	53 Agriculture, stock-farming,
14 Roman Emperors from	Magna (Libya)	land surveying
Macrinus to Justinian	35 Social relations	54 Hunting, fishing, food
15 Christianity	36 Schools	55 Commerce
16–19 The Roman army	37 Model of Rome in the time	56–58 Roman art (outstanding
20–21 The Roman navy	of Constantine the Great	examples)
22 Ports	38 Plans of Roman towns	59 Column of Marcus Aurelius

*Museo Nazionale delle Arti e Tradizioni Popolari

The National Museum of Folk Arts and Traditions has ten sections – an extension is planned – devoted to Italian folk art and the traditions and customs of the different parts of Italy, illustrated with displays of flags, costumes, musical instruments and models. The museum is at present closed. Normal opening times are 9 a.m.–2 p.m., public holidays 9 a.m.–1 p.m. Closed Mon.

Situation
EUR, Piazza Marconi 10

Underground stations
EUR-Marconi or EUR-Fermi (line B)

*Museo Nazionale Etrusco di Villa Giulia   B3
(National Etruscan Museum)

Situation
Piazzale de Villa Giulia

Bus
26

Trams
19, 30

Opening times
9 a.m.–2 p.m., Sun. 9 a.m.–
1 p.m.

Closed
Mon.

The Villa Giulia, built by Vignola for Pope Julius III in 1550–55, has housed the national collection of Etruscan art since 1889. The museum provides a comprehensive survey of the high standard of art and culture attained by this mysterious people, whose achievements the Romans deliberately obscured. Particularly notable are the finds from Etruscan cemeteries (cinerary urns, reconstruction of a tomb from Cerveteri), fine small sculpture and everyday utensils, statuary (in particular the Apollo of Veii) and the famous sarcophagus from Cerveteri (c. 530 B.C.) with the reclining figures of a husband and wife. The museum contains much else of interest – figures and figurines, grave goods and votive offerings, pottery, glass, gold and silver jewellery.

Museo Nazionale Romano o delle Terms

See Terme di Diocleziano

Museo di Roma (Museum of Rome), Palazzo Braschi   C2/3

Situation
Piazza San Pantaleo 10

Buses
46, 62, 64

Opening times
9 a.m.–2 p.m., Sun. 9 a.m.–
1 p.m., Tues. and Thurs. also
5–8 p.m.

Closed
Mon.

The Palazzo Braschi, built from 1792 onwards for the Braschi family, relatives of Pope Pius VI, has housed since 1952 a collection of pictures, drawings, watercolours and prints illustrating the history of the city of Rome, together with sculpture, terracotta figures, majolica, tapestries and costumes. The exhibits also include Pope Pius IX's private train (1850) and two state carriages. The museum's 51 rooms contain a wealth of material illustrating life in medieval and modern Rome and the history and development of the city.

Museo Torlonia   C2

Situation
Via Corsini 5

Buses
23, 28, 65

The Museo Torlonia is one of the largest private collections of antiquities in Europe, with some 600 pieces of sculpture. The collection was begun by Giovanni Raimondo Torlonia (1754–1928), a wealthy Roman, who acquired a number of private collections and added to them material found in excavations on his estates.
The museum can be seen by appointment only: apply to the Amministrazione Torlonia, Via della Conciliazione 30.

Obelisco de Axum (Obelisk of Axum)   C3/4

Underground station
Circo Massimo (line B)

The Obelisk of Axum, 24 m (80 ft) high, which stands in the Piazza di Porta Capena was brought from Axum, the holy city of Ethiopia, in 1937, during the Italian war of conquest in Abyssinia.

Oratorio dei Filippini   C2

Immediately to the left of the Chiesa Nuova (see entry) is the Oratory, a residential house of prayer of the Congregation of Oratorians founded by St Philip Neri. The house was built for the Oratorians – an order which was very popular in Rome – by Borromini (1637–50), and was designed as a place where they could live, work and pray in common. A notable feature of the building is the finely articulated façade, which contrasts with the adjoining church in height, form and colouring.

The Sala del Borromini, in the former Oratory, is now used as a concert hall. The Oratory also contains the Biblioteca Vallicelliana, the oldest library open to the public in Rome.

Situation
Piazza della Chiesa Nuova

Buses
46, 62, 64

Oratorio di San Giovanni in Oleo   D4

The Oratory of St John "in the Oil" is a small octagonal chapel built by Bramante at the beginning of the 16th c. on the remains of an earlier building and later embellished by Borromini. Here, according to legend, St John was thrown into boiling oil but emerged unharmed, thereafter being banished to Patmos.

If the Oratory is closed apply to the missionary college at No. 17.

Situation
Via di Porta San Sebastiano

Bus
118

*Ostia Antica

No site in the neighbourhood of Rome gives such a vivid and comprehensive impression of an ancient city as Ostia Antica, the excavated remains of Roman Ostia.

According to Roman legend it was here, at the mouth (*ostium*) of the Tiber, that Aeneas, forefather of the Latins, landed in Italy and King Martius established a settlement in the 7th c. B.C. Archaeological investigation has shown, however, that it was only about 335 B.C. that a little fishing and trading town grew up here on the banks of the Tiber and on the sea coast. This settlement flourished and developed along with Rome, and under the Empire became one of the busiest and most important Roman commercial and naval ports, with a population of some 10,000: a status which is clearly reflected in the extensive surviving remains.

In later centuries the town fell into oblivion, for a variety of reasons. The importance of Rome as a political and commercial centre showed a steady decline, with the division of the Empire in the reign of Constantine, the fall of the Western Empire in the 5th c. and the troubles of the medieval period; the Tiber deposited increasing quantities of silt around its mouth, so that the sea moved steadily farther away from Ostia; the area was plagued by malaria; and finally the construction of a canal at Fiumicino in 1613 deprived the town of its maritime trade.

Excavations carried out since the 19th c. have brought to light more than half the town's area of 66 ha (165 acres), revealing streets and dwelling-houses, theatres and administrative buildings, temples and barracks, shops and workshops, tombs and warehouses, baths and city gates, inns and hostels, sports

Railway
Rome–Ostia Lido
branch of Underground
line B
Station Ostia Antica

Opening times
9 a.m. to an hour before
sunset

Closed
Mon.

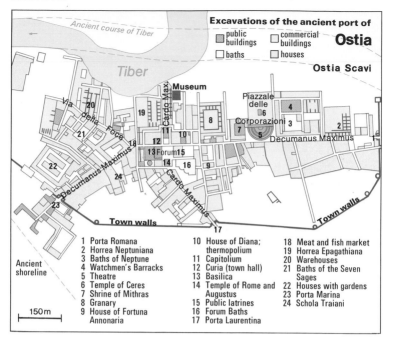

Excavations of the ancient port of Ostia

- public buildings
- commercial buildings
- baths
- houses

Ostia Scavi

Tiber

Ancient course of Tiber

Museum

Piazzale delle Corporazioni

Decumanus Maximus

Via della Foce

Decumanus Maximus

Cardo Maximus

Cardo Max.

Town walls

Town walls

Ancient shoreline

150m

1 Porta Romana
2 Horrea Neptuniana
3 Baths of Neptune
4 Watchmen's Barracks
5 Theatre
6 Temple of Ceres
7 Shrine of Mithras
8 Granary
9 House of Fortuna Annonaria
10 House of Diana; thermopolium
11 Capitolium
12 Curia (town hall)
13 Basilica
14 Temple of Rome and Augustus
15 Public latrines
16 Forum Baths
17 Porta Laurentina
18 Meat and fish market
19 Horrea Epagathiana
20 Warehouses
21 Baths of the Seven Sages
22 Houses with gardens
23 Porta Marina
24 Schola Traiani

facilities and port installations, statues and mosaics. The excavations have yielded not merely a series of unrelated remains but the layout of a complete urban organism, with its division into five wards or districts and its rectangular street plan.

It is possible to drive into the excavation site (Scavi) and leave your car in the car park. Alternatively you can start your tour on foot from the main entrance. In the latter event you follow the Via dei Sepolcri (Street of Tombs), pass through the Porta Romana and continue along the Decumanus Maximus (part of the Via Ostiense, the road from Rome) to the theatre, passing on the way the Piazzale della Vittoria (with a statue of Minerva Victoria, the goddess of victory), baths, warehouses (*horrea*) and dwelling-houses.

Even a brief tour should include at least the following:

First, the theatre. Built in the reign of Augustus, altered under Septimius Severus and Caracalla and restored some years ago, it can accommodate an audience of some 2700. Performances are given here during the summer. From the auditorium there is a view of the Piazzale delle Corporazioni behind the theatre, with the offices of 70 business firms and shipping agents, their business and place of origin being indicated by mosaics on the floor. In the centre of the square is the Temple of Ceres. To the right can be seen the Caserma dei Vigili (Watchmen's Barracks), a palaestra (a sports and athletic ground) and the Baths of Neptune. On the opposite side of the Decumanus

Ostia Antica: the Great Baths

A fish merchant's shop

Maximus are the Warehouses of Hortensius and beyond these an area which has not yet been excavated.

Beyond the theatre are the handsome House of Apuleius (Casa di Apuleio) and a mithraeum (shrine of Mithras), and on the opposite side of the main street the Collegium Augustale and the House of Fortuna Annonaria, amid a closely packed complex of dwelling-houses. From here continue S to the temple of the Magna Mater (Cybele) and return to the main street, passing on the way the Forum Baths, the Temple of Rome and Augustus and the Casa dei Triclini. In the Forum, adjoining the Temple of Rome and Augustus, is the Basilica, and at the far end of the Forum, dominating the scene, is the Curia.

The tour of the site can be extended to take in the Tempio Rotondo, the Scuola di Traiano, the Piazzale della Bone Dea, the Casa a Giardino (dwelling-houses, gardens and arcades), the Baths of Mithras, temples of the republican period, the House of Amor and Psyche, the Little Market, the Casa dei Dipinti and the Casa di Diana.

There is also an interesting museum containing finds from the site.

Palatino (Palatine Hill)

C3

The Palatine occupies a leading place among the seven hills of Rome. It is associated with the legend of the foundation of the city, and has yielded evidence of the earliest settlement in this area, strategically situated 50 m (165 ft) above the Tiber, near

Underground station
Colosseo (line B)

Palatino

The Palatine

Buses
11, 15, 27, 85, 87, 88, 90,
90b, 118, 673

Trams
13, 30

Opening times
Summer 9 a.m.–6 p.m.,
winter 9 a.m.–3 p.m.
Sun. 9 a.m.–1 p.m.

Closed
Tues.

the Isola Tiberina. Under the Empire palaces (the very word
"palace" comes from the Palatine) were built here by the
Emperors and great aristocratic families of Rome; and although
the remains of these buildings give only a very inadequate
impression of their former magnificence, a walk over the
Palatine nevertheless takes us into the heart of Roman history.
History
Politicians such as Agrippa, the great art patron, and writers
including Cicero had houses on the Palatine. Augustus, who
was born here, enlarged his father's mansion, and under
Augustus and his successors a whole series of splendid
palaces, temples and public buildings were erected, reaching in
the reign of Domitian the form in which we see their remains
today. Since each generation carried out alterations and
rebuildings it is now difficult to disentangle the different
periods of construction.

During the Middle Ages the splendours of the Palatine fell into
eclipse. Numbers of convents and churches – the oratory of
Caesarius, Santa Anastasia, Santa Lucia, San Sebastiano –
were built over the remains of the pagan buildings, and the
noble Frangipane family used them to establish a fortified
stronghold. In the 16th c. wealthy families, including the
Ronconi, Mattei, Spada, Magnani and Barberini, laid out
gardens and vineyards on the hill, and Cardinal Alessandro
Farnese commissioned famous architects to give the Palatine
park its final form.

The Palatine began to attract archaeological interest in the 18th
c. The names of many buildings on the Palatine were known
from the works of Roman writers, but some buildings of major

importance could not be located on the ground, and even today have not been found. The Palatine was frequently ravaged by fire; and as a result of these and other vicissitudes in its history it is now reduced, like the Forum, to a great field of ruins – but highly impressive and evocative ruins. The most important and most interesting of the structures on the hill are described below.

Access

There are four routes of access to the Palatine. The first leads from Via San Gregorio Magno through the gateway designed by Vignola as the entrance to the Farnese Gardens. The other three start from the Forum (see Foro Romano): the Clivus Capitolinus, which leads past the Arch of Titus; the flight of steps at the House of the Vestals; and the large vaulted passage at Santa Maria Antiqua. (Plan, see Foro Romano.)

Criptoportico (Cryptoporticus)

To the N of the House of Livia are the remains of the Cryptoporticus, a semi-subterranean barrel-vaulted corridor 130 m (430 ft) long which linked the various Imperial palaces (the palaces of Tiberius, Livia and Flavians) with one another. Tradition has it that the Emperor Caligula was murdered by conspirators in this corridor in A.D. 41.

Tempio de Cibele (Temple of Cybele)

The Temple of Cybele (or of Magna Mater, the Great Mother) in the Farnese Gardens was built in 204 B.C. to house the "Black Stone" of the goddess, following guidance given by the Sibylline Books. Rock-cuttings found in front of the temple represent the earliest evidence of human settlement on the Palatine (9th–8th c. B.C.), a dwelling site of the early Iron Age which has been christened the "House of Romulus".

Casa di Livia (House of Livia)

The House of Livia (Augustus' wife) was part of the palace of Augustus and is so called because the inscription "Livia Augusta" was found on a lead pipe in one of the rooms. Augustus himself may have lived in these apartments.

Palazzo dei Flavi (Palace of the Flavians)

The ruins of the Palace of the Flavians lie in the centre of the Palatine hill. Built by an architect named Rabirius at the end of the 1st c. A.D. for the Emperor Domitian (a member of the Flavian dynasty), the Domus Flavia was designed to provide a setting for the increased splendour and display which the Emperors now demanded. The building undoubtedly met these enhanced requirements, with its large pillared courtyard (peristyle), the spacious dining-room (*triclinium*) to the S, the throne room (*aula regia*) to the N, a rectangular hall 30·5 by 38·7 m (100 by 127 ft) with an apse at one end, the shrine of the domestic gods (*lararium*) and a basilica which probably served as a law court.

Stadium near the Palace of the Flavians on the Palatine

Domus Augustana (House of Augustus)

The Domus Augustana seems to have been not so much the house of Augustus himself as the residence of the Imperial house (*augusta*). Although not yet fully excavated, this building of two and three storeys is still immensely impressive, with its monumental and yet harmonious dimensions. Built, like the Palace of the Flavians, in the reign of Domitian, it was at first the residence of successive Emperors but later, right down to Byzantine times, was occupied by high dignitaries of the Empire as their residence and place of work.

Orti Farnesiani (Farnese Gardens)

The Farnese Gardens were laid out in the 16th c. by Vignola for Cardinal Alessandro Farnese and were completed by Rainaldi. Like the gardens of the Villa d'Este at Tivoli (see entry), these gardens, with their terraces and pavilions, their lawns and flowerbeds, their groves of trees and fountains, were designed to provide a kind of stage-setting for gatherings of like-minded people.

The Arcadia literary academy met here in the 17th c., leaving a small nymphaeum as its memorial. The stucco decoration is of interest as well as the fountains themselves.

The remains of the palace of Tiberius lie under the gardens. Excavations – still very far from complete – have brought to light remains of an atrium.

Stadio Domiziano (Stadium of Domitian)

Among the main buildings erected by Domitian (A.D. 81–96) on the Palatine was his Stadium, a running track 160 m ,(525 ft) long and 47 m (155 ft) across. It is not known whether the public were admitted to the contests and displays in this stadium or whether it was reserved for the entertainment of the Emperor and his personal guests; indeed, it is not even certain whether it was actually used for sporting contests at all or whether it was merely designed as a garden in the form of a stadium.

According to tradition St Sebastian was martyred in this stadium.

Terme di Settimio Severo (Baths of Septimius Severus)

The remains of these baths are the most imposing ruins on the Palatine. The piers and arches of the building were supported on massive substructures which have outlasted the centuries in massive bulk. Remains of the heating system can still be seen in some of the rooms and corridors.

From a rectangular terrace near the baths there is the finest view of Rome from the Palatine (particularly impressive at sunset), with the Colosseum (see Colosseo), the Baths of Caracalla (see Terme di Caracalla), the Caelian, the Aventine, the Janiculum and on the low ground below it the Circus Maximus (Circo Massimo), a huge structure which could accommodate 185,000 spectators.

*Palazzo Barberini and Galleria Nazionale d'Arte Antica   B4
(National Gallery of Ancient Art)

Pope Urban VIII (Maffeo Barberini), that great builder and art patron, was fortunate in having the two greatest architects of the Baroque period, Borromini and Bernini, available to work for him during his reign (1623–44). The bees which featured in the Barberini coat of arms are found on buildings all over Rome, and so many ancient buildings were destroyed to make room for these new creations that the epigram "Quod non fecerunt barbari, fecerunt Barberini" ("What the barbarians did not destroy was destroyed by the Barberini") became current in Rome.

The palace, rearing high above the Piazza Barberini (entrance in Via delle Quattro Fontane), was begun by Carlo Maderna, with the help of Borromini, in 1625 and completed by Bernini in 1633. The complex layout of rectangular and oval staircase halls, suites of rooms and state apartments can be more easily appreciated on a plan than on the ground. The central feature of the palace is the Salone, two storeys high, with a ceiling painting of the "Triumph of Divine Providence" by Pietro da Cortona (1632–9), mainly designed to glorify the Papacy and the Barberini family.

In the Palazzo Barberini, modelled on the palaces of northern Italy, the High Baroque found its fullest expression.

Situation
Via delle Quattro Fontane 13

Underground station
Barberini (line A)

Buses
60, 61, 62, 71, 415

Opening times
9 a.m.–2 p.m., Sun.
9 a.m.–1 p.m.

Closed
Mon.

Galleria Nazionale d'Arte Antica

The Palazzo Barberini now houses the Galleria Nazionale d'Arte Antica (National Gallery of Ancient Art). After the unification of Italy in 1870 the Italian state acquired many famous works of art by the expropriation of the Papal State, and also took over various private collections and acquired other works by gift and purchase, thus building up a great store of art treasures. Since the Second World War the National Gallery has acquired mainly works of the 13th–16th c. and also of the Baroque period.

Among the painters represented are Giovanni da Rimini, Simone Martini, Fra Angelico, Filippo Lippi (Madonna and Child), Piero della Francesca, Antoniazzo Romano, Pietro Perugino, Sodoma, Andrea del Sarto, Girolamo Sermoneta, Pietro da Cortona, Raphael ("La Fornarina", the portrait of a baker's daughter of Trastevere – though there is some controversy about this identification), El Greco (Adoration of the Shepherds, Nativity and Baptism of Christ), Jacopo and Domenico Tintoretto, Titian (Venus and Adonis), Hans Holbein (portrait of Henry VIII, perhaps a copy) and Caravaggio (Narcissus).

Palazzo Bonaparte   C3

Situation
Via del Corso

Buses
46, 56, 60, 62, 64, 65, 70, 71, 75, 81, 85, 88, 90, 95

The Palazzo Bonaparte – still bearing the name on the façade – stands at the end of the Corso nearest Piazza Venezia. In this 17th c. palace Napoleon's mother Letizia Ramorino lived until her death in 1836.

---

*Palazzo Borghese   B3

Situation
Piazza Borghese

Buses
26, 28, 70

Like other noble Roman families, the Borghese family, to which Pope Paul V (1605–21) belonged, had to have both a palace in the city and a summer or "weekend" residence in the country (see Villa Borghese). Cardinal Camillo Borghese accordingly bought a palace near the Tiber and, becoming Pope as Paul V, presented it to his brothers Orazio and Francesco. The palace, begun by the architect Martino Lunghi, was completed for the Borghese family by Flaminio Ponzo to a plan which earned it the name of "Cembalo" ("harpsichord"), with the "keyboard" towards the Tiber. The sumptuous appointments of the palace reflected all the magnificence of a Papal family. The courtyard with its double row of arcades, its ancient statues, its garlands, its figures of youths and putti is a haven of peace for the visitor coming in from the noise and bustle of the streets.

---

*Palazzo della Cancelleria (Papal Chancery)   C2

Situation
Piazza della Cancelleria

In the 15th c. the leadership of Italy in the fields of art and culture was at first held by Florence under the Medici. Rome

In the Palazzo Borghese

suffered during this period from the troubles in which the Papacy was involved (the Pope's exile at Avignon, the schism during which various Cardinals contested the Papal throne), and only gradually recovered its dominant position as the city of the Popes and the centre of Christendom during the second half of the century – in spite of a further setback when the Eastern churches broke away from Papal control in 1452.

The magnificent Palazzo della Cancelleria (originally the palace of Cardinal Riario, later the Papal Chancery and seat of the government of the Papal State) marked a major step in this development. It was built between 1483 and 1513, partly with blocks of travertine from the Colosseum (see Colosseo), for Cardinals Scarampo and Mezzarota and Raffaelle Riario (the latter of whom used on this project the 60,000 scudi he won in gaming from Franceschetto Cybo, nephew of Pope Innocent VIII). The architects were Andrea Bregno (Montecavallo) and Bramante. Fortune, however, turned against Cardinal Riario: having taken part in a conspiracy against Pope Leo X, he lost his property and the palace was confiscated. The external elevations of the palace are very characteristic of Renaissance architecture with their clear geometric lines and their uniformity of pattern; the stonework is plain and uncluttered, without superfluous ornament.

The most notable feature of the interior is the large Sala dei Cento Giorni (Hall of a Hundred Days), with paintings (1546) commissioned by Cardinal Alessandro Farnese and completed by Vasari and a team of assistants in a hundred days – leading Michelangelo to make the sarcastic remark, "You can see that."

Buses
46, 62, 64

Palazzo della Cancelleria (Papal Chancery)

The square inner courtyard, surrounded by three-storeyed ranges of rooms, is also notable for the clarity and regularity of its structure.

Palazzo Cenci   C3

Situation
Piazza Cenci

Buses
23, 26, 44, 56, 60, 65, 75,
170, 710, 718, 719, 774

The Palazzo Cenci was built in the 16th c. on the site of the ruined Circus Flaminius (221 B.C.). According to popular tradition Francesco Cenci embellished the palace chapel in 1575 to house the tombs of his children Giacomo and Beatrice, whom he had resolved to have killed; but it was the children who murdered their father and were beheaded for the murder on the Ponte Sant'Angelo in 1599. The story provided Shelley with the theme of his verse drama "The Cenci".

*Palazzo dei Conservatori   C3

Situation
Campidoglio

Underground station
Colosseo (line B)

The Palazzo dei Conservatori, built by Giacomo della Porta in 1564–75 to the design of Michelangelo, contains reception rooms used by the municipality of Rome on ceremonial occasions and also houses part of the Capitoline Museum (see Museo Capitolino). Notable exhibits in the museum include fragments of a colossal statue of the Emperor Constantine (in the courtyard); the Capitoline She-Wolf, an Etruscan work of

Palazzo dei Conservatori, Campidoglio

the 6th c. B.C. (the hindquarters were damaged by lightning in 65 B.C.; the figures of Romulus and Remus were added at the Renaissance); parts of the Fasti Consulares et Triumphales, a list of consuls and their victories; and the "Boy with a Thorn", a Hellenistic copy in bronze of a 5th c. original. One room in the palace, the Sala delle Oche, is named after the geese whòse cackling was said to have saved Rome from capture by the Gauls in 385 B.C. The palace also contains the Capitoline Picture Gallery (Pinacoteca Capitolina), with paintings by Titian, Tintoretto, Rubens, Van Dyck and Velázquez.

Buses
57, 85, 87, 88, 90, 90b, 92, 94, 95, 716, 718, 719

Opening times
Tues.–Sat. 9 a.m.–2 p.m., Sun. 9 a.m.–1 p.m., Tues. and Thurs. also 5–8 p.m., Sat. also 8.30–11 p.m.

Closed
Mon.

Palazzo Corsini   C2

The Palazzo Corsini was built in the 15th c. for Cardinal Domenico Riario, a nephew of Pope Sixtus IV. In the 17th c. it was occupied by Queen Christina of Sweden after her conversion to the Roman Catholic faith and her abdication, and here she brought artists and men of learning together in an academy which later became the famous Arcadia. After coming into the possession of the Corsini family the palace was completely rebuilt by Ferdinando Fuga (1723–36). It now houses part of the collections of the National Gallery of Ancient Art (the former Corsini Gallery), mainly European painting of the 17th and 18th c. Much of the Corsini collection is now in the main part of the National Gallery in the Palazzo Barberini (see entry).

Situation
Via della Lungara 10

Buses
23, 28, 28b, 65

*Palazzo Doria Pamphili (Galleria Doria Pamphili)   C3

Situation
Via del Corso
(entrance to Gallery at Piazza
del Collegio Romano 1A)

Buses
46, 56, 60, 62, 64, 65, 71,
75, 81, 85, 88, 90, 90b, 95,
170

Opening times
Tues., Fri., Sat. and Sun.
10 a.m.–1 p.m.

The Palazzo Doria, one of Rome's largest palaces, is bounded by the Corso, Via del Plebiscito, Via della Gatta, Piazzo del Collegio Romano and Via Lata, with the Palazzo Bonaparte (see entry) forming an enclave at the SE corner.
In the course of its three centuries of existence the palace, with its varied façades and courtyards, has been fashioned by a number of different architects and owned by different families – first the della Rovere, then the Aldobrandini and finally the Pamphili, from whom it descended to the Doria family.

Galleria Doria Pamphili

The Galleria Doria Pamphili contains a collection of pictures, mainly from the private collections of the Pamphili and Doria families. They include works by Titian, Tintoretto, Correggio, Raphael (?), Lippi, Lotto, Bordone, Caravaggio (including his masterly "Rest on the Flight into Egypt"), Velázquez (the famous portrait of Pope Innocent X Pamphili), Claude, Breughel, Domenichino and Solimena as well as some fine marble sculpture (including a bust of Innocent X by Bernini). Visitors are also shown the private and state apartments of the palace, with pictures and sculpture.

*Palazzo Farnese   C2

Situation
Piazza Farnese

Buses
23, 28, 28b, 46, 62, 64, 65

The effect of the Palazzo Farnese is enhanced by the fact that it can be viewed across an open square. In this palace, the handsomest of all the 16th c. Roman palaces, Renaissance architecture, which had begun in Rome with the Palazzo Venezia (see entry), reached its magnificent culmination.
Cardinal Alessandro Farnese, later Pope Paul III (1534–49), commissioned Antonio da Sangallo the Younger in 1515 to build the palace. After Sangallo's death it was continued by Michelangelo (from 1546) and completed by Giacomo della Porta in 1580. The palace later passed into the hands of the Bourbons of Naples, and it is now the French Embassy.
The exterior is of majestic effect with its massive structure of ashlar masonry and its restrained articulation, mainly based on simple geometrical forms. The façade, 46 m (150 ft) long, has three storeys of contrasting design which are almost completely dominated by the fenestration. These rows of windows with their different surrounds, the main entrance doorway and the central window on the first floor create a total harmony, so that nothing could be altered, added or taken away without reducing the perfection of the whole.
The side elevations repeat the structure of the main front, but the narrowness of the streets deprives them of their full effect. The rear façade faces the Tiber.
The interior courtyard follows ancient models in having Doric columns and pillars on the ground floor, Ionic on the first and Corinthian on the second. Stones from the Colosseum (see Colosseo) were used in the construction of the palace.

A notable feature of the interior of the palaces is the gallery on
the first floor, 20 m (65 ft) long and 6 m (20 ft) wide, with
frescoes ("The Triumph of Love in the Universe") by Annibale
Caracci (1597–1604).

Palazzo Laterano (Lateran Palace)   C4

The Lateran Palace was the residence of the Pope from the time
of Constantine until 1309, when Clement V was compelled to
transfer the seat of the Papacy to Avignon. After the Pope's
return from exile in France the Apostolic Palace in the Vatican
became the Papal residence.
The original palace dating from the time of Constantine was
destroyed on a number of occasions, and in 1558 it was
completely rebuilt by Sixtus V.
The palace is now occupied by the Roman diocesan
administration.

Situation
Piazza San Giovanni in
Laterano

Underground station
San Giovanni (line A)

Trams
16, 85, 87, 88, 93, 218, 650

Palazzo Massimo alle Colonne   C2/3

The Palazzo Massimo, a master work by Baldassare Peruzzi
built in 1532–6, lies between the Piazza Sant'Andrea della
Valle and Piazza Pantaleo. The residences of the Massimo
which had previously stood here were destroyed in 1527
during the famous Sack of Rome, the plundering of the city by
Charles V's troops.
The palace is a characteristic example of the Mannerist school
of architecture (between the Renaissance and Baroque),
which relieves the weight of the masonry by breaking up and
transforming the basic geometric forms and giving them an
elegant and playful effect.

Situation
Corso Vittorio Emanuele II

Buses
46, 62, 64

Palazzo Montecitorio

See Camera dei Deputati

*Palazzo Pallavicini-Rospigliosi   C3

This palace, on the way up to the Quirinal hill (Via XXIV
Maggio), was built by Vasanzio and Maderna in 1603 for
Cardinal Scipione Borghese and later enlarged for the French
statesman Cardinal Mazarin, who was of Italian origin. It now
belongs to the Pallavicini-Rospigliosi family and contains the
Pallavicini picture collection, which includes early works by
Rubens.
In the small garden is the Casino Pallavicini, the principal room
in which has a famous ceiling painting of Aurora by Guido
Reni.

Situation
Via XXIV Maggio

Buses
57, 64, 65, 70, 71, 75, 81,
170

Opening times
Casino
First day of month, 10 a.m.–
noon and 3–5 p.m.

83

Palazzo di Propaganda Fide B3

Situation
Piazza di Spagna

Underground station
Piazza di Spagna (line A)

Bus
115

Diagonally opposite the Palazzo di Spagna, now the Spanish Embassy to the Holy See (see Piazza di Spagna), is the Palazzo di Propaganda Fide, built for Popes Gregory XV and Urban VIII by Bernini and Borromini. This is the headquarters of the Congregation for the Propagation of the Faith, an organisation established in the 16th c. to promote the missionary activities of the Church. In front of the two palaces is an ancient column bearing a figure of the Virgin, the Column of the Immaculate Conception, around the base of which are the prophets Isaiah and Ezekiel, together with Moses and David. Every year on 8 December the Pope comes to the column to commemorate the proclamation of the dogma of the Immaculate Conception in 1854.

Palazzo del Quirinale C3

Situation
Piazza del Quirinale

Buses
57, 64, 65, 70, 71, 75, 81, 170

In Roman times the Quirinal hill, which had legendary associations with Romulus, was occupied by a residential district of the city with numerous handsome mansions. In the 16th c. Pope Gregory VIII selected this as the site of a Papal summer residence, which was begun in 1574 and later extended stage by stage (such famous architects as Fontana, Maderna and Bernini being involved in the work), until by the time of Pope Clement XII (1730–40) it formed a gigantic complex, with long ranges of buildings surrounded by gardens. From 1870 to 1946 the Quirinal was the official residence of the king; it is now occupied by the President of Italy.

Palazzo dei Senatori (Senatorial Palace) C3

Situation
Campidoglio

Underground station
Colosseo (line B)

Buses
57, 85, 87, 88, 90, 90b, 92, 94, 95, 716, 718, 719

The Palazzo dei Senatori, situated at the far end of the Piazza del Campidoglio (see entry), above the Forum, was built in the 16th c. on the remains of the Tabularium, the record office of ancient Rome, and is now the seat of the Mayor and Municipal Council of the city. The double staircase leading up to the entrance was designed by Michelangelo, who also set up here two ancient statues of the river gods of the Nile and Tiber. In the centre is a fountain with an ancient statue of Minerva, which was revered as an image of Rome. The handsome bell-tower, modelled on a medieval campanile, was erected in 1580.

Palazzo Spada (Galleria Spada) C2

Situation
Piazza Capo di Ferro

Buses
23, 28, 28b, 65

The Palazzo Spada was built by Giulio Mersi da Caravaggio in 1540–50 for Cardinal Girolamo Capo di Ferro. Later it passed into the hands of Cardinal Spada and was restored by Borromini. It is now the seat of the Italian Council of State, and also contains the Galleria Spada.
The most notable feature of the palace is the *trompe-l'œil* colonnade built by Borromini about 1635 to link two

Quirinal Palace, residence of the President of Italy

courtyards. In this passage with its twin rows of columns and coffered ceiling the apparent length is increased by a reduction in size of the structural elements from one end to the other.

The four-storeyed façade of the palace has elegant stucco decoration (by Giulio Mazzoni, 1556–60) and eight statues of famous Romans (from left to right Trajan, Pompey, Fabius Maximus, Romulus, Numa Pompilius, Marcellus, Caesar and Augustus). The rooms have rich stucco ornament, and in one room is a statue, said to be the statue of Pompey beside which Caesar was murdered.

Galleria Spada

This gallery consists mainly of the private collection of pictures assembled by Cardinal Bernardino Spada (1594–1661); they are displayed in rooms with graceful stucco decoration. Among the fine pictures to be seen here are portraits of Cardinal Spada by Guido Reni and Guercino, Andrea del Sarto's "Visitation", Titian's unfinished "Musician" and a "Landscape with Windmill" by Pieter Breughel.

Opening times
9 a.m.–2 p.m., Sun. 9 a.m.–1 p.m.

Closed
Mon.

* Palazzo Venezia   C3

The Palazzo Venezia, begun in 1451 by Cardinal Pietro Barbo, later Pope Paul II, continued under a number of architects and completed in 1491, stands next to the church of San Marco in

Situation
Piazza Venezia

Palazzo (Casa) Zuccari

Underground station
Colosseo (line B)

Buses
46, 57, 85, 87, 88, 90, 90b,
92, 94, 95, 716, 718, 719

Opening times
9 a.m.–2 p.m., Sun. 9 a.m.–
1 p.m.

Closed
Mon.

the Piazza Venezia (see entry), one of the busiest traffic intersections in the world. The palace is now occupied by the Palazzo Venezia Museum and the National Institute of Archaeology and Art History, and is also frequently used for temporary art exhibitions.

This elegant and harmoniously proportioned palace belonged between 1594 and 1797 to the Republic of Venice – hence its name – and then became the Austrian Embassy. During the Fascist period it was the official residence of Mussolini, who used to deliver his rhetorical speeches from the central balcony. Adjoining the Palazzo Venezia, with its massive façade and tower, is the smaller Palazzetto Venezia, which was moved to its present site when the National Monument to Victor Emmanuel II (see Monumento Nazionale a Vittorio Emanuele II) was built.

The Palazzo Venezia Museum (not all open to the public at present) contains a varied collection – wood and marble sculpture, weapons and textiles, tapestries and pictures, busts and terracotta models, applied arts and printed books, a map of the world in the Sala del Mappamondo, porcelain and glass – from many different periods, nations and cultures.

Palazzo (Casa) Zuccari B3

Situation
Via Gregoriana

Underground station
Piazza di Spagna (line A)

Bus
115

The Palazzo or Casa Zuccari, built by the painter Federico Zuccari about 1600 as a residence and studio, stands at the E end of Piazza Trinità dei Monti, between Via Sistina and Via Gregoriana. It was later occupied by the widowed Queen Maria Kasimira of Poland and is now the seat of the Biblioteca Hertziana, an institute of art history attached to the German Max-Planck-Gesellschaft. The doorway and windows of the palace (Via Gregoriana 30) are formed by the jaws of monsters.

**Pantheon C3

Situation
Piazza della Rotonda

Buses
26, 87, 94

Opening times
9 a.m.–1 p.m., 2–5 p.m.
Sun. 9 a.m.–1 p.m.

The architectural form of the Pantheon, the largest and best preserved monument of Roman antiquity, is so simple that the structure has survived the hazards of the centuries almost intact. The name of its builder is inscribed above the entrance: Marcus Agrippa, son-in-law of the Emperor Augustus, who dedicated it to the "most holy" (Greek *pantheon*) planetary gods – hence the dome, representing the firmament, with its opening for the sun – and not to all the gods as the name seems to imply. The Pantheon is the place of burial of the Italian kings (Victor Emmanuel II, second niche on right; Umberto I, second niche on left); the greatest Cardinal Secretary of State of modern times, Consalvi (tomb by Thorvaldsen, 1824, third niche on left) and the great Renaissance painter Raphael (between second and third niches on left) are also buried here. The Pantheon was damaged by fire in A.D. 80 and was rebuilt in the reign of Hadrian (120–125); the brickwork of this period

The Pantheon ▶

demonstrates the extraordinarily high standard of technical mastery achieved by the Romans. In the course of the centuries the building suffered further damage and plundering: Pope Gregory III removed the gilded bronze roof-tiles, while Urban VIII used the heavy bronze roofing of the porch in the construction of Bernini's Confessio in St Peter's (see San Pietro in Vaticano). The building was, however, regularly restored, and also received some structural additions, since removed.

The first Christian Emperors forbade the use of this pagan temple for worship, and it remained disused until Pope Boniface IV dedicated it to the Virgin and all the Christian martyrs on 1 November 609 – the origin of the feast of All Saints.

From the Piazza della Rotonda, from which the Pantheon is seen hemmed in by buildings and the semicircular dome appears much flatter than it really is, steps lead down into the porch: formerly there were steps up to the entrance, but the ground level has risen considerably since then. The porch, 33 m (108 ft) wide and 13·50 m (44 ft) high, has 16 granite columns

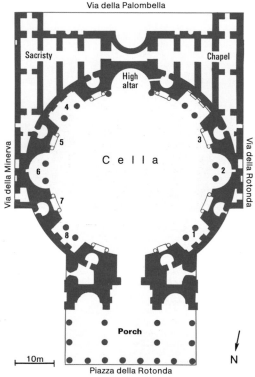

Via della Palombella

Sacristy

Chapel

High altar

4

5

C e l l a

3

Via della Minerva

6

2

7

8

1

Porch

10m

N

Piazza della Rotonda

Pantheon
St Maria ad Martyres

1 "Annunciation", a fresco by Melozzo da Forlì (15th c.)
2 Tomb of Victor Emmanuel II, first king of Italy (1820–78)
3 "St Anne and the Virgin", sculpture by Lorenzo Ottoni (?: 17th c.)
4 Monument to the Papal diplomat Cardinal Ercole Consalvi (1757–1824: tomb in San Marcello)
5 Tomb of Raphael (Raffaello Santi or Sanzio, 1483–1520)
6 Tomb of Umberto I, second king of Italy (1844–1900: assassinated at Monza); below it the tomb of Queen Margherita (d. 1926)
7 Tomb of Baldassare Peruzzi (1481–1536), architect and painter
8 On the altar "St Joseph with the Boy Jesus" by Vincenzo de' Rossi; on either side the tombs of the painters Perin del Vaga (1501–47) and Taddeo Zuccari (1529–66) and the architect and sculptor Flaminio Vacca (1538–1605); on the walls "Joseph's Dream" and "Flight into Egypt", stucco reliefs by Carlo Monaldi (c. 1720)

with Corinthian capitals (12·50 m (41 ft) high, 4·50 m (15 ft) apart) and two massive ancient bronze doors.

The mighty dome of the Pantheon was the supreme achievement of Roman interior architecture. The overwhelming effect of the interior results from the harmonious proportions of the whole vast structure: the height is the same as the diameter (43·20 m – 142 ft), while the walls of the cylinder supporting the dome measure half the diameter (21·60 m – 71 ft). In the walls of the cylinder (6·20 m (20 ft) thick) are semicircular and rectangular niches. The interior of the dome is coffered. The only lighting for the interior comes from a circular opening, 9 m (30 ft) wide, in the dome.

The restrained decoration of the interior enhances the effect of the architecture. The harmony and perfect proportions of the Pantheon – built in the image of the earth with the vault of the firmament above it – have impressed artists and visitors down the centuries. (The magnificent acoustics will be demonstrated for a small consideration.)

*Passeggiata del Gianicolo   C2

The Passeggiata del Gianicolo, lined with busts of Italian patriots, extends along the Janiculum from the Porta San Pancrazio to the Piazza della Rovere (near the Vatican), offering magnificent views of the whole of central Rome and the outlying districts, extending to the surrounding hills.

Bus
41

In Piazza Garibaldi is a monumental equestrian statue of Giuseppe Garibaldi, one of the great figures of the fight for Italian unity in the 19th c. Every day on the stroke of noon an Austrian cannon in this square fires a shot which resounds far over the city to announce the time. The terraces around the square offer what is perhaps the finest panoramic view of Rome.

A little way N is a statue of Garibaldi's wife Anita, her hair streaming in the wind.

*Piazza Bocca della Verità   C3

The Piazza della Bocca della Verità occupies the site of the ancient Forum Boarium or cattle market, situated conveniently close to the Tiber, which provided a ready means for the disposal of refuse. From this square there is a view, scarcely to be equalled anywhere else in Rome, which takes in both ancient and Christian buildings: the church of Santa Maria in Cosmedin (see entry), a Romanesque building with a modestly proportioned porch and a graceful campanile; the Arch of Janus (see Arco di Giano) and beyond it the handsome church of San Giorgio in Velabro (see entry) and the Arco degli Argentari, the arch of the merchants and bankers; the church of San Giovanni Decollato (see entry); the Casa dei Crescenzi, the residence of the most powerful family in Rome during the early medieval period; and two ancient temples, the Tempio della Fortuna Virile and the Tempio di Vesta (see entries), with the Baroque Fountain of the Two Tritons.

Buses
15, 23, 57, 90, 92, 94, 95, 716

Piazza di Campo dei Fiori (Flower Market) C2

Buses
46, 62, 64

It is difficult to remember that this cheerful square, in which the flower market of Rome is held every morning, was a place of execution (rarely used though it might be) during the period of Papal rule. Here on 7 February 1600 Giordano Bruno, a monk found guilty of heresy by the Inquisition and condemned to death when he refused to recant, was burned at the stake. He is commemorated by a bronze statue, under which are medallions of other heretics condemned by the Church, including Erasmus, Wycliffe and Hus.

*Piazza Navona and Fontana dei Fiumi C2/3
(Fountain of the Four Rivers)

Buses
26, 46, 62, 64, 70, 81, 88, 90

The Piazza Navona is one of the most characteristic Baroque squares in Rome, constantly filled with crowds of visitors as well as Romans. The palaces and churches around the square still mark out the area of the stadium (240 m (790 ft) long, 65 m (215 ft) across) constructed here by Domitian. During the Middle Ages the arena was used for water festivals and horse races. It was rebuilt, with its magnificent series of palaces and churches (including Sant'Agnese – see entry) by Borromini during the Baroque period.

*Fontana dei Fiumi (Fountain of the Four Rivers)

There are three fountains in the square, the most notable being the Fontana dei Fiumi (1647–51), with which Bernini won the favour of Pope Innocent X. This is a masterly and spirited composition with a large basin from which emerges a rocky crag bearing an obelisk, surrounded by plants and animals. At the four corners are figures personifying the Nile, Ganges, Danube and Rio de la Plata – the rivers then believed to be the largest in the four known continents. Each figure is accompanied by appropriate flora and fauna.

According to a traditional Roman joke the Nile has his head veiled because the source of the river was not known, or alternatively – alluding to the bitter rivalry between the two famous architects, Bernini and Boromini – the Nile is covering his eyes to avoid seeing the structural defects in Borromini's church of Sant'Agnese (see entry), facing the fountain.

The other two fountains in the square, the Fontana del Moro in front of the Palazzo Pamphili and the Fontana del Nettuno with its figure of the sea god, cannot compare with the Fontana dei Fiumi in beauty and artistic quality.

Piazza del Popolo B3

Underground station
Flaminio (line A)

Before the demolition of the city walls visitors arriving in Rome from the N on the Via Cassia or Via Flaminia, two of the old Roman consular highways, received their first impression of the magnificence of the city when they passed through the

Fountain of the Four Rivers, Piazza Navona

Porta del Popolo into the Piazza del Popolo. On the E, under the Pincio hill (see entry), and on the W, above the Tiber, the square is enclosed by semicircular walls built by Giuseppe Valadier in 1809–20. The square was enlarged in the 16th c., during the reign of Pope Sixtus V, and the Via di Ripetta and Via del Babuino were laid out, radiating on either side of the Via del Corso. Some decades later the twin churches of Santa Maria dei Miracolo and Santa Maria in Monte Santo (see entries) were built flanking the end of the Corso. In the centre of the square is the Obelisco Flaminio, an Egyptian obelisk from the Circus Maximus, originally brought to Rome by Augustus. Beside the Porta del Popolo is the church of Santa Maria del Popolo (see entry).

Buses
2, 90, 90b, 115

---

*Piazza del Quirinale and Fontana dei Dioscuri   C3
(Dioscuri Fountain)

The square in front of the Quirinal Palace (see Palazzo del Quirinale), residence of the President of Italy, is one of the most beautiful in Rome, offering a panoramic view of the city extending W to St Peter's (see San Pietro in Vaticano). In the centre of the square is the famous Dioscuri Fountain, with the 14 m (46 ft) high obelisk which formerly stood at the entrance to the Mausoleum of Augustus and the 5·60 m (18 ft) high figures of the Dioscuri (Castor and Pollux as horse-tamers) from the nearby Baths of Constantine.
Opposite the Quirinal Palace is the sumptuously decorated Palazzo della Consulta, built by Ferdinando Fuga in 1734 for

Buses
57, 64, 65, 70, 71, 75, 170

Pope Clement XII to house the Papal court, the Tribunale della Sacra Consulta. The palace is now occupied by the Corte Costituzionale, the Italian supreme court.

Piazza San Giovanni in Laterano C4

Underground station
San Giovanni (line A)

Buses
16, 85, 87, 88, 93, 93b, 93c, 218, 650

The Piazza San Giovanni in Laterano, at the end of Via Merulana, is bounded by the Lateran Palace, the side entrance to the church of St John Lateran (see San Giovanni in Laterano) and the baptistery of San Giovanni in Fonte (see entry). It is dominated by an Egyptian obelisk, the tallest (31 m (102 ft) high, or 47 m (154 ft) including the base) and also the oldest in Rome. It was brought from Thebes to Rome in a specially constructed ship in A.D. 357 and set up in the Circus Maximus. In 1587, during the reign of Sixtus V, it was transferred to its present site, and the equestrian statue of Marcus Aurelius which stood here was moved to the Capitol (see Campidoglio).

*Piazza di Spagna and Scalinata della Trinità dei Monti B3
(Spanish Steps)

Underground station
Piazza di Spagna (line A)

Bus
115

The Piazza di Spagna, a large irregularly shaped square named after the Spanish Embassy to the Holy See which was established here in the 17th c., is one of Rome's most typical squares and a special attraction for every visitor.

Spanish Steps

The feature which first catches the tourist's eye is the elegant Scalinata della Trinità dei Monti or Spanish Steps, constructed by Francesco de Sanctis in 1723–5 in a bewildering pattern of steps and landings, now wider and now narrower, now turning this way and now that, with a terrace on which to rest and enjoy the view half-way up. The steps were paid for by the French ambassador, Gueffier: hence the fleurs-de-lis which can be seen here and there.

Trinità dei Monti

At the top of the steps is the French church of the Trinità dei Monti, begun by Louis XII in 1502 and consecrated by Pope Sixtus V in 1585. It was restored after the Napoleonic occupation of Rome. The interior still preserves some of the original Gothic arches and contains an "Entombment" by Daniele da Volterra.

Via del Babuino

The Via del Babuino, from the Piazza di Spagna to the Piazza del Popolo, is a busy street with many art galleries and antique shops. Parallel to it, below the slopes of the Pincio, is the Via Margutta, the haunt of artists and intellectuals.

Via Condotti

From the Piazza di Spagna the Via Condotti leads SW to the Corso. This is Rome's most fashionable shopping street, with the famous Caffè Greco, long frequented by artists, writers and musicians. Among its patrons have been Goethe, Gogol, Schopenhauer, Mendelssohn, Berlioz, Wagner and Liszt.

The Spanish Steps ▶

*Barcaccia Fountain

The fountain at the foot of the Spanish Steps, in the shape of a boat, is known as the "Barcaccia". It is said that Pietro Bernini, Gian Lorenzo's father, who created the fountain in 1627–9, got the idea when the Tiber overflowed its banks and a boat was stranded in the square.

Piazza Venezia   C3

Buses
46, 56, 57, 60, 62, 64, 65, 70, 71, 75, 81, 85, 87, 88, 90, 90b, 92, 94, 95, 170, 716, 718, 719

The Piazza Venezia is one of the busiest traffic intersections in Europe, at the meeting of five roads – the Via del Corso, the main street of the city, running NW to the Piazza del Popolo; Via del Plebiscito, running SW to St Peter's (see San Pietro in Vaticano); the Piazza Aracoeli, leading to the Capitol (see Campidoglio); the Via dei Fori Imperiali, running SE to the Imperial fora (see Foro di Traiano, Foro di Cesare, Foro di Augusto, Foro di Nerva, Foro di Vespasiano), The Forum Romanum (see Foro Romano) and Colosseum (see Colosseo); and Via Battista, climbing to the Quirinal.

The square is dominated by the Palazzo Venezia (see entry) and the church of San Marco, an early 20th c. office building similar in proportions to the Palazzo Venezia and the National Monument to Victor Emmanuel II (see Monumento Nazionale a Vittorio Emanuele II).

*Pincio Gardens   B3

Underground station
Flaminio (line A)

Buses
1, 2b, 90b, 95, 115, 202, 203, 205, 490, 492, 495

The Pincio Gardens, lying above the Piazza del Popolo below the grounds of the Villa Medici (see entries), were laid out at the beginning of the 19th c. by the architect Giuseppe Valadier, in an area occupied by gardens belonging to old Roman families, including the Pinci after whom they are named.

The paths in the gardens are lined with busts of Italian patriots. The views from the terraces, looking down on the Piazza del Popolo and across the whole of central Rome to St Peter's (see San Pietro in Vaticano), are among the finest in the city, particularly at sunset.

Piramide di Caio Cestio (Pyramid of Cestius)   D3

Situation
Piazza di Porta San Paolo/ Piazza Ostiense

Buses
11, 23, 27, 57, 94, 95, 318, 673, 716

Trams
13, 30, 30b

The Pyramid of Cestius, more steeply pitched than the Egyptian pyramids on which it was modelled, was built in 12–11 B.C. as the tomb of Caius Cestius, who had been praetor, tribune of the people and one of the Septemviri Epulones (the committee of seven which organised religious festival banquets). It was later incorporated, together with the Porta San Paolo (the ancient Porta Ostiense), in the Aurelian Walls.

The pyramid, 22 m (72 ft) square and 27 m (89 ft) high, is faced with Carrara marble and was built, as the inscription records, within the space of 330 days. The tip of the pyramid is said to have originally been gilded. It contains a tomb chamber measuring 6 by 4 m (20 by 13 ft).

Pyramid of Cestius

Ponte Milvio

*Ponte Milvio (Ponte Molle, Milvian Bridge)

Buses
1, 32, 201, 202, 203, 204, 205, 220, 301, 391, 446, 911

This bridge, to the N of the city in a direct line from the Forum (see Foro Romano) and the Piazza del Popolo (see entry) by way of the Via Flaminia, was originally constructed over the Tiber during the republican period. Four of the piers are ancient.

The Ponte Milvio was the scene of the fateful battle on 28 October A.D. 312 in which Constantine defeated his fellow Caesar Maxentius. Attributing his victory to the God of the Christians, Constantine showed his gratitude by granting them freedom of worship.

*Ponte Sant'Angelo   B2

Buses
23, 28, 28b, 34, 41, 42, 46, 46b, 62, 64

The Ponte Sant'Angelo, the finest of Rome's bridges, was built by Hadrian in A.D. 136 to give access to his Mausoleum (see Castel Sant'Angelo) and was known as the Pons Aelius after one of the Emperor's forenames. The figures of angels which now line the bridge were carved by pupils of Bernini to his design (1660–7).

Porta Maggiore   C5

Situation
Piazza di Porta Maggiore

Buses
152, 153, 154, 155, 156, 157

Trams
13, 14, 19, 19b, 30, 30b, 516, 517

The Porta Maggiore, now surrounded by the swirl of modern traffic, was one of the most imposing structures in ancient Rome. It was built by the Emperor Claudius in A.D. 52 at the point where two important roads, the Via Praenestina (the road to Praeneste, present-day Palestrina) and the Via Casalina (the road to Labici), left the city, passing under two aqueducts, the Aqua Claudia and the Anio Novus (the River Aniene). They were later incorporated in the Aurelian Walls.

Adjoining the gate is the tomb of a Roman master baker, Virgilius Eurysaces, and his wife.

Porta Pia   B4

Situation
Piazza di Porta Pia

Buses
36, 37, 60, 61, 62, 63, 65, 136, 137, 490, 495

The Porta Pia, a town gate in the Aurelian Walls (see Mura Aureliane) near the ancient Porta Nomentana, was built by Michelangelo for the Medici Pope Pius IV in 1561–4. Near here on 20 September 1870 Italian troops entered the Papal city, an event which heralded the end of the Pope's temporal authority in the Papal State.

Porta San Sebastiano (formerly Porta Appia)   D4

Situation
Via Appia Antica

Bus
118

This gate in the Aurelian Walls was refortified at the end of the 4th c. A.D. in view of the increasing threat to Rome from the Germanic tribes, and was again renovated in the 6th c. by Belisarius and Narses. The Porta Appia, later renamed after the church of San Sebastiano outside the city on the Via Appia (see entry), was the principal entrance to the ancient city.

The so-called Arch of Drusus (Arco di Druso) inside the Porta

San Sebastiano probably dates from the time of Trajan; in the reign of Caracalla it was used to support an aqueduct.

Porta Tiburtina

The Porta Tiburtina, the city gate on the road to Tivoli (see entry), the Via Tiburtina, was originally built in the reign of Augustus as an arch supporting the Marcia, Tepula and Julia aqueducts. A gate flanked by towers was built in front of the arch in the reign of Honorius (beginning of 5th c.).

Situation
Via Tiburtina

Buses
11, 71

Portico di Ottavia (Portico of Octavia)   C3

The Portico of Octavia was originally built by Quintus Metellus Macedonius in 149 B.C., renovated by Augustus in 27 B.C., and dedicated to his sister Octavia, whose name it now bears; it was later rebuilt by Septimius Severus and Caracalla. It is now represented by a number of columns and remains of the entablature, which are incorporated in the porch of the church of Sant'Angelo in Peschiera. The portico, adjoining the Theatre of Marcellus (see Teatro di Marcello), originally covered an area 115 by 135 m (375 by 445 ft) in extent and contained numerous pieces of Greek and Roman sculpture.

Situation
Via del Progresso

Buses
15, 23, 57, 90, 90b, 92, 94, 95, 716, 774

San Bernardo alle Terme (church)

See Terme di Diocleziano

San Carlo ai Catinari (church)   C3

St Charles Borromeo, to whom this church is dedicated, was born at Arona in 1538. In 1560 he was made Cardinal Archbishop of Milan by his uncle Pope Pius IV. He died in 1584 and was canonised in 1610. Soon after his canonisation this church, built by Rosato Rosati, was dedicated to him by the Barnabite order. |
San Carlo ai Catinari (named after the manufacturers of wash-tubs, *catinari*, whose workshops were near here) has an imposing travertine façade and a very fine interior.

Situation
Piazza Benedetto Cairoli

Buses
26, 44, 46, 56, 60, 65, 75, 87, 94, 170, 710, 718, 719

San Carlo al Corso (church)   B3

Although officially dedicated to St Ambrose and St Charles Borromeo, both bishops of Milan, this church is always known simply as San Carlo al Corso.
This "national church" of the Lombards was given its present form by Onorio and Martino Lunghi, together with Pietro da Cortona and Carlo Fontana, in the 17th c. Its most impressive feature is the dome, whether this is seen from within the church (which has a 72 m (236 ft) long nave)' or from outside in a general prospect of central Rome, above which it rears up in imposing bulk.

Situation
Via del Corso

Buses
2, 26, 81, 90, 90b, 115, 911, 913

San Carlo alle Quattro Fontane (church)   C3

Situation
Via del Quirinale

Buses
57, 64, 65, 70, 71, 75, 170

This masterpiece by Borromini, situated at the intersection of Via del Quirinale and Via delle Quattro Fontane, is only a short distance away from a masterpiece by Bernini (see Sant'Andrea al Quirinale). It is named after the four Baroque fountains at the intersection, with reclining figures representing respectively the Tiber, the River Aniene, Fidelity and Valour.

Borromini began building this church, his first church in Rome, in 1638. Its total area is no greater than one of the piers at the crossing in St Peter's (see San Pietro in Vaticano). The building shows a lively interplay of convex and concave lines with no attempt at regular form. "Harmony and divergence, symmetry and assymmetry, passion and serenity blend here into an inexhaustible play of forms" (Anton Henze).

The façade of the church is strongly articulated. In the interior, an elongated oval, the richness of the decoration largely conceals the basic architectural structure.

Borromini died in 1667, shortly before the church was completed.

*San Clemente (church)   C4

Situation
Via San Giovanni in Laterano

Buses
85, 88

San Clemente is one of the most venerable and beautiful of Rome's churches.

On a site previously occupied by a house containing a shrine of Mithras – now far below street level – an early Christian church was built at some time before A.D. 385 and dedicated to St Clement, third bishop of Rome after Peter. After the destruction of this church by the Normans in 1084 a new basilican church was built over its ruins at the beginning of the 12th c.

The upper church reflects the old basilican structure with its sequence of entrance porch, atrium with a fountain, the nave where the congregation worshipped and the area reserved for the clergy (the *schola cantorum*), with the high altar and the apse. Notable features of the interior are the ancient columns and the intarsia work by the Cosmati family in the marble pavement, the screens, the Easter candlestick, the tabernacle and the bishop's throne. The triumphal arch and apse are decorated with mosaics of Old and New Testament scenes, the most richly decorated in Rome, with the Tree of Life and the Cross, saints and symbolic devices, animals and plants combined in intricate patterns.

In the little St Catherine's Chapel at the W end of the N aisle are early Renaissance frescoes by Masolino (before 1431) depicting scenes from the life of St Catherine of Alexandria, of particular importance as showing the earliest use of perspective painting in Rome.

The lower church, a three-aisled pillared basilica of the 4th c., has frescoes dating from different centuries in the Romanesque period. Notable among them are an Ascension in the central aisle, in which the donor, Pope Leo IV, is shown with a square nimbus, indicating that he was still alive; episodes from the Passion; and scenes from the life of St Clement.

San Carlo alle Quattro Fontane   *San Giorgio in Velabro*

San Crisogono (church)   C3

The church of San Crisogono, situated at the end of the Viale
di Trastevere nearest the Tiber, was originally built at some time
before 499 in honour of St Chrysogonus, martyred in the reign
of Diocletian, and rebuilt in 1129. Situated in the busy Piazza
Sonnino, the church attracts large numbers of worshippers.
The two porphyry columns of the triumphal arch are the largest
in Rome.

Situation
Viale di Trastevere/Piaza
Sonnino

Buses
26, 44, 56, 60, 75, 170, 710,
718, 719

San Francesco a Ripa (church)   C3

The present church of San Francesco a Ripa was built in 1231,
replacing an earlier chapel belonging to the pilgrim hospice of
San Biagio, in which St Francis was said to have stayed when
visiting Rome. The church was rebuilt by Mattia de' Rossi in
1682–89. In the fourth chapel in the N aisle is a famous statue
of the Blessed Ludovica Albertoni, a major late work by Bernini
(1674).

Situation
Piazza San Francesco a Ripa

Buses
23, 26, 28, 97, 170, 718,
719

Trams
13, 30

San Giorgio in Velabro (church) and Arco degli Argentari   C3

The name Velabro refers to the marshy area on the banks of
the Tiber where according to Roman legend Faustulus found

Situation
Via del Velabro

99

Buses
15, 23, 57, 90, 90b, 92, 94, 95, 716, 774

the twins Romulus and Remus. The first church on the site was built by Leo II (682–683), the second by Gregory IV (827–844); the campanile and porch were added in the 12th c. The present church, a handsome Romanesque building incorporating ancient elements (columns and capitals), stands near the Arch of Janus (see Arco di Giano). It is a popular wedding church.

Adjoining the church is the Arco degli Argentari (Arch of the Money-changers), erected in honour of Septimius Severus, his wife Julia Domna and their sons Caracalla and Geta, by merchants and bankers of the Forum Boarium and later incorporated in the church of San Giorgio. It has reliefs, some of them remarkably well preserved, depicting the Imperial family attending a sacrifice and barbarian prisoners. Some of the names in the original dedication were later erased.

San Giovanni Decollato (Church of the Beheading of St John)   C3

Situation
Via di San Giovanni Decollato

Buses
15, 57, 90, 90b, 92, 94, 95, 716

There was in Papal Rome a "Fraternity of Mercy" (Confraternità della Misericordia), established in 1488 (of which Michelangelo was a member), which had undertaken responsibility for accompanying condemned prisoners to execution and had the right, once a year, to secure the pardon of a prisoner. This body erected the church of San Giovanni in honour of the beheading (decollation) of St John the Baptist; begun in 1535, the church was completed in 1555. The paintings in the church and in the oratory adjoining the cloisters depict scenes from the life of the saint as it is described in the Bible, with particular emphasis on his beheading.

San Giovanni dei Fiorentini (church)   C2

Situation
Via Giulia

Buses
23, 28, 28b, 41, 42, 46b, 62, 64, 65, 98, 98c, 881

Pope Leo X, a member of the Florentine ruling dynasty of the Medici, being desirous of providing a church for his fellow-countrymen in Rome, held an architectural competition in which both Michelangelo and Raphael took part. The competition was won, however, by Sansovino, who enlisted other architects in the building of the church – Sangallo, Michelangelo (in an advisory capacity), della Porta, Maderna and Alessandro Galilei, who was responsible for the façade. The church is impressive for its size, the exactly contrived spatial effect of the interior and the rich Baroque decoration and furnishings, including many fine paintings.

---

*San Giovanni in Fonte (bapstistery)   C4

Situation
Piazza San Giovanni in Laterano

Underground station
San Giovanni (line A)

Buses
16, 85, 87, 88, 93, 218, 650

The baptistery of St John was built by Constantine on the site of a Roman nymphaeum in the Lateran Palace. This octagonal building, the oldest baptistery in Christendom, provided a model for later baptisteries.

The doors of the chapel of St John the Baptist emit a ringing sound when they are open or shut.

*San Giovanni in Laterano (Basilica of St John Lateran)   C4

The inscription on the façade of St John Lateran claims the status of "Mater et caput omnium ecclesiarum urbis et orbis" ("Mother and head of all the churches of the City and the world").

A beginning was made A.D. 313 with the building of a large church dedicated to the Saviour on the ruins of the palace of the Laterani and of a barracks. This was accordingly the first of the four "patriarchal" basilicas – the others being St Peter's (see San Pietro in Vaticano), San Paolo fuori le Mura and Santa Maria Maggiore (see entries) – and the most venerable of the seven pilgrimage churches of Rome (the four patriarchal churches, together with Santa Croce in Gerusalemme, San Sebastiano and San Lorenzo fuori le Mura – see entries). This status was confirmed by the holding of general councils of the Church in St John Lateran in 1123, 1139, 1179, 1215 and 1512.

Before the Popes established their residence in the Apostolic Palace in the Vatican after their return from exile in Avignon they lived mainly in the Lateran; and St John Lateran has remained the episcopal church of the Pope. Various additions and alterations were carried out in the 5th, 8th, 10th, 13th and 15th c., and in the 16th and 17th c. the church was almost completely rebuilt. The W porch, the interior and the main façade were completely refashioned at this period. During medieval times the church was put under the patronage of St John the Baptist and St John the Evangelist.

The basilican plan of the church, with its porch, narthex, five-aisled apse, presbytery and apse, was established in the original Constantinian church and respected in the Baroque rebuilding. The wide façade with its huge statues by

Situation
Via Vittorio Emanuele Filiberto (main entrance); Piazza San Giovanni in Laterano (side entrance)

Underground station
San Giovanni (line A)

Buses
16, 85, 87, 88, 93, 218, 650, 673

Opening times
7 a.m.–6.30 p.m.

San Giovanni in Laterano

San Giovanni in Fonte

Coro

Chiostro

100 m

N

1 Bronze doors (Roman)
2 Holy Door
3 Statue of Constantine the Great
4 Frescoes by Giotto (Boniface VIII)
5 Orsini Chapel
6 Torlonia Chapel
7 Massimo Chapel
8 St John's Chapel
9 Papal altar
10 Tomb of Pope Martin V (crypt)
11 Baroque organ
12 Side door
13 Monument of Pope Leo XIII Entrance to Portico of Leo XIII
14 Choir chapel
15 Sacristies
16 Chapterhouse
17 St Hilary's Chapel. Entrance to cloister
18 Chapel of St Francis of Assisi (monument of 1927)
19 Santorio Chapel
20 Chapel of Assumption
21 Corsini Chapel
22 Baptistery

San Giovanni in Laterano

Interior view

Alessandro Galilei (*c.* 1735) is a masterpiece of late Baroque architecture. Note also the bronze doors of the main doorway, which came from the ancient Curia in the Forum, and the Holy Door (far right). The interior, 130 m (427 ft) long, was refashioned by Borromini on the occasion of Holy Year 1650, with massive piers along the nave and tall figures of Apostles (4·25 m (14 ft) high), by various sculptors, in the niches. The magnificent timber ceiling dates from the 16th c.

Above the Papal altar (Altare papale) is a tabernacle-like baldachin in which the heads of the Apostles Peter and Paul are preserved (shown by custodian: tip). Here, too, is a wooden altar at which the earliest Popes, Peter's immediate successors, are said to have officiated. In the Confessio at the foot of the altar is the bronze tomb of Pope Martin V (on which it is a Roman custom to throw a coin) – one of the numerous tombs of great persons, both ecclesiastical and lay, which the church contains.

In the apse (beyond the presbytery), which was widened by Pope Leo XIII (1878–84), are some very fine mosaics – faithful copies of early Christian originals, renewed by Torriti in the 13th c. – depicting Christ surrounded by angels and (below, on either side of a jewelled cross) various saints, including St Francis of Assisi and St Antony of Padua.

The valuable decoration and furnishings of the church have given it an air of rather cold magnificence.

The Cloister (Chiostro: entrance in left-hand aisle), a masterpiece of 13th c. architecture by a family of Roman artists, the Vassalletti, should not be missed.

San Giovanni a Porta Latina (church)   D4

This early Romanesque church lies hidden behind the ancient
city walls in Via di Porta Latina.
The basilica of "St John at the Latin Gate" was founded in the
5th c., rebuilt around 720 and restored in 1191, during the reign
of Pope Celestine III. It is in the familiar form of the Roman
basilica, 'with a portico supported by columns and a tall
campanile of classical type.
The church contains an important cycle of early 13th c.
frescoes depicting 46 Old and New Testament scenes which
are among the finest medieval frescoes in Rome.

Bus
118

San Girolamo (degli Illirici or degli Schiavoni)   B3

After the Turkish victory in the battle of Kosovo in 1387 many
refugees from Dalmatia and Albania fled to Rome, and this
church (built during the reigns of Sixtus IV and V and
completed in 1588) was thereafter known as the church "degli
Illirici" or "degli Schiavoni". It is now the Croatian national
church and has a priests' college attached to it.

Situation
Via Ripetta/Via Tomacelli

San Gregorio Magno (church)   C4

The church of San Gregorio, which is approached by a large
flight of steps, was founded in 575 – before he became Pope –
by Gregory the Great, a member of the Antitii family, who
converted his family house on this site into a convent. It was
rebuilt in the medieval period and completely refashioned in
the Baroque period on the model of the church of Sant'Ignazio,
though on a smaller scale. The atrium, the church itself, the
oratory and the three chapels of St Andrew, St Silvia and St
Barbara combine to form a unity of impressive effect.

Situation
Via de San Gregorio

Buses
11, 15, 27, 118, 673

Trams
13, 30, 30b

San Lorenzo in Lucina (church)   B3

The church of San Lorenzo in Lucina, dedicated to the martyr
St Lawrence, who is much venerated in Rome, has had an
eventful history. Originally built in the 4th and 5th c. over the
house of a Roman woman named Lucina, it was rebuilt in the
12th c. and received its present form in 1650.
On the high altar is a "Cruciform" by Guido Reni, one of his
finest works. The fourth chapel in the S aisle, the Fonseca
Chapel, was designed by Bernini.

Situation
Piazza di San Lorenzo in
Lucina

Buses
52, 53, 56, 58, 60, 61, 62,
71, 81, 88, 90, 95, 115

*San Lorenzo fuori le Mura (St Lawrence without the Walls)   B5

This early Christian basilica, one of the seven pilgrimage
churches of Rome, is dedicated to St Lawrence, who was

Situation
Piazza San Lorenzo

San Luigi dei Francesi

Buses
11, 71, 109, 111, 309, 311, 411, 415, 492

Trams
19, 19b, 30, 30b

Opening times
7 a.m.–noon, 3–6 p.m.

martyred in A.D. 238 by being roasted on a gridiron. (The other pilgrimage churches are San Giovanni in Laterano, San Pietro in Vaticano, San Paolo fuori le Mura, Santa Maria Maggiore, San Sebastiano and Santa Croce in Gerusalemme – see entries.) The church was founded by Constantine the Great and thereafter frequently rebuilt and restored – most recently after suffering damage in an Allied air raid on Rome in July 1943.

San Lorenzo, situated beside the Campo Verano, Rome's largest cemetery, has preserved through all rebuildings (particularly in the 13th c.) the structure of an early Christian basilica, with its porch (containing ancient sarcophagi), its wide, high nave with narrow lateral aisles, its chancel on a higher level and its handsome columns. Lower down, on the level of the first basilica, is the tomb of Pope Pius IX (1846–78). Particularly fine is the Cosmatesque work (coloured stones inlaid in marble) on the two marble ambos (pulpits for the reading of the Gospels and Epistles: the one on the epistle side, to the right, is the finest in Rome), the Easter candlestick, the floor, the tabernacle, the bishop's throne and the tomb of Cardinal Fieschi.

The mosaics on the triumphal arch depict Christ surrounded by saints, with elaborate representations, to left and right, of Jerusalem and Bethlehem.

There is a plain cloister dating from the late 12th c.

---

*San Luigi dei Francesi (church)   C3

Situation
Piazza di San Luigi dei Francesi

San Luigi dei Francesi, dedicated to St Louis (Louis IX of France), is the French national church in Rome. It was begun by Cardinal Giulio de' Medici, later Pope Clement VII, but work was then suspended and not resumed until 1580 (under the direction of Domenico Fontana). The church was dedicated in 1589.

The Renaissance façade was probably the work of Giacomo della Porta (c. 1540–1602). The church itself, a three-aisled pillared basilica, contains three major pictures (scenes from the life of St Matthew) by Caravaggio (c. 1597). Masterpieces of realistic painting, with Caravaggio's new composition of light and shade and striking chiaroscuro effects, they were not universally admired at the time.

---

*San Paolo fuori le Mura (St Paul without the Walls)

Situation
Piazzale San Paolo

Underground station
San Paolo (line B)

Buses
23, 123, 170, 223, 673, 707, 766

Opening times
7 a.m.–6 or 6.30 p.m.

Few remains have so far been found of the early Christian chapel built in the time of Constantine (4th c.) over the grave of St Paul, well outside the city on the road to Ostia; but it seems certain that Paul – who according to tradition was beheaded in A.D. 67 and buried by the Via Ostiensis – was venerated in early times at the site of the present church. In order to do honour to the Apostle the Emperors of the 4th and 5th c. built a basilica which until the rebuilding of St Peter's (see San Pietro in Vaticano) was the largest in the world. This church was damaged on various occasions by earthquake and fire, and finally was completely destroyed by fire, as a result of the

San Lorenzo fuori le Mura

San Paolo fuori le Mura

carelessness of a plumber, on 15 July 1823. Thereafter it was rebuilt, with financial assistance from many countries, and reopened in 1854. San Paolo is one of the four patriarchal churches of Rome (the others being St John Lateran, St Peter's and Santa Maria Maggiore) and one of the seven pilgrimage churches (the patriarchal churches together with Santa Croce in Gerusalemme, San Lorenzo fuori le Mura and San Sebastiano).

Following its 19th c. rebuilding San Paolo is notable particularly for its basilican plan, following the early Christian model, and for a number of fine works of art. The church is entered by way of a colonnaded forecourt which leads into the porch (19th c. mosaics high up on the façade), with the Holy Door, on the inner side of which can be seen the old bronze door, cast in Constantinople in the 11th c. The interior of the church is dark, since the alabaster windows admit little light. The nave (120 m (395 ft) long, 60 m (195 ft) wide, 23 m (75 ft) high) is divided into five aisles by a forest of 80 columns, leading up to the triumphal arch (5th c. mosaic), the altar with its ciborium and the apse (mosaics). The apse mosaic is a 19th c. copy of the destroyed 13th c. original. High up on the walls of the church are portrait medallions of all the Popes from Peter onwards.

Particular features which should not be missed are the ciborium (by Arnolfo di Cambio, 1285) over the Papal altar, which, like the altar in St Peter's, probably marks the spot where the Apostle was buried; a magnificent medieval Easter candlestick, 5 m (16 ft) high, to the right of the altar; the Chapel of the Crucifix and the baptistery.

San Pietro in Vincoli

In the sacristy is the entrance to the cloister of the Benedictine abbey, decorated with mosaics by the Vassalletti family (1204–41). The variety of form of the columns and the colour of the mosaics make this one of the most attractive cloisters in the West.

*San Pietro in Montorio (church) and Tempietto di Bramante   C2

The church of "St Peter on the Golden Mountain" (from the name of Mons Aureus or Monte d'Oro which was given in early times to the Janiculum), an early Renaissance building of the late 15th c., owes its foundation to the medieval legend – without historical foundation – that the Apostle Peter was crucified on this spot. The church was built for King Ferdinand IV of Spain by Baccio Pontelli (after 1481). The chapels on the left-hand side contain notable pictures ("Scourging of Christ" by Sebastiano del Piombo, 1519–25) and monuments.
In a court to the right of the church is the famous Tempietto di Bramante (a small round pillared temple), a chapel built in 1502 to commemorate the crucifixion of St Peter which is recognised as a classic example of High Renaissance architecture, demonstrating the characteristic return to antiquity and the revival of Greco-Roman architectural forms. The harmony of its proportions and symmetry of its forms make this little temple an architectural delight.

Situation
Via Garibaldi

Buses
41, 44, 75, 710

*San Pietro in Vincoli (St Peter in Chains)   C4

San Pietro in Vincoli is one of the oldest churches in Rome, having been begun in 431. It was originally dedicated to SS. Peter and Paul, but when Pope Leo the Great was presented with the chains which Peter was traditionally believed to have worn in the Mamertine Prison, St Peter became sole patron of the church; the chains are now preserved as a precious relic in the high altar. The church has been considerably altered by later additions. Its most notable features are the 20 columns with Doric capitals in the nave; the tomb of Cardinal Nicholas of Cusa (Kues on the Mosel, Germany: d. 1465) in the N aisle; and above all the monument of Pope Julius II in the S transept. This monument to the great Pope of the della Rovere family (1503–13) was originally conceived by Michelangelo on a larger scale for erection in St Peter's. Of the sculpture originally planned Michelangelo himself executed only three figures – the central figure of Moses, together with Rachel and Leah, the two wives of Jacob. The statues of Rachel and Leah, symbols of the active and the contemplative life, are late works of outstanding quality; but the figure of Moses (1513–16), designed also to celebrate the great Pope and Prince of the Renaissance, ranks among the finest achievements in the sculpture of the world. Moses is depicted at the moment when he has received from God the tables of the Law, which he holds under his right arm, and is watching his people dancing round the golden calf, his face reflecting both divine illumination and wrath over the faithlessness of his people. (The horns on his forehead reflect a mistranslation of the Biblical text.)

Situation
Piazza San Pietro in Vincoli

Underground station
Cavour (line B)

Buses
11, 27, 81

Opening times
7 a.m.–1 p.m., 2.30–5.30 p.m.

San Sebastiano (church)

Situation
Via Appia Antica

Bus
118

Opening times
8.30 a.m.–noon, 2.30–5 p.m.

The church of St Sebastian on the Via Appia is one of the seven pilgrimage churches of Rome (the others being San Giovanni in Laterano, San Pietro in Vaticano, San Paolo fuori le Mura, Santa Maria Maggiore, Santa Croce in Gerusalemme and San Lorenzo fuori le Mura – see entries), built in the 4th c. on the site of old cemeteries and catacombs. According to tradition the remains of the Apostles Peter and Paul were kept here during the persecutions in the reigns of Decius and Valerian, and St Sebastian, a Christian officer in the Praetorian Guard who was martyred in the reign of Diocletian, was buried here. In the 13th and early 17th c. three Roman tombs and a series of Christian catacombs were brought to light. Also found here were the foundations of the Constantinian basilica and remains of Roman houses. (A conducted tour of the whole underground complex of catacombs is to be strongly recommended.) Beneath the centre of the church is a meeting-hall (*triclia*) in which commemorative services were held, with large numbers of scratched inscriptions dating from the turn of the 3rd–4th c. Here can be seen numerous examples of the symbolic language of the early Christians – the fish (Greek *ichthys*, made up of the initials of the words "Jesus Christ, Son of God, Saviour"); the lamb, referring to Christ's sacrificial death; the anchor, a sign of trust; the dove as a symbol of peace. It is believed that the remains of Peter and Paul, who are particularly venerated here, were brought from the Vatican and the Via Ostiense for safe keeping in St Sebastian's during the persecution of the year 258, in the reign of Valerian.

Here, too, are tomb chambers on several levels (1st c. A.D.) with fine paintings, stucco decoration and inscriptions.

From the apse steps lead down to the Platonia, the tomb of the martyr Quirinius. To the left of this is a cell known as the Domus Petri (4th c. wall paintings).

*Sant'Agnese (church)   C2

Situation
Piazza Navona

Buses
46, 62, 64, 70, 81, 88, 90

The church of Sant'Agnese, on the W side of the Piazza Navona (see entry), is dedicated to the Roman martyr St Agnes. It is built on the foundations of one side of the Stadium of Domitian, on the spot where, according to legend, the saint was about to be exposed naked to the populace when her hair suddenly and miraculously grew long to cover her nakedness. The church, which adjoins the Palazzo Pamphili (see entry), was founded by Pope Innocent X, a member of the Pamphili family, and built by a succession of architects – first Girolamo Rainaldi (1652), then Borromini (1653–7) and finally Carlo Rainaldi (1672). The façade, campanile and dome (heightened by Borromini) present a lively interplay of convex and concave forms, gables, canopies, windows, columns and piers. The interior shows the same sense of movement and yet of unity. There are fine 7th c. mosaics in the apse.

Sant'Agnese provided a model which was followed in many churches of the Baroque and Rococo periods, both in Italy and in other countries.

*Sant'Agnese fuori le Mura (St Agnes without the Walls)   A5

According to the legend Agnes was a young and beautiful Roman girl who steadfastly refused to marry the son of the pagan governor of the city and was martyred for her faith. Constantine's daughter Constantia built a church in her honour in the 4th c. outside the city on the Via Nomentana. The present church was built by Pope Honorius I (625–638), but has undergone much alteration and restoration since then.
Notable features of this church, a basilica with a high, narrow nave, are the 16 antique columns, the richly decorated wooden ceiling (17th c.), the marble candelabra and the bishop's throne in the chancel. Finest of all, however, is the apse mosaic, which depicts St Agnes with Popes Honorius and Symmachus. Beneath the church are the Catacombe di Sant'Agnese (A.D. 300), part of the complex being preserved in its original state.

Situation
Via Nomentana 349

Buses
36, 37, 60, 136, 137, 310

Opening times
8 a.m.–noon and 3–6.30 p.m.

*Sant'Agostino (church)   C3

Sant'Agostino, situated near the Piazza Navona (see entry), is noted for its image of the Madonna del Parto (Madonna of Childbirth), who is invoked by pregnant women seeking a safe delivery and married couples wanting a child. The church, built between 1479 and 1483 (probably by Giacomo da Pietra-santa) and rebuilt in 1750, has a severe travertine façade, one of the earliest Renaissance façades in Rome.
The interior, with a high nave barely wider than the aisles, is dominated by the dome, which is flanked by the transepts. In addition to the Madonna del Parto (by Jacopo Sansovino, 1421) the church has a painting of the Prophet Isaiah by Raphael (1512: third pillar on left) and Caravaggio's Madonna of the Pilgrims (1605: first chapel in N aisle).
To the right of the church is the Biblioteca Angelica (state-owned since 1873), a library specialising in philology.

Situation
Piazza Sant'Agostino

Buses
26, 70

*Sant'Andrea al Quirinale (church)   C3

Sant'Andrea al Quirinale, built by Bernini (1658–71) for Cardinal Camillo Pamphili as the church of a Jesuit seminary, is a jewel among the smaller churches of Rome, and forms a counterpoint with the nearby church of San Carlo alle Quattro Fontane (see entry), built by Bernini's great rival Borromini.
Sant'Andrea, which was the court chapel of the Italian royal house from 1870 to 1946, is notable both for the consummate perfection of its design and the richness of its decoration. The circular ground plan of the Renaissance is here extended into the oval which was favoured by Baroque architects, and this, opened out still further by eight lateral chapels, creates the sense of space and movement which appealed to the Baroque taste.
The lively architectural pattern is matched by the lavish interior decoration with its pilasters and friezes, arches and recesses,

Situation
Via del Quirinale

Buses
57, 64, 65, 70, 71, 75, 170

Sant'Andrea al Quirinale

coffered domes, cornices and windows, marble and stucco of many colours (old rose, white, gold). There are also fine frescoes and pictures, mainly of the Baroque period.

Sant'Andrea della Valle (church)　　　　　C3

Situation
Corso Vittorio Emanuele

Buses
46, 62, 64, 70, 81, 88, 90

The beauty of the façade and dome of the church of Sant'Andrea della Valle is best seen from the Corso del Rinascimento; a distinctive feature is the angel with outspread wings on the left-hand side, taking the place of a volute (there is no corresponding feature on the right-hand side). Sant'Andrea, served by the Theatines (a preaching order), is very popular with the people of Rome – as is evidenced by the fact that Puccini sets the first act of "Tosca" in the Cappella Allavanti, the first chapel in the S aisle of the church.

The architects responsible for Sant'Andrea (Francesco Grimaldi, Giacomo della Porta, Carlo Maderna and Carlo Rainaldi) followed the model of the Gesù church, some 500 yd away; many features are clearly reminiscent of that church – the two-storey travertine façade with its plastic structure, the nave (high and wide, but yet creating an effect of harmony and unity) with its side chapels, transept, choir and apse, and the mighty dome (the second largest in Rome after the dome of St Peter's) – and indeed the ground plan of Sant'Andrea is almost indistinguishable from that of the Gesù.

The side chapels contain some fine pictures and statues, but the most notable features of the interior are the tombs of two

Popes belonging to the Piccolomini family of Siena which were brought here from St Peter's in 1614 and now stand in the nave near the N transept: the humanist Pope Pius II (Aeneas Silvius Piccolomini, d. 1464) on the left and Pope Pius III (Francesco Todeschini Piccolomini, d. 1503) on the right. Both tombs were the work of Paolo Taccone and Andrea Bregno.

The magnificent frescoes in the dome and the semi-dome of the apse were painted by Domenichino (1624–8).

Sant'Ignazio (church) C3

The Society of Jesus, founded by Ignatius Loyola in 1540, soon attracted an increasing following and a large membership in Rome and throughout Europe; and to honour the memory of their founder, who died in 1556 and was canonised in 1622, the Jesuits built the church of Sant'Ignazio – the second Jesuit church in Rome, following the Gesù (see entry) – between 1626 and 1650, with financial assistance from Cardinal Ludovico Ludovisi, a nephew of Pope Gregory XV. Both the architect, Orazio Grassi, and the painter, Andrea Pozzo, were Jesuits.

The square in which the church stands, with something of the air of a stage set, and its imposing façade are very much in the Baroque spirit, the interior even more so. The spacious wide nave (equally suitable for preaching purposes and for conducting the service from one central spot), the linked side chapels and the sumptuous decoration and furnishings, with their use of precious materials and elaborate ornamental patterns, were all calculated to draw the faithful back to the church (this was the period of the Counter-Reformation). The harmony of the interior does not suffer from the fact that the central dome originally planned was not built: in its place and on the ceiling Andrea Pozzo created a *trompe l'œil* painting celebrating the triumph of St Ignatius, his entry into Paradise and the four missionary regions of the world, in which the painted representation of Heaven appears to break up the illusionist architecture and the sham dome. (A marble disc in the floor marks the spot from which the illusion is most effective.) In Sant'Ignazio architecture, sculpture and painting merge into one another: the eye of the believer was to be caught and held by art, his heart to be opened to the teaching of the Church.

In the S transept is the tomb of St Aloysius (Luigi Gonzaga, 1568–91), in the N transept that of St John Berchmans – both Jesuit saints.

Situation
Piazza di Sant'Ignazio

Buses
26, 56, 60, 62, 71, 81, 85, 87, 88, 90, 90b, 94, 95

Santa Cecilia in Trastevere (church) C3

St Cecilia, described in her Life as "Coeli Lilia" (the Lily of Heaven), was one of the early Christian martyrs who were always much venerated in Rome and became the subject of numerous legends.

Traditionally the church occupies the site of the house belonging to Cecilia's husband Valerian. Originally founded in

Situation
Piazza di Santa Cecilia

Buses
23, 26, 28, 44, 75, 97, 170, 710, 718, 719, 774

the 5th c., it was much altered and rebuilt in later centuries. It is of basilican type, with forecourt, porch (façade by Ferdinando Fuga, 1725), a Romanesque campanile, a wide nave with rows of columns, chancel and apse.

In the chancel are a marble ciborium by Arnolfo di Cambio (1283) and a figure of St Cecilia carved by Stefano Maderna in 1600 (a year after the discovery of a tomb containing the body of a young girl in this position). The apse has a mosaic dating from the reign of Pope Paschal I (9th c.). In the crypt can be seen the excavated foundations of a Roman house.

Special permission is required to visit the adjoining convent, which contains a magnificent "Last Judgment" by Pietro Cavallini (1293).

Santa Costanza (church)   A5

Situation
Via Nomentana

Buses
36, 37, 60, 136, 137, 310

Close to the church of Sant'Agnese fuori le Mura (see entry), on the Via Nomentana, is a church with one of the most beautiful interiors of all the Roman churches – Santa Costanza, a round church erected at the beginning of the 4th c. as a mausoleum for Constantine's daughters Constantia (or rather Constantina) and Helen, wife of Julian the Apostate. This little architectural masterpiece, measuring 22·50 m (74 ft) in diameter, is simple in conception, with an unpretentious brick-built exterior, but constructed internally with costly and valuable materials (12 double columns with capitals). The mosaics depict both sacred and pagan figures, with animals playing amid vines. In this church Roman architecture, the mosaic art of late antiquity and early Christian symbols are blended into a harmonious whole.

Santa Croce in Gerusalemme (church)   C5

Situation
Piazza Santa Croce in
Gerusalemme

Underground station
San Giovanni (line A)

Buses
3, 9, 15, 81

Opening times
7.45 a.m.–1 p.m., 3.30–
7 p.m.

Santa Croce in Gerusalemme is one of the seven pilgrimage churches of Rome, the others being San Giovanni in Laterano, San Pietro in Vaticano, San Paolo fuori le Mura, Santa Maria Maggiore, San Sebastiano and San Lorenzo fuori le Mura (see entries). Pilgrims like to attend services at these churches on the eve of important Catholic festivals.

The church was built in the reign of Constantine for the purpose – so the legend goes – of housing the relics of Christ's Passion which Constantine's mother Helen had brought from the Holy Land. It received its present late Baroque form in the 18th c. (architect, Domenico Gregorini).

Santa Francesca Romana (church)   C3

Underground station
Colosseo (line B)

Buses
11, 27, 81, 85, 87, 88

To replace the church of Santa Maria Antiqua a new church dedicated to the Virgin, Santa Maria Nuova, was built in the second half of the 10th c. on the other side of the Forum, on what is now the Via dei Fori Imperiali. The church occupied part of the site of the old temple of Venus and Rome. The tower, a characteristic example of a medieval Roman campanile, was

added in the 13th c. The church received its present name
when it was dedicated to the foundress of the Oblates, St
Frances of Rome.
Notable features of the interior, which is richly decorated with
marble, stucco and pictures, are the Confessio, the apse mosaic
and the 6th c. Madonna on the high altar (ascribed to St Luke).

Santa Maria degli Angeli (church)

See Terme di Diocleziano

Santa Maria dell'Anima (church)   C2

Pilgrims to Rome expected to find a hospice where they could
stay and a church belonging to their particular nation. Santa
Maria dell'Anima, situated near the Piazza Navona (see entry),
was built in 1501–14 for German pilgrims – that is, all pilgrims
from the Holy Roman Empire – and it is still the church of the
German Catholic community in Rome.
Soon after the church was built Pope Adrian VI (1522–3) – a
native of Utrecht and the last non-Italian Pope before John
Paul II – was buried here. His tomb, on the S side of the choir, is
flanked by allegorical figures representing the four cardinal
virtues, Prudence, Justice, Fortitude and Temperance. The
experience of this sorely tried Pope, who reigned during the
early days of the Reformation, is summarised in a Latin
inscription referring to the effect on a man's life of the age into
which he is born. The interior of this tall hall-church is richly
decorated.

Situation
Via di Santa Maria del-
l'Anima (entrance in Piazza
della Pace)

Buses
26, 70, 81, 88, 90

Santa Maria in Aracoeli (church)   C3

The church of Santa Maria in Aracoeli occupies a venerable
sacred site on the Capitol (see Campidoglio), having been built
by Franciscans in the 13th c. on the foundations of the ancient
temple of Juno Moneta, which dated from the 6th c. B.C. The
steep flight of 124 steps leading up to the church (which
young couples like to climb after their wedding) was
constructed in 1348. In the Middle Ages the church was at the
centre of Roman political life, being the meeting-place of the
municipal parliament. The interior was redecorated after the
defeat of the Turkish fleet at Lepanto in 1571.
The majestic flight of steps leads up from the Via del Teatro di
Marcello to a bare brick façade which makes the interior appear
all the more sumptuous, in spite of its simple basilican plan
(with side chapels added later). Notable features of the church
are the 16th c. wooden ceiling, the Cappella Bufalini at the near
end of the S aisle, which has frescoes by Pinturicchio (1485),
and the numerous grave-slabs and monuments in the floor and
on the walls.
In the N transept is an elegant aedicula (miniature temple)
marking the spot where the Sibyl prophesied to Augustus that
a virgin would bear a divine child who would overthrow the
altars of the gods: whereupon the Emperor set up an altar on

Situation
Via del Teatro di Marcello

Buses
57, 90, 90b, 92, 94, 95, 716,
718, 719

the spot with the inscription – now on the triumphal arch – "Ecce ara primogeniti Dei" ("Behold the altar of the firstborn of God").

Beneath the aedicula are the remains of St Helen, Constantine's mother, who searched for the True Cross and the relics of Christ's Passion in the Holy Land and brought them back to Rome.

In the sacristy can be seen the "Santo Bambino", a figure of the Child Jesus which legend says was carved from the wood of an olive-tree in the garden of Gethsemane and which is popularly credited with miraculous qualities. At Christmas the image is set up in the nave, and children preach "sermons" in front of it.

*Santa Maria in Cosmedin (church)   C3

Situation
Piazza Bocca della Verità

Buses
15, 23, 57, 90, 90b, 92, 94, 716

On the S side of the Piazza Bocca della Verità, overlooking the Tempio di Fortuna Virile, the Arco di Giano and the church of San Giorgio in Velabro (see entries), is the church of Santa Maria in Cosmedin (probably given this name by Byzantines after a square in their city).

This is one of the finest examples of medieval church architecture in Rome. Begun in 772, during the reign of Pope Adrian I, and completed in its present form in about 1124, under Calixtus II, it is an architectual gem (suggesting an alternative derivation of the name Cosmedin from the Greek *cosmos*, which means "perfect order" or "ornament").

The noble harmony of the church's proportions begins with the seven-storey campanile and is continued in the wide two-storey porch with its projecting canopy; it reaches even sublimer heights in the interior, with its tall nave and carefully structured layout to meet liturgical needs, and is infinitely repeated in the intarsia (inlaid marble) work by the Cosmati.

The alternation of columns and piers, the irregular dimensions, the three apses, the aisles with their famous frescoes, the Cosmatesque work in the floor and the marble screens of the *schola cantorum* (the area reserved for the clergy), the marble ambos (reading pulpits), the bishop's throne with its two lions' heads and the ornamental disc behind it, the twisted Easter candlestick, the ciborium over the altar: all these details combine to make Santa Maria in Cosmedin one of the most beautiful of the smaller churches of Rome.

In the crypt are early Christian tombs and the foundations of a pagan temple.

At the left-hand end of the porch is the large stone mask known as the Bocca della Verità, the "Mouth of Truth". According to the popular belief, the Romans when taking an oath would put their right hand into the mouth of the mask, which would then close and hold them fast if they perjured themselves. Nowadays the "Mouth of Truth" serves only as a threat to troublesome children.

*Santa Maria Maggiore (church)   C4

Situation
Piazza di Santa Maria Maggiore

Santa Maria Maggiore is the largest of the 80 Roman churches dedicated to the Virgin. It is also one of the four patriarchal basilicas (coming after San Giovanni in Laterano, San Pietro in

Santa Maria in Aracoeli

Santa Maria in Cosmedin

Bocca della Verità

Santa Maria sopra Minerva

Underground station
Termini (lines A and B)

Buses
3, 4, 16, 27, 70, 71, 93, 93b,
93c

Trams
14, 516, 517

Opening times
7 a.m.–7 p.m.

Vaticano and San Paolo fuori le Mura – see entries) and one of
the seven pilgrimage churches (the patriarchal churches
together with Santa Croce in Gerusalemme, San Lorenzo fuori
le Mura and San Sebastiano – see entries). It is the only church
in Rome in which mass has been celebrated every day without
interruption since the 5th c.

According to legend on the night of 4–5 August in the year 358
the Virgin appeared to Pope Liberius and a Roman patrician
named Johannes and told them to build a church on the spot
where snow fell on the following day (in the month of
August!). Snow did fall on the following morning on the
Esquiline hill, outlining the plan of a basilica; and since then the
feast of Our Lady of the Snow has been celebrated on 5
August. Archaeological research has been unable to establish,
however, whether the church was erected in the 4th or the
5th c. The original church was added to in later centuries: a new
apse was built in the 13th c.; the campanile (75 m (245 ft) high,
the tallest in Rome) in 1377; Alexander VI built the golden
coffered roof with the first gold from America; two side
chapels, the Cappella Sistina and the Cappella Paoline, were
added; and between the 16th and 18th c. the church was
surrounded by a whole series of extensions (prelates' houses).

From the square with the obelisk (14·80 m (49 ft) high) from
the Mausoleum of Augustus (see Mausoleo di Augusto) an
imposing flight of steps leads up to the entrance at the chancel
end of the church. The main entrance (façade by Ferdinando
Fuga, 1743) is reached by way of the column from the Basilica
of Maxentius, now crowned by a figure of the Virgin (see
Basilica di Massenzio).

The interior is perhaps the finest and most majestic church
interior in Rome: 86 m (282 ft) long, three-aisled, with 36
marble and four granite columns, mosaics (4th or 5th c., the
oldest in Rome) on the upper part of the walls and a coffered
ceiling.

The Cappella Sistina on the right and Cappella Paolina on the
left are in effect transepts. The Cappella Sistina, built by
Domenico Fontana (1594–90) for Pope Sixtus V, contains
relics of the manger in Bethlehem, a bronze tabernacle and the
tombs of Sixtus V and his predecessor Pius V. The Cappella
Paolina was built for Pope Paul V by Flaminio Ponzo; on the
altar is a much venerated image of the Virgin (the "Salus Populi
Romani"), traditionally attributed to St Luke but in fact a
13th c. work.

A further contribution is made to the magnificence of the
decoration by the mosaics on the triumphal arch and in the
apse, depicting Old and New Testament themes, scenes from
the life of the Virgin and a "Coronation of the Virgin" by
Jacopo Torriti (end of 13th c.), the supreme achievement of
the art of the Roman mosaic-workers (best light early in the
morning).

The canopy over the Papal altar is supported on four porphyry
columns from Hadrian's Villa at Tivoli (see entry).

---

*Santa Maria sopra Minerva (church)   C3

Situation
Piazza della Minerva

The Piazza della Minerva, behind the Pantheon (see entry), is
graced by a charming monument – the marble elephant by

Bernini which Ercole Ferrata (1667) used as the base supporting a small Egyptian obelisk (6th c. B.C.). The inscription on the plinth of the monument is to the effect that great strength is required to bear wisdom.

The church, served by the Dominican order (the headquarters of which are to the left of the church), is built on the site of a temple of Minerva: hence its name. It was begun, in Gothic style, about 1280 but was completed only in 1453 with the vaulting of the nave. It is thus the only Gothic complex of any size in Rome.

Situated in the centre of the city and served by St Dominic's preaching order, the church was popular with the people of Rome, and the number of grave slabs and monuments in the floor and on the walls of this three-aisled basilica and in the side chapels with their numerous pictures bears witness to the part it played in the religious life of the city. The best known of the funerary chapels is the Caraffa Chapel at the end of the S transept, also known as the Chapel of the Annunciation of St Thomas, which contains the tomb of Cardinal Oliviero Caraffa and is famous for its frescoes by Filippo Lippi (1489). These glorify both the Virgin (Annunciation and Assumption) and St Thomas Aquinas, a member of the Dominican order (the triumph of the saint and scenes from his life).

The high altar contains the relics of St Catherine of Siena (1347–80), author of numerous letters to the exiled Popes at Avignon urging them to return to Rome. In front of the altar, to the left, is a statue of the Risen Christ by Michelangelo (1521), which has been unjustly depreciated in comparison with his other works. It was criticised during Michelangelo's lifetime for looking more like a youthful pagan god than the founder of Christianity, and later a loincloth was added to cover its nakedness. Quiet contemplation is needed to appreciate the full expressiveness of the statue, but the masterly skill with which the marble is fashioned is evident at the first glance. Michelangelo's genius so impressed other artists that the painter Sebastiano del Piombo, for example, maintained that Christ's knees were worth more than all the buildings in Rome. In a passage to the left of the presbytery is the tomb of the painter Fra Angelico, a member of the Dominican order.

Buses
26, 87, 94

Santa Maria di Monserrato (church)   C2

About the same time as the church of Santa Maria dell'Anima (see entry) was built for the Germans this church was built by Antonio da Sangallo the Elder (1495 onwards) for the Aragonese and Catalans. The initiative came from the famous (or notorious) Pope Alexander VI, a member of the Spanish family of Borja (which became in Italian Borgia), who is buried in the church. Santa Maria di Monserrato (named after the famous Marian pilgrimage centre of Montserrat near Barcelona) has been since 1875 the Spanish national church in Rome.

Notable features of the church are the tombs of the two Borgia Popes, Calixtus III and Alexander VI, and a number of marble statues, including a bust of Cardinal Pietro Montoya by Bernini (1621).

Situation
Via di Monserrato/
Via Giulia 151

Buses
23, 28, 28b, 65

*Santa Maria della Pace (church)   C2

Situation
Via della Pace

Buses
26, 70, 81, 88, 90

Santa Maria della Pace, one of Rome's most beautiful churches, reached its present form in a number of stages. In 1482 Pope Sixtus IV rebuilt an earlier church of the Virgin on this site in thanksgiving for the peace with Milan. The architect is thought to have been Baccio Pontelli, who created a rectangular church to which another architect, perhaps Bramante, added an octagonal structure and a cloister. In 1656 Pietro da Cortona restored the church, adding the Baroque façade and a semicircular porch (pronaos). This spirited entrance gives access to the nave and octagon, which contains famous frescoes by Raphael (1415) depicting the ancient Sibyls, to which figures of prophets and saints were later added by other painters.

The admirably proportioned cloister, built for Cardinal Oliviero Caraffa in 1504, was Bramante's first work in Rome.

*Santa Maria del Popolo (church)   B3

Situation
Piazza del Popolo

Underground station
Flaminio (line A)

Below the pines of the Pincio Gardens (see entry) stands the church of Santa Maria del Popolo, with its fine Renaissance façade, dome and campanile. Legend has it that there was once a chapel here, built to drive away the evil spirit of Nero, which Pope Sixtus IV (1471–84) enlarged into a church. This was extended by Bramante in 1505, occupied by Augustinian

Santa Maria del Popolo

canons and later restored by Bernini. Martin Luther, an Augustinian, lived in the Augustinian house during his visit to Rome in 1510–11; and after the Reformation the altar at which he had celebrated mass was shunned by other members of the order.

As a parish church Santa Maria del Popolo, built on a Latin cross plan with three aisles and many side chapels, contains numerous tombs, including those of Cardinal Ascanio Sforza (d. 1505) and Cardinal Girolamo Basso della Rovere (d. 1507), both by Andrea Sansovino, in the choir. On the vaulting of the choir are frescoes by Pinturicchio depicting the Coronation of the Virgin, with Evangelists, Sibyls and Fathers of the Church. The side chapels are particularly fine. The first on the right was built for the Papal family of della Rovere, the second (by Carlo Fontana, 1682–7) for Cardinal Cybo, the second on the left (designed by Raphael, 1513–15) for the Chigi family. The Cesari Chapel, in the N transept, contains two famous pictures by Caravaggio, the "Conversion of St Paul" and the "Crucifixion of St Peter".

Buses
1, 2, 2b, 90, 90b, 95, 115, 202, 203, 205, 490, 492, 495

Santa Maria in Trastevere (church)   C2

Santa Maria in Trastevere (the densely populated part of Rome on the right bank of the Tiber, see Trastevere) is the oldest church of the Virgin in Rome. According to legend it stands on the spot where a spring of oil flowed 38 years before Christ's birth as an intimation of the future Saviour. This may also be the

Situation
Piazza Santa Maria in Trastevere

Buses
23, 28, 28b, 56, 60, 65

Santa Maria in Trastevere

Santa Maria della Vittoria

Opening times
7.30 a.m.–noon, 4–7 p.m.

place where Christians were able for the first time to hold services in public. (Photograph, p. 119.)

The building of the church began between 221 and 227, in the reign of Pope Calixtus I, and was completed in 340, in the reign of Julius I. It was rebuilt by Innocent II (1130–43), who came from the Trastevere district, and redecorated in the Baroque period. It is now one of the finest and most imposing churches in Rome.

The church has a Romanesque campanile, a façade decorated with mosaics (the Virgin with ten female saints) and a portico containing early Christian sarcophagi and various medieval fragments.

Notable features of the interior are the Cosmatesque (marble intarsia) work in the floor; the coffered wooden ceiling, partly gilded, by Domenichino (1617); the 22 massive Ionic columns in the nave; and a 15th c. tabernacle by Mino del Reame (at W end of nave, on right).

The mosaics in the apse are masterpieces of medieval art. In the conch (c. 1140) are Christ, the Virgin and saints, above a frieze of lambs, and below this are scenes from the life of the Virgin – Nativity, Annunciation, Nativity of Christ, Three Kings, Presentation in the Temple, Assumption (by Pietro Cavallini, c. 1291).

---

*Santa Maria della Vittoria (church)   B4

Situation
Via XX Settembre

Underground station
Repubblica or Barberini
(line A)

Buses
60, 61, 62, 415

Santa Maria della Vittoria commemorates the Emperor Ferdinand II's victory in the battle of the White Mountain near Prague in 1620, during the Thirty Years War, which was attributed to the intervention of the Virgin. The church, previously dedicated to St Paul, then received an image of the Virgin found at Pilsen and reputed to be miraculous and was re-dedicated under its present name.

This attractive Baroque church, built by Carlo Maderna in 1608–20 for Cardinal Scipione Borghese, is of imposing effect with its finely contrived decoration of coloured marble, rich stucco ornament and paintings. The most impressive thing in the church, however, is the altar of St Teresa of Avila (fourth chapel on left) created by Bernini in 1646 for Cardinal Cornaro. St Teresa (1515–82), the mystic and writer who re-founded the order of Carmelite nuns, is depicted in a state of ecstatic rapture, pierced by the love of God which is symbolised by the arrow of the angel who hovers over her.

In the sacristy are pictures and flags commemorating the battle of the White Mountain.

---

*Santa Prassede (church)   C4

Situation
Via San Martino ai Monti

Buses
16, 93, 93b, 93c

Opening times
By appointment

A legend relates that the two daughters of a Roman senator named Pudens, Pudentiana (see Santa Pudenziana) and Praxedes, were converted to the Christian faith by St Peter. The church dedicated to St Praxedes has gone through a number of different building stages but has preserved the spatial character of an early Christian basilica, its high pillared nave rising into the presbytery with its triumphal arch and apse mosaics (9th c.,

Santa Maria della Vittoria

in the reign of Pope Paschal I). The mosaics are among the finest in Rome. On the triumphal arch is a representation of the heavenly Jerusalem, in the apse is the apocalyptic Lamb of the Revelation, and in the conch of the apse, above a frieze of lambs, Christ with SS. Peter and Paul leading Praxedes and Pudentiana, accompanied by Pope Paschal as the donor and by St Zeno. In addition to glorifying the saints the representations had a didactic purpose: the object, as in other religious painting, was to instruct the worshippers, who in the Middle Ages were mostly illiterate, in the doctrines of the faith. The Chapel of St Zeno (in the S aisle), built by Pope Paschal I (817–824) to house the tomb of his mother Theodora, is like a medieval picturebook, every part of the walls and vaulting being covered with mosaics depicting saints and Biblical symbols.

*Santa Pudenziana (church)   C4

Santa Pudenziana is said to occupy the house of the Roman senator Pudens, whose daughters Pudentiana and Praxedes (see Santa Prassede) were converted by St Peter while staying in the house. The church was originally built in the reign of Pope Siricius (384–399); it has undergone much subsequent alteration, but the original apse with its mosaic decoration has been preserved.

The church, now lying below the present street level, is entered from Via Urbana. Externally its most notable features are the

Situation
Via Urbana

Buses
27, 70, 71, 81

Opening times
By appointment

121

campanile and the remains of a Romanesque doorway. The finest thing in the interior is the mosaic in the apse (end of 4th c.), now rather cramped by later building. It shows Christ surrounded by Apostles and women against a lively background based on ancient models, with a skilful use of perspective. Above the central group are the buildings of a city, a cross and the (partly obliterated) symbols of the four Evangelists, the man, the lion, the bull and the eagle.

---

*Santa Sabina (church)   C3

Situation
Piazza Pietro d'Illiria

Buses
23, 57, 92, 94, 95, 716

Both externally and internally the church of Santa Sabina preserves the character of an early Christian basilica. Built by Peter of Illyria in 425–432 over the house of a Christian woman named Sabina, it was embellished with marble by Pope Eugenius II in 824. In 1222 Pope Honorius III presented the church to the Dominicans.

The central doorway in the porch has the oldest carved wooden doors in Christian art (432), with delicate and expressive reliefs by unknown artists depicting Old and New Testament scenes. Of the original 28 panels 18 have survived, though not in their original positions. The scenes can be readily identified (from top to bottom and left to right):

1st row: Crucifixion, Healing of the Blind Man, Multiplication of the Loaves, Marriage in Cana, Doubting Thomas, Moses and the Burning Bush, Christ before Pilate.

2nd row: Resurrection, Miracles of Moses, Christ's Appearance to the Women.

3rd row: Three Kings, Ascension, Peter's Denial, Crossing of the Red Sea, Miracle of the Serpent.

4th row: Christ between Peter and Paul, Triumph of Christ, Assumption of Elijah, Moses before Pharaoh.

The nave is flanked by 20 Corinthian columns (20 m (65 ft) high) of Parian marble. On the wall above the entrance is one of the oldest mosaics in Rome – two female figures symbolising the Church of the Gentiles (pagans) and the Church of the Circumcision (Jews), with an inscription commemorating the erection of the church. The choir has fine marble screens with intarsia ornament.

Adjoining the church is a Dominican monastery in which St Thomas Aquinas was a monk, with a beautiful Romanesque cloister.

---

*Santi Apostoli (church)   C3

Situation
Piazza SS. Apostoli

Buses
56, 57, 60, 62, 64, 65, 70, 71, 75, 81, 85, 88, 90, 95, 170

The Church of the Apostles in the Palazzo Colonna, originally dedicated to SS. Philip and James, was probably founded by Pope Pelagius I (556–561) after the expulsion of the Goths from Rome. It was altered and renovated by later Popes and finally rebuilt by Francesco and Carlo Fontana (1702 onwards) as the last basilican church erected in Rome. In the porch, which lies at an angle to the church, are examples of ancient and medieval art. Notable features of the interior (63 m (207 ft) long) are the ceiling frescoes (Triumph of the Franciscan

Order), the tomb of Pope Clement XIV, a masterpiece by Canova (1787), and the tomb of Cardinal Pietro Riario (d. 1474).

* Santi Cosma e Damiano (church)   C3

This church, dedicated to the two Oriental doctor saints Cosmas and Damian, was converted in the 6th c. from a Roman building in Vespasian's Forum of Peace (see Foro di Vespasiano): hence its aisleless ground plan. In the 17th c. the interior was redecorated in Baroque style.

The church has a fine wooden ceiling of 1632 and a medieval Easter candle with Cosmatesque decoration. It is, however, notable mainly for the mosaics on the triumphal arch and in the apse, which date from the reign of Pope Felix IV (526–530). On the triumphal arch are scenes from the Book of Revelation, in the apse the "Transmission of the Divine Law", in which Christ is depicted handing the scroll of the Law to Peter and Paul, flanked by SS. Cosmas and Damian, St Theodore and Pope Felix IV.

The Christmas crib (Nativity scene) in the vestibule is one of the largest in Rome and of considerable artistic quality.

Situation
Via dei Fori Imperiali

Underground station
Colosseo (line B)

Buses
11, 27, 81, 85, 87, 88

Santi Giovanni e Paolo (church)   C4

According to tradition a church was built on this site in the 5th c. by a Roman senator named Byzantius and his son Pammachius in honour of the martyrs John and Paul, officers in the Roman army who were executed in the time of Julian the Apostate. The church is said to have been built over the remains of the house on the Caelian hill in which they were killed. Around 1150 it was rebuilt by Cardinal Giovanni di Sutri, with the addition of the porch, the campanile and the dwarf gallery in the apse. During the Baroque period the interior was redecorated.

Excavations in the present century have revealed the Roman house under the church, so that it is now possible to follow the history of the site in an unbroken line from the original Roman house wtih its fine brick masonry and lively frescoes (the best preserved ancient wall paintings in Rome, depicting Venus and a male divinity), the antique columns and the two lions in the porch, by way of the medieval building, with its marble columns and the campanile built over the walls of the large temple of Claudius on the Caelian, to the basilica we see today.

Situation
Piazza dei Santi Giovanni e Paolo

Buses
11, 15, 27, 118, 673

Trams
13, 30, 30b

Santi Quattro Coronati (church)   C4

The first church on this site was built in the 4th c. in honour of four martyrs. According to one legend they were Roman soldiers who refused to do honour to a statue of Aesculapius; another version states that they were sculptors from Pannonia who refused to carve a pagan idol. By virtue of the second of these legends the church is popular with stonemasons. The

Situation
Via dei Santi Quattro Coronati

Buses
15, 81, 85, 87, 88, 118, 673

Santo Stefano Rotondo

Trams
13, 30, 30b

martyrs are said to have been killed by having an iron crown driven on to their heads: hence they are "crowned" martyrs.

The present church was erected in the reign of Pope Paschal II (c. 1100) after the destruction of an earlier church by the Normans in 1084.

The principal features of the church are the nave and apse, with the tall campanile; the Cappella di San Silvestro, with scenes from the life of Constantine, selected for their relevance to the conflict between the Pope and the Emperor in the Middle Ages; the crypt and the famous cloister.

Santo Stefano Rotondo (church)   C4

Situation
Via di Santo Stefano
Rotondo

Buses
85, 88, 673

Santo Stefano Rotondo was, architecturally, one of the great churches of Rome, but its state of dilapidation destroys the full effect of this imposing structure, with its ground plan of a Greek cross set within a circle. The church dates from the 5th and 7th c. (Popes Simplicius and Adrian I). In addition to St Stephen the Protomartyr (feast 26 December) St Stephen of Hungary is honoured here.

The church of Santo Stefano Rotondo merits thorough renovation, and although a beginning has been made with this work progress is lamentably slow.

Scala Santa (Holy Staircase)   C5

Situation
Piazza San Giovanni in
Laterano

Underground station
San Giovanni (line A)

Buses
16, 85, 87, 88, 93, 218, 650,
673

Diagonally across the main front of San Giovanni in Laterano (see entry) is the church of the Scala Santa, on the position of the dining-room (triclinium) of the Lateran Palace (see Palazzo Laterano). It contains the Papal chapel of the palace (Capella Sancta Sanctorum, with 13th c. mosaics) and the Holy Staircase, a flight of 28 marble steps (now clad with wood) which is believed to be a staircase from Pilate's palace in Jerusalem, brought to Rome in the 4th c. by St Helen. It is the practice for the faithful to climb the steps on their knees in memory of Christ's Passion.

Spanish Steps

See Piazza di Spagna

*Teatro di Marcello (Theatre of Marcellus)   C3

Situation
Via del Teatro di Marcello

Buses
15, 23, 57, 90, 90b, 92, 94,
95, 716, 774

The Romans had seen in Greece how theatres with a semicircular auditorium could be built against the slope of a hill, thus avoiding the necessity of a costly building operation to provide support for the tiers of seating; and the same technique could well have been applied in Rome, which had plenty of hills. The desire to display Roman power, artistic achievement and technological skill, however, led Pompey to erect a free-standing theatre in 55 B.C., and Augustus followed

In the Scala Santa church

Theatre of Marcellus

his example in the theatre built for his nephew and son-in-law Marcellus, predestined to be the Emperor's successor had he not died before his time.

The theatre, originally planned by Caesar, was begun in 13 B.C. and completed two years later. The auditorium was now supported by a massive system of arcades, and the disposition of the stage and the tiers of seating was matched to the external elevation. The remains are still impressive, in spite of the fact that the theatre was converted into a fortress and residence by the Fabi, Savelli and Orsini families during the Middle Ages.

In the 16th c. a new palace was built by Baldassare Peruzzi for the Savelli family on the ruins of the theatre, but this still preserved the form of the original structure. (Photograph, p. 125.)

On a high platform in front of the Theatre of Marcellus (to right) are three corner columns from the Temple of Apollo Sosianus, originally built in 435–433 B.C., restored in 179 B.C. and rebuilt in 32 B.C. by the consul Sosianus.

Tempietto di Bramante

See San Pietro in Montorio

*Terme di Caracalla (Baths of Caracalla)   D4

Situation
Via delle Terme di Caracalla

Underground station
Circo Massimo (line B)

Buses
11, 27, 90, 90b, 94, 118, 673

Trams
13, 30, 30b

Opening times
9 a.m.–4 p.m.; Sun. & Mon.
9 a.m.–1 p.m.

The Baths of Caracalla to the S of the city, begun by Septimius Severus in A.D. 206 and completed by Caracalla in 216, were much more than public baths. Nowadays they would be called a "leisure centre", containing as they did a whole system of baths (hot and cold baths, a swimming pool, sweat-baths with both dry and damp heat), facilities for gymnastics and sport, pleasant rooms for social intercourse, gardens to walk in, lecture rooms and libraries, hairdressers and shops.

These various needs were met in a massively imposing structure covering an area 330 m (1100 ft) square, a complex of gigantic halls with huge columns and piers, domes and semi-domes, barrel vaulting and cross vaulting, which could accommodate some 1500 people at a time. The floors and walls were covered with marbles, mosaics and frescoes. The leisure needs of the population have never been catered for with such magnificence as in the Roman baths: even in ruin their splendour is still apparent.

Terme di Diocleziano (Baths of Diocletian)   B4

Situation
Piazza dei Cinquecento/
Piazza dell'Esedra

Underground stations
Repubblica or Termini
(line A)

Diocletian built these baths to serve the northern districts of the city, the southern districts having been catered for by the Baths of Caracalla. (For the functions of Roman baths, see Terme di Caracalla.) The Baths of Diocletian, measuring 356 by 316 m (1170 by 1035 ft), were even bigger than those of Caracalla. Their huge scale can be appreciated when it is seen how widely separated from one another are the surviving parts of the

Baths of Caracalla

structure, many of them now incorporated in later buildings – the Museo Nazionale Romano or Museo delle Terme (National Museum, Baths Museum), with a collection of Greek and Roman art; the church of Santa degli Angeli, built by Michelangelo; the round church of San Bernardo; the Planetarium; the Piazza dell'Esedra, in an exedra of the Baths; and the cloister and other structures belonging to a Carthusian monastery.

Buses
3, 4, 16, 36, 37, 38, 57, 60, 61, 62, 63, 64, 65, 170, 319, 910

The baths could no longer be used after the Acqua Marcia aqueduct was cut in A.D. 536, and thereafter the building fell into decay.

**Museo Nazionale Romano or Museo delle Terme
(National Museum, Baths Museum)

This museum, housed in part of the Baths of Diocletian, has the largest collection of ancient art in Rome after that of the Vatican Museums (see Vatican, Musei Vaticani).

Among the most notable exhibits are pre-Christian and Christian sarcophagi and a great range of Greek, Hellenistic and Roman sculpture, including a fine Apollo, a Nereid, the "Young Dancing-Girl", the "Discus-Thrower" from Castle Porziano, the "Wounded Niobe" from the Gardens of Sallust (5th c. B.C.), the Venus of Cyrene (4th c. B.C.), the Ephebe of Subiaco (3rd c. B.C.), a "Defeated Boxer" (3rd c. B.C.), the "Maiden of Anzio", the Lancellotti "Discus-Thrower" (an excellent copy of the statue by Myron), the Ostia Altar, etc.

Underground station
Repubblica or Termini
(line A)

Buses
3, 4, 16, 36, 37, 38, 57, 60, 61, 62, 64, 65, 170, 319, 910

Opening times
9 a.m.–2 p.m., Sun. and public holidays 9 a.m.–1 p.m.

Closed
Mon.

Museo delle Terme – courtyard

The Museum also contains the Ludovisi Collection, with the "Ludovisi Throne" (5th c. B.C.) and statues of the "Dying Galatian", Ares, Athena Parthenos (a copy of Phidias' statue in the Parthenon), Juno and Orestes and Electra.

The Great Cloister (Grande Chiostro) of 1565, with a fountain, contains marble sculpture, architectural fragments, sarcophagi, mosaics and inscriptions.

On the 1st floor of the Museum are a collection of mosaics, stucco work and frescoes and wall paintings from the Villa of Livia at Prima Porta.

San Bernardo alle Terme (church)

Situation
Piazza di San Bernardo

Underground station
Repubblica (line A)

In a rotunda at the NW corner of the Baths is the church of San Bernardo alle Terme, built at the end of the 16th c. The dome is similar to that of the Pantheon but only half its size (22 m (72 ft) in diameter as compared with 43·20 m – 142 ft).

Santa Maria degli Angeli (church)

Situation
Piazza della Repubblica
(Piazza dell'Esedra)

Underground station
Repubblica (line A)

The central complex of the Baths was preserved by being incorporated in this 16th c. church dedicated to the Virgin and her attendant archangels. It was designed by Michelangelo, taking in parts of the ancient structure, in particular the tepidarium (warm bath), a hall 90 m (295 ft) long, 27 m (90 ft) wide and 30 m (100 ft) high. The church is in the form of a Greek cross (with arms of equal length), with chapels at the angles. In order to keep the church dry its floor was raised 2 m (6½ ft) above ground level, so that the bases of the ancient columns were buried. The building of the church was continued after Michelangelo's death, and thereafter it was restored and redecorated on a number of occasions.

Many well-known personalities are buried in the church, which is also used by the State for solemn services on special occasions

Buses
57, 60, 61, 62, 65, 75, 415, 910

Fontana delle Naiadi (Fountain of the Naiads)

The Fountain of the Naiads in the Piazza della Repubblica – also known as the Piazza dell'Esedra since it is laid out on the site of an exedra of the Baths – was erected between 1885 and 1914. It consists of four groups of female figures playing with marine animals, with a figure of "Man Victorious over the Hostile Forces of Nature" in the middle.

Situation
Piazza della Repubblica

*Tivoli

Tivoli, the ancient Tibur, situated on the Via Tiburtina 31 km (19 miles) from Rome and now a town of 50,000 inhabitants, has two main tourist attractions – the Villa d'Este and the Villa Adriana.

Buses
Buses to Tivoli from Via
Gaeta (Stazione Termini)

Villa d'Este

The Villa d'Este, situated in its beautiful gardens, ranks as the "Queen of Villas". Originally laid out by Pirro Ligorio for Cardinal Ippolito d'Este, of the great Ferrara family of Este, in the 16th c., the whole complex blended the natural landscape (a gently sloping hillside), the play of water in fountains and cascades and the architectural forms of the buildings into a harmonious and refreshing whole. The villa was completed in the early 17th c. by Luigi and Alessandro d'Este. It later passed into the hands of the Habsburg family, and in 1918 was taken over by the State.

From the villa itself a series of terraces and flights of steps lead down into the spacious gardens, in which hundreds of fountains, cascades and basins toss water into the air, collect it or allow it to pass on its way downhill. The gardens are filled with the sound of plashing and running water. The whole system, with its playful sculptural forms, is designed with a single purpose in mind – to please the eye and delight the senses.

Opening times
9.30 a.m. to 1½ hours before sunset; from the end of April the Villa is also open 8.30– 11.30 p.m., during summer 9 p.m. to midnight; closed Mon.

Villa Adriana (Villa of Hadrian)

The mightly ruins of Hadrian's Villa give an overwhelming impression of Imperial grandeur and the splendour of the Roman Empire in its heyday. In the extensive grounds of the villa Hadrian built small-scale copies of all the places and buildings which had particularly impressed him on his wide travels about the Empire, including the vale of Tempe in

Teatro Marittimo, Tivoli

Thessaly, a canal at the Egyptian town of Canopus and the Academy of Athens. Here, too, everything was provided to meet the needs of the Imperial court. Visitors can now walk about the site and see the remains both of the reproductions of famous buildings and the residences of the Emperor and his court. Of particular interest are the Greek Theatre (at the entrance); the "garden room" of a small palace showing the restless architectural style of the period with its interplay of convex and concave lines; the Piazza d'Oro (Golden Square), which was surrounded by 60 columns; the Teatro Marittimo ("Maritime Theatre"); a small villa with a marble colonnade and the "Island of Solitude"; two sets of baths, one large and one small; the Canopus, a long basin or canal, with the Temple of Serapis and the Academy; the Stadium; the Caserma dei Vigili (Watchmen's Barracks); the Library; and the Imperial palace proper. A general impression of the whole complex is provided by a model housed in a building near the entrance.

*Tomba di Cecilia Metella (Tomb of Caecilia Metella)

Situation
Via Appia Antica

Bus
118

The tomb of Caecilia Metella and her husband, one of the best known of ancient Roman monuments, stands in a conspicuous position in the picturesque setting of the Via Appia Antica.
This tall cylindrical structure, 20 m (65 ft) in diameter, was erected by the famous family of the Metelli in the 1st c. B.C. Caecilia Metella was the daughter of a general and her husband

was a son of the Crassus who was a member of the Triumvirate together with Caesar and Pompey.
In 1302 the Caetani family incorporated the tomb in their castle and equipped it with battlements.

Opening times
9.30 a.m.–3.30 p.m.

Closed
Mon.

Torre delle Milizie   C3

The Torre delle Milizie is one of the oldest and strongest fortified towers in Italy and the largest in Rome. It is popularly believed that Augustus is buried under the tower and that Nero watched the burning of Rome from the top.
The tower was built by Pope Gregory IX in the 13th c., and probably takes its name from a nearby barracks of Byzantine militia. It belonged to a succession of different noble families and played a part in their endless feuds. In 1312 the German king Henry VII used it as his base during his successful attempt to secure his coronation as Emperor in spite of the hostility of the Roman nobility. The tower began sinking on one side soon after its erection, so that Rome, like Pisa, has its leaning tower. From the top of the tower there are magnificent views of central Rome and the ancient remains.

Situation
Via Quattro Novembre

Buses
46, 56, 57, 60, 62, 64, 65, 70, 71, 75, 81, 88, 90, 95, 170

Trastevere   C/D2/3

Trastevere (from *trans Tiberim*), the district of Rome beyond the Tiber, has preserved much of the character of old Rome, with its narrow and irregular streets, its little squares and its venerable churches, such as Santa Maria in Trastevere (see entry).
The people of Trastevere claim that their district is older than Rome. There is a constant bustle of life and activity in the Viale Trastevere and the little lanes and square opening off it. This liveliness is at its height in the evening; but visitors who go across to Trastevere for their evening meal in one of its numerous trattorie should take care to give thieves no opportunity to ply their trade.

Buses
26, 28, 44, 56, 60, 75, 97, 170, 710, 718, 719

Città del Vaticano (Vatican City)   B1/2,C1

The extensive territories of the Papal States in central Italy, originally presented to the Pope by the Frankish king Pippin the Short, father of Charlemagne, were incorporated in the new kingdom of Italy in 1870. The Pope thereafter regarded himself as a prisoner in the Vatican, and this rift between Church and State was not finally healed until 1929, when Mussolini concluded the Lateran Treaty with the Holy See under which the Pope gained full sovereignty over the more restricted territory of the Vatican State.
The Vatican State is the smallest independent state in the world, with an area of 0·44 sq. km (110 acres) and a population of 1000. It consists essentially of the Vatican palace and gardens, St Peter's and St Peter's Square, most of the area being enclosed by the Vatican walls, with a white strip across

Underground
Ottaviano (line A)

Buses
23, 34, 41, 42, 46, 49, 62, 64, 65, 98, 492, 881, 907, 991

Trams
19, 30

131

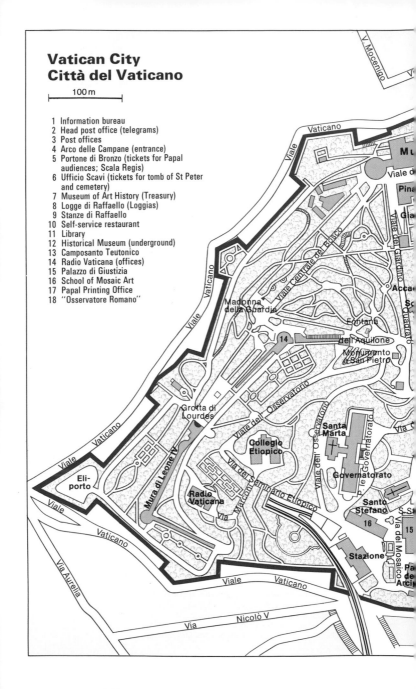

Vatican City
Città del Vaticano

|———— 100 m ————|

1 Information bureau
2 Head post office (telegrams)
3 Post offices
4 Arco delle Campane (entrance)
5 Portone di Bronzo (tickets for Papal
  audiences; Scala Regis)
6 Ufficio Scavi (tickets for tomb of St Peter
  and cemetery)
7 Museum of Art History (Treasury)
8 Logge di Raffaello (Loggias)
9 Stanze di Raffaello
10 Self-service restaurant
11 Library
12 Historical Museum (underground)
13 Camposanto Teutonico
14 Radio Vaticana (offices)
15 Palazzo di Giustizia
16 School of Mosaic Art
17 Papal Printing Office
18 "Osservatore Romano"

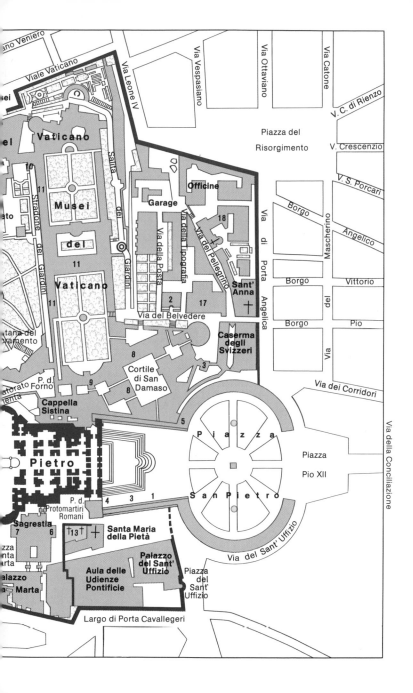

St Peter's Square marking the boundary on that side. (During the period of German occupation in the Second World War this line was of some significance.)

The Pope (since 1978 John Paul II, formerly the Polish Cardinal Karol Wojtyla), supreme head of the Roman Catholic Church (membership over 700 million), is invested with legislative, executive and judicial powers. In external affairs he is represented by the Cardinal Secretary of State, while the administration is headed by a Governor responsible only to the Pope.

Since the dissolution of the Guardia Nobile and Guardia Palatina in 1970 the Pope's bodyguard consists only of the Gendarmeria and the Swiss Guard. Membership of the Swiss Guard is restricted to Roman Catholic citizens of Switzerland aged between 19 and 25, who must be unmarried and of a minimum height of 1·74 m (5 ft 8½ in.). The period of service is from 2 to 20 years. The present strength of the Swiss Guard is 90, including officers. Members of the Guard wear medieval uniforms in the colours of the Medici Popes (yellow, red and blue).

The Vatican City has its own currency (1 Vatican lira=1 Italian lira), postal service (issuing stamps which are valid throughout Rome), telephone and telegraph services, newspapers and periodicals (in particular the "Osservatore Romano", with a circulation of 60,000–70,000), radio station (Radio Vaticana: transmissions on medium and short waves in some 35 languages), a fleet of about a hundred vehicles (registration letters SCV), and its own railway station and helicopter pad.

The Vatican flag has vertical stripes of yellow and white, with two crossed keys below the Papal tiara (triple crown) on a white ground.

Papal possessions outside Vatican City – the basilicas of San Paolo fuori le Mura and Santa Maria Maggiore (see entries), the Papal administrative offices and the Pope's summer residence at Castel Gandolfo (see entry) – enjoy extra-territorial status and are not subject to Italian law.

The territory of Vatican City, with the exception of certain permitted areas (St Peter's, the museums, the Camposanto Teutonico, etc.) can be entered only with special permission. Vehicles are subject to a speed limit of 30 km p.h. (18½ m.p.h.) within Vatican City.

Musei Vaticani (Vatican Museums)   B1

Underground station
Ottaviano (line A)
Buses
23, 32, 49, 51, 81, 907, 990, 991; shuttle service from Piazza San Pietro (south side)
Trams 19, 30
Opening times
Eastertide and July–Sept.
Mon.–Fri. 9 a.m.–4 p.m., Sat. & last Sun. in month 9 a.m.–1 p.m.; other months 9 a.m.–1 p.m., closed Sun.
Admission fee

The Vatican Museums, which occupy much of the Vatican Palace (see Palazzi Vaticani) in Viale Vaticano, contain one of the world's greatest art collections.

The history of the museums goes back to 1506, when Pope Julius II, pursuing the ideals of the Renaissance, began to collect ancient works of art. The collections were increased over the centuries by art treasures from the territories of the Papal States, works of art presented to the Popes and items related to the work of the Roman Catholic Church.

Vatican City: Governor's Palace ▶

In addition there are works of art created specifically for the Vatican Palace, including the paintings in the Sistine Chapel and the Stanze di Raffaello.

The museums are closed on Sundays and public holidays.

**Pinacoteca (Picture Gallery)

The Pinacoteca, founded by Pius VI and later robbed of many of its treasures by Napoleon, contains in its 16 rooms a collection of pictures, ranging in date from the Middle Ages to the present day, which gives an excellent survey of the development of Western painting. The pictures are arranged in chronological order.

Pictures of particular note include the following:

Room I: medieval art (Byzantine, Sienese, Umbrian and Tuscan), including a liturgical vestment (*pluviale*) which belonged to Pope Boniface VIII (13th c.).

Room II: triptych of Cardinal Stefaneschi (Giotto).

Room III: "Madonna" and "St Nicholas of Bari" by Fra Angelico, triptych by Filippo Lippi.

Room V: "Pietà" by Lucas Cranach the Elder.

Room VII: "Coronation of the Virgin" by Pinturicchio, "Madonna" by Perugino.

Room VIII: tapestries from cartoons by Raphael, and Raphael's famous "Transfiguration" (1517: his last picture) and "Madonna of Foligno" (1512–13).

Room IX: "St Jerome", an unfinished work by Leonardo da Vinci.

Room X: "Madonna" by Titian.

Room XII: "Entombment" by Caravaggio.

Room XIV: Dutch and Flemish masters (school of Rubens).

Room XV: portraits of Popes.

Museo Gregoriano Egizio (Egyptian Museum)

The Egyptian Museum in the Cortile della Pigna, re-founded by Pope Gregory XVI (the first collection having been assembled by Pius VII), contains a small but valuable collection of Egyptian art from the 3rd millennium B.C. to the 6th c. B.C., including basalt and wooden sarcophagi, heads of gods and pharaohs, mummified heads, stelae, statues of gods and animals and papyri.

*Museo Pio-Clementino

The Vatican Museums have the largest collection of ancient sculpture in the world, mailnly found in Rome and the surrounding area. The collection was arranged on a systematic basis by Popes Clement XIV (1769–74) and Pius VI (1775–99). Among outstanding items are the following:

Sala a Croce Greca: the porphyry sarcophagi of Constantia (Constantine's daughter) and St Helen (his mother), richly decorated with figures and symbols.

Sala Rotonda: Zeus of Otricoli, a copy of a work by Bryaxis (4th c. B.C.).

Sala delle Muse: Belvedere Torso, a work by Apollonius of

Vatican Museums
Musei Vaticani

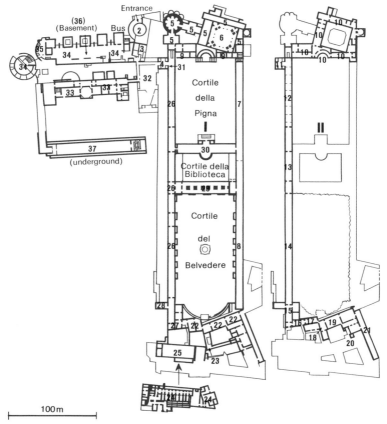

100 m

1 Lift	14 Galleria delle Carte Geografiche (Map Gallery)	25 Sistine Chapel
2 Stairs	15 Pius V's Chapel	26 Vatican Library
3 Vestibule (tickets, information)	16 Sala Sobieski	27 Museo Sacro della Biblioteca
4 Atrio dei Quattro Cancelli	17 Sala dell'Immacolata	28 Sala delle Nozze Aldobrandine
5 Museo Pio-Clementino	18 Urban VIII's Chapel	29 Salone Sistino
6 Cortile Ottagono	19 Stanze di Raffaello	30 Braccio Nuovo
7 Museo Chiaramonti	20 Nicholas V's Chapel (Beato Angelico)	31 Museo Profano della Biblioteca
8 Galleria Lapidaria	21 Logge di Raffaello (Loggias of Raphael)	32 Cortile della Pinacoteca
9 Museo Gregoriano Egizio (Egyptian Museum)	22 Appartamento Borgia	33 Pinacoteca (Picture Gallery)
10 Museo Gregoriano Etrusco (Etruscan Museum)	23 Salette Borgia	34 Museo Gregoriano Profano (Museum of Secular Art)
11 Sala della Biga	24 Collezione d'Arte Religiosa Moderna (Museum of Modern Religious Art)	35 Museo Pio Cristiano
12 Galleria dei Candelabri		36 Museo Missionario Etnologico
13 Galleria degli Arazzi (Tapestry Gallery)		37 Museo Storico (Historical Museum)

Athens (1st c. B.C.) which was admired by Michelangelo; statues of Apollo and the Muses.

Sala degli Animali: numerous realistic marble and alabaster statues of animals; statue of Meleager with dog and a wild boar's head (Roman copy).

Galleria delle Statue: Apollo Sauroctonus (Apollo the Lizard-Killer: Roman copy of a bronze original by Praxiteles); the Candelabri Barberini (the finest ancient candelabras known), from the Villa Adriana at Tivoli.

Gabinetto delle Maschere (Cabinet of Masks): Cnidian Venus, a Roman copy of the Aphrodite of Praxiteles (4th c. B.C.).

Cortile del Belvedere: the most famous statues in the Vatican – the Apollo Belvedere (Roman copy of an original by Leochares c. 330 B.C.), Canova's Perseus, a Hermes of the Hadrianic period (copy of an original by Praxiteles) and above all the celebrated Laocoön group, a masterpiece of Hellenistic sculpture (at the finding of which in 1506 Michelangelo was present) depicting the Trojan priest Laocoön and his sons in a mortal struggle with two huge snakes.

Gabinetto del Apoxyomenos: the Athlete Apoxyomenos, a copy of a famous bronze statue by Lysippus, found in Trastevere in 1849.

*Museo Chiaramonti

The Museo Chiaramonti, founded by Pope Pius VII (1800–23), a member of the Chiaramonti family, is housed in a long gallery leading to the Papal palace and contains numerous works of Greek and Roman art, of varying quality.

There are also works of Greek and Roman sculpture in the Galleria Lapidaria and the Braccio Nuovo, which links the two long wings extending from the entrance to the museums to the Palazzi Vaticani.

Notable items in the Braccio Nuovo are the Augustus of Prima Porta, a statue of the Emperor found in 1863 in the country villa of his wife Livia; a statue of the god of the Nile; and the Doryphorus ("Spear-Carrier"), a copy of a work by Polycletus. In the Sala della Biga, near the entrance, are two Discus-Throwers, copies of works by Myron and Polycletus (5th c. B.C.).

*Museo Gregoriano Etrusco (Etruscan Museum)

The Etruscan Museum, founded by Pope Gregory XVI (1831–46), contains in its 18 rooms works of art and everyday objects which throw light on the life of the Etruscans and their ideas of the afterlife. The collection also includes Greek and Roman works.

Particularly notable items are the rich grave goods from the Regolini-Galassi tomb at Cerveteri, the Mars of Todi, the Stele del Palestrita (from Attica, 5th c. B.C.), a head of Athena and numerous fine vases.

*Museo Gregoriano Profano (Museum of Secular Art)

This museum of secular art was also founded by Gregory XVI. Until 1963 it was housed, along with the Museo Pio Cristiano and the Museo Epigrafico Cristiano, in the Lateran Palace (see Palazzo Laterano). It now occupies a modern museum building adjoining the Pinacoteca which was built during the reigns of Popes John XXIII (1958–63) and Paul VI (1963–78). The works of ancient sculpture in this excellently arranged museum were mostly found in the territories of the Papal States. It includes Roman copies of Greek sculpture and originals of Roman Imperial sculpture – statues, reliefs, funerary monuments and sarcophagi, together with works of political and religious content.

First section: Roman copies and re-workings of Greek originals.

2nd section: Roman sculpture (1st and early 2nd c. A.D.).

3rd section: sarcophagi.

4th section: Roman sculpture (2nd and 3rd c. A.D.)

*Biblioteca Apostolica Vaticana (Vatican Library)

Judged by the value of its contents, the Vatican Library is the richest in the world. Since its foundation by Nicholas V in 1450 the library has been systematically built up, and now contains, in addition to books printed since the end of the 15th c., some 7000 incunabula, 25,000 medieval hand-written books and 80,000 manuscripts. In the library hall, 70 m (230 ft) long, built by Domenico Fontana, are cases displaying some of its greatest treasures – Biblical codices, illuminated Gospel books, finely printed books, valuable parchments and ancient papyri and scrolls.

Museo Sacro

At the end of the long range housing the Vatican Library is this Museum of Sacred art, containing material found during the excavation of catacombs and early Christian churches in Rome and the surrounding area. Pope Pius XI (1922–39) showed a particular interest in the smaller works of Christian art. In a side room is the "Aldobrandini Wedding" (Nozze Aldobrandine), a sensitively painted and well-preserved ancient fresco which was found about 1600 and until 1818 was kept in the Aldobrandini Gardens.

*Appartamento Borgia

The Borgia Pope Alexander VI (1492–1503) had a private residence built for himself and his family within the Vatican Palace, and commissioned Pinturicchio to decorate it with wall and ceiling paintings. Between 1492 and 1495 the painter and his assistants and pupils painted a series of scenes, combining Renaissance, humanist and ancient themes with Christian subjects:

1st room: prophets and Sibyls.

2nd room: the Creed, with prophets and Apostles.

3rd room: allegories of the seven liberal arts.

4th room: legends of saints.

5th room: scenes from the life of Christ and the Virgin.

The Papal portraits formerly in the 6th room have not survived.

**Stanze dì Raffaello (Raphael Rooms)

These rooms above the Appartamento Borgia, built by Pope Nicholas V, contain a magnificent series of frescoes by Raphael, who was commissioned by the art-loving Pope Julius II in 1508 to repaint the rooms.

Room 1 (Sala dell'Incendio di Borgo, Room of the Burning of the Borgo):
Ceiling painting by Perugino, and four paintings of historical scenes by pupils of Raphael (1517 onwards): Leo IV and the burning of the Borgo (the district around St Peter's) in 847; coronation of Charlemagne by Leo III in 800; Leo IV's naval victory over the Saracens off Ostia in 849; and Leo III's oath (denying false accusations) in 800. These paintings, commemorating his predecessors of the same name, were commissioned by Pope Leo X (1513–21).

Room 2 (Sala della Segnatura, the meeting-place of an ecclesiastical tribunal):
The frescoes in this room, painted by Raphael in 1508–11, represent the supreme achievement of Renaissance painting. They depict the culture of the period in all its richness and splendour.
The Disputa del Sacramento, a theological disputation on the doctrine of transubstantiation, depicts the world of religious faith. In the lower zone, around the altar, are Popes, bishops, teachers and theologians, including Pope Innocent III, St Bonaventure and Dante. Above them, under God the Father, are Christ with the Virgin and John the Baptist, attended by saints.
The Scuola d'Atene (School of Athens), set in the newly built St Peter's, represents the field of the natural sciences – attainable without divine revelation – and depicts representatives of philosophy (the two central figures, Plato and Aristotle, together with Socrates), architecture (Bramante), history (Xenophon) and mathematics (Archimedes, Pythagoras, Euclid), together with Raphael himself (in the corner, second from right).
Above one window is an associated scene depicting Parnassus, with Apollo playing a violin, the blind Homer, the Muses and other ancient poets (Virgil, Sappho, Ovid, Catullus and Horace). Above the other are a scene depicting the glorification of canon and civil law and allegorical representations of the virtues of Prudence and Temperance. On the ceiling, corresponding to the scenes on the walls below, are allegories of theology, philosophy, poetry and justice.

Room 3 (Sala d'Eliodoro, Room of Heliodorus):
The paintings by Raphael in this room (1512–14) show still greater expressive power and a livelier sense of movement than those in the Sala della Segnatura. They depict four scenes: Leo the Great repulsing Attila, the Mass of Bolsena (in which an unbelieving priest was convinced of the truth of the doctrine of transubstantiation), the expulsion of Heliodorus from the Temple and the liberation of St Peter from prison.

Room 4 (Sala di Costantino, Room of Constantine):
The painting dates almost entirely from the reign of Clement VII, after Raphael's death. On the long wall is a fine picture (by pupils of Raphael) of Constantine's victory over Maxentius at the Milvian Bridge.

*Cappella di Niccolò V (Nicholas V's Chapel)

Nicholas V's Chapel, near the Stanze di Raffaello, has frescoes by Fra Beato Angelico on the life and martyrdom of SS. Stephen and Lawrence (1447–9).

Galleria delle Carte Geografiche/Galleria dei Candelabri e degli Arazzi
(Map Gallery/Gallery of Candelabras and Tapestries)

The Map Gallery, 120 m (395 ft) long, has maps of all the different parts of Italy, often with views of cities and prospects of scenery. Beyond this gallery (when coming from the Vatican Palace) is the Gallery of Candelabras and Tapestries, with valuable tapestries of the 15th–17th c. and Roman marble candelabras.

**Cappella Sistina (Sistine Chapel)

The Sistine Chapel, built by Pope Sixtus IV in 1473–84, is a plain rectangular hall 40·50 m (133 ft) long, 20·70 m (68 ft) wide and 13·20 m (43 ft) high with large wall and ceiling surfaces, divided into two by a marble balustrade (by Mino da Fiesole and Andrea Bregno). The chapel is the Pope's domestic chapel, and is also used for services and special occasions. After the death of a Pope the conclave to elect his successor is held here. There are frescoes on the side walls, the ceiling and the altar wall. Restoration will take until 1992.

The side walls are covered with large frescoes painted for Sixtus IV (1481–3) by the most celebrated painters of the day – Perugino, Botticelli, Rosselli, Pinturicchio, Signorelli and Ghirlandaio – depicting Biblical scenes against the background of the Umbrian and Tuscan scenery familiar to the artists. These late 15th c. paintings already reflect the discovery of man as an individual and his importance in the historical process, and with consummate artistic skill depict him acting within an architectural and landscape setting, thus preparing the way for the further development of this trend by Michelangelo. *Paintings on side walls*

The left-hand wall has scenes from the life of Moses, liberator of the Jewish people from their captivity in Egypt; the circumcision of Moses; Moses with the shepherds and the burning bush; the crossing of the Red Sea; Moses receiving the tables of the Law on Mount Sinai; the destruction of the company of Korah; and the death of Moses.

The right-hand wall depicts events in the life of Christ, the liberator of mankind from sin – his baptism in the Jordan; the cleansing of lepers (a magnificent work by Botticelli); the calling of Peter and Andrew; the Sermon on the Mount; Christ giving the keys to Peter; and the Last Supper.

The frescoes on the ceiling were painted by Michelangelo in the reign of the great Pope and Renaissance prince Julius II, most of them being his own unaided work. They were painted between the autumn of 1508 and August 1510 and, after a pause, completed in 1511–12. Michelangelo's idea was an ambitious one, never attempted on such a scale before: no less than to depict the Creation as it is described in Genesis. *Paintings on ceilings*

The central part of the ceiling (beginning at the near end) depicts God separating light from darkness, creating the sun and the moon, separating land and sea, creating Adam and then Eve; the Fall; Noah's thank-offering; the Flood; and Noah's drunkenness. In the lower ranges of the vaulting are colossal figures of the prophets and Sibyls who conveyed God's message to the Jews and the Gentiles.

Michelangelo confines himself to restrained colours, with a predominance of soft blues, greens, ochres, reds and whites. The figures are depicted in vigorous and passionate movement.

Painting on altar wall

Michelangelo began work on the large fresco on the altar wall 22 years later (1534), in the reign of Pope Paul III, when he was 59. As a counterpart to his depiction of the Creation on the ceiling he painted on this wall the final scene in the story of the world, the Last Judgement, depicting Christ returning as the Judge to summon the righteous to paradise and consign the damned to hell. The theme in all its details is based on the scriptural account. With its dramatic presentation of its subject, which Michelangelo sees as a judgment on the life of the individual human being, this ranks as one of the greatest achievements of European painting.

In the Last Judgment Christ is depicted as a powerful youthful god standing on a cloud, surrounded by the Virgin, the Apostles and other saints. The righteous (to the left) rising up into heaven and the damned (on the right) tumbling into hell form a powerful upward and downward movement which determines the eternal fate of mankind, while below the dead are seen rising from their graves. In the middle are angels blowing their trumpets to summon all men to judgment, and up above other angels carry in triumph the instruments of the Passion.

The 391 figures are represented with athletic forms, and many of them have readily recognisable attributes (Peter with his key, Sebastian with his arrows, Lawrence with his gridiron, Bartholomew with his flayed skin, which bears a portrait of Michelangelo himself, Catherine with her wheel).

Museo Profano

This collection of secular art includes a variety of Etruscan, Roman and medieval material.

Museo Pio Cristiano

This museum, founded by Pope Pius IX in 1854, contains material which until 1963 was housed in the Lateran Palace (see Palazzo Laterano). There are two sections, one devoted to architecture, sculpture and mosaics, the other to inscriptions.

Museo Missionario Etnologico

Objects brought back from the various mission fields of the Church were originally (from 1926 onwards) displayed in the

Sistine Chapel ▶

Sistine Chapel: Michelangelo's "Creation of Adam"

Sistine Chapel: Botticelli's "Destruction of the Company of Korah"

Palazzo Laterano (see entry). Pope Pius XI directed that they should be brought together in a systematic arrangement, and in 1970 all material of interest (to scholars as well as to the general public) was transferred to the Museo Missionario Etnologico.

Museo Storico

This Historical Museum, housed in a large building under the Giardino Quadrato (Square Garden), near the Pinacoteca, displays material on the history of the Papal States, Papal carriages and weapons and uniforms of the Papal guards.

Collezione d'Arte Religiosa Moderna

Pope Paul VI (1963–78) was interested in modern religious art, and made available 55 rooms in the Vatican for the display of works of art presented to the Popes or acquired by them. The collection contains more than 800 works by artists of many different countries, including Rodin, Barlach, Matisse, Modigliani, Kokoschka, Dali, Munch, Vlaminck, Feininger, Ernst, Beckmann, Nolde, Le Corbusier, Kandinsky, de Chirico, Greco, Marini, Rouault, Hartung and Hansing.

*Palazzi Vaticani (Vatican Palace)   B1

Some impression of the size of the Vatican Palace, which lies immediately to the right of St Peter's Square (see Piazza San Pietro) and St Peter's itself (see San Pietro in Vaticano), can be gained by starting from the fountain on the left-hand side of St Peter's Square, from which the huge bulk of the main range of buildings can be seen rearing up above the square, and then continuing along outside the walls to the entrance to the Vatican Museums (see Musei Vaticani).

There would no doubt be some form of lodging for the Bishop of Rome near Old St Peter's (then well outside the city) as early as the 6th c.; but the Papal residence was for long in the Palazzo Laterano (see entry). The first Pope to consider the Vatican as a residence was Nicholas III (1277–80); and this alternative seemed all the more attractive when the Pope returned from exile in Avignon in 1377 and found the Lateran Palace in a state of dilapidation. From 1450 onwards successive Popes systematically embellished and enlarged the Vatican, enlisting in this task the best architects in Rome. The most notable contributions were made by Nicholas V, Sixtus IV (Sistine Chapel), Alexander VI (Appartamento Borgia), Julius II (Cortile del Belvedere, Loggias in the Cortile di San Damaso), Paul III (Cappella Paolina, with frescoes by Michelangelo), Pius V and Sixtus V (the present private apartments, reception rooms and library).

The total area covered by buildings, excluding the gardens, is 55,000 sq. m (13½ acres), of which 25,000 sq. m (6 acres) are accounted for by courtyards. The total number of rooms and chapels is 1400. And surely no other palace in the world can

Underground station
Ottaviano (line A)

Buses
23, 32, 41, 47, 62, 64, 492, 990

Trams
19, 30

compare with the Vatican in historical and artistic importance. In addition to the Pope's own residential apartments and offices the palace houses a number of ecclesiastical bodies as well as the Vatican Museums (see Musei Vaticani). The main entrance is the bronze door at the end of the right-hand colonnade, which leads into the Corridorio del Bernini and, at the far end of this, Bernini's Scala Regia.

*Giardini Vaticani (Vatican Gardens)

The Vatican Gardens, behind St Peter's and the Vatican Palace, occupy a large part of the area of Vatican City. In the gardens are a variety of buildings serving particular purposes, churches and offices, towers and fountains, the Casina di Pio IV (seat of the Pontifical Academy of Sciences) and a coffee-house. The N end of the gardens is bounded by the Leonine Walls, the railway station, the radio transmitter and the Vatican Museums.

**Piazza San Pietro (St Peter's Square)   B2

Buses
23, 32, 41, 47, 62, 64, 492, 990

The Piazza San Pietro in front of St Peter's was laid out by Bernini between 1656 and 1667 to provide a setting in which the faithful from all over the world could gather; and the square he created – perhaps the most famous square in the world – has maintained its fascination right down to our own day. It is in two parts – a large ellipse measuring 340 by 240 m (1115 by 785 ft) and a smaller trapezoid area, the Piazza Retta, from which a broad flight of steps, flanked by statues of the Apostles Peter and Paul, leads up to the church. The oval is enclosed at each end by semicircular colonnades formed by 284 columns and 88 pillars of travertine in four rows. Around the balustrade on the roof of the colonnades are set 140 statues of saints. On either side of the oval are fountains 8 m (26 ft) high with large granite basins; the one on the right, erected in 1613, is by Maderna, the one on the left (1675) probably by Bernini. Two discs set into the paving mark the focal points of the ellipse.

In the centre of the oval, towards which the square slopes gently down, is an Egyptian obelisk 25·50 m (87 ft) high. This was brought from Heliopolis to Rome by Caligula in A.D. 39 and set up in his circus (later known as the Circus of Nero). Throughout the Middle Ages this obelisk remained in its original position – the only one in Rome to do so – until Pope Sixtus V directed in 1586 that it should be moved to St Peter's Square. Domenico Fontana was charged with the very difficult task of transporting this huge mass of stone, weighing 350 tons, to its new site. The operation took four months (from 30 April to 10 September 1586) and involved the employment of 900 workmen, 140 horses and 44 winches. It is said that at one point the ropes were on the point of breaking under the strain when one of the workmen, disregarding the Pope's strict order that there should be absolute silence, shouted "Pour water on them!" and saved the situation. The story goes that the Pope then granted him and his family the privilege of supplying the palm branches used in the Palm Sunday services, a practice which his descendants have maintained until the present day. On 13 May 1981 there was an attack here on Pope John Paul II.

Piazza San Pietro (St Peter's Square) and Via della Conciliazione

Papal guards: the Swiss Guard (left) and the Gendarmeria (right)

San Pietro in Vaticano (St Peter's Church) B1

Situation
Piazza San Pietro

Underground station
Ottaviano (line A)

Buses
23, 32, 41, 47, 62, 64, 492, 990

Trams
19, 30

Opening times
7 a.m.–6 or 7 p.m.

The most famous church in Christendom is St Peter's, dedicated to the Apostle who is believed to have been the first Bishop of Rome, and whose successor each Pope, as supreme head of the Roman Catholic Church, feels himself to be. The history of St Peter's reflects the history of the Papacy.

The original church of St Peter was dedicated by Pope Sylvester I in A.D. 326, thanks to the patronage of the Emperor Constantine. It must have been evident at that time that the site, on the slopes of the Vatican hill, was a difficult one to build on, involving considerable differences of level which had to be allowed for in the foundations; and in addition it was well outside the city. That this inconvenient site was nevertheless selected for the building of St Peter's suggests – with some archaeological evidence in support – that it was honoured in the long memory of Rome as the position of the Apostle's tomb; for Peter was traditionally believed to have been martyred in 64 or 67 in the Imperial gardens on the Vatican hill. Old St Peter's, a five-aisled basilica of the classical type which we know from medieval descriptions, was frequently restored and richly embellished, but after the Pope's return from exile in Avignon and the western schism (when there were a number of Popes at the same time) it was in an advanced stage of dilapidation.

Pope Nicholas V accordingly resolved in 1452 to build an entirely new church and to seek the help of all Christendom in building it. (One source of income for this purpose was the sale of indulgences, which provoked Martin Luther to his protest.) Construction began in 1506 and was pushed ahead with all speed, but the completion and embellishment of the church involved every Pope from Julius II (1503–13) to Pius VI (1775–99). A number of architects took part in the work. The first plan was prepared by Bramante, who was accused of embezzlement of funds and the use of poor materials; then followed Raphael, Fra Giocondo, Giuliano da Sangallo, Baldassare Peruzzi, Antonio da Sangallo and finally Michelangelo, who took over in 1547 at the age of 72. He was responsible in particular for the design of the dome, the drum of which was completed by the time he died in 1564. Other architects were Vignola, Ligorio, della Porta, Fontana and Maderna (who, at Paul V's request, extended the original centralised building towards the square by the addition of a nave).

Façade

In addition to calling for the lengthening of the church towards the square Paul V desired that St Peter's should be linked with the Palazzo Apostolico (Vatican Palace); and for the sake of symmetry this involved a corresponding extension on the other side, giving the façade a total length of 114·70 m (376 ft). The height (45·50 m – 149 ft) could not be increased, however, since this would have hidden still more of Michelangelo's dome. Maderna sought to palliate these unfortunate proportions by an elaborately articulated pattern of columns and pillars, doorways, balconies and windows.

From the central balcony on the façade the senior member of the college of cardinals proclaims the name of a new Pope

St Peter's ▶

elected by the conclave, and from this balcony, too, the Pope pronounces his blessing "urbi et orbi" on certain festivals, and beatifications and canonisations are announced. On the top of the façade are statues of Christ flanked by Apostles, 5·70 m (19 ft) high. The two clocks at the ends of the façade were added by Giuseppe Valadier in the 19th c.

Portico

The portico (71 m (233 ft) long, 13·50 m (44 ft) deep, 20 m (66 ft) high) is entered through five doorways with bronze grilles. On the outer side are two equestrian statues – Charlemagne to

St Peter's Church
San Pietro in Vaticano

| 50 m |

St Peter's Square

1 Principal entrance
2 Porta Santa
3 Michelangelo's Pietà
4 Monument to Christina of Sweden
5 St Sebastian's Chapel
6 Monument to Margravine Mathilda of Tuscany
7 Chapel of the Sacrament
8 Gregorian Chapel
9 Altar of St Jerome
10 Statue of St Peter
11 Altar of the Archangel Michael
12 Altar of St Peter (restoring Tabitha to life)

13 Tomb of Pope Urban VIII
14 Throne of St Peter (by Bernini)
15 Tomb of Pope Paul III
16 Chapel of the Column
17 Altar of St Peter (healing the lame man)
18 Grave of Pope Alexander VII
19 Altar of the Crucifixion of St Peter
20 Statue of St Andrew: entrance to Sacre Grotte Vaticane
21 Tomb of Pope Pius VIII; entrance to Sacristy and Museum

22 Clementine Chapel
23 Altar of St Gregory
24 Monument to Pope Pius VII
25 Choir Chapel
26 Tomb of Pope Pius X
27 Tomb of Pope Innocent VIII
28 Chapel of the Presentation
29 Monument to Maria Clementina Sobieska; entrance to dome
30 Baptistery
31 Sacristy
32 Museo Storico-Artistico (Tesoro)
33 Canons' Sacristy

the left, Constantine (by Bernini) to the right. Above the main doorway are fragments of a mosaic by Giotto from Old St Peter's, the "Navicella" (the Apostles' ship in the storm). The double bronze doors, also from Old St Peter's, were the work of the Florentine sculptor Filarete (1433–45); they depict Christ and the Virgin, the Apostles Peter and Paul and their martyrdom, and historical scenes. To the left is the "Door of Death", a modern work by Giacomo Manzù. To the right is the Porta Santa, which is kept closed except in Holy Years.

The huge dimensions of the interior are of overwhelming effect. The church is 186 m (610 ft) long, rises to a height of 46 m (150 ft) in the nave and 119 m (390 ft) in the dome, covers an area of 15,000 sq. m (18,000 sq. yd) and can accommodate a congregation of 60,000. In the pavement of the nave, for purposes of comparison, are marked the lengths (measured from the apse) of other great churches. In spite of its enormous size, however, the simple architectural plan (in the form of a Latin cross, with the nave longer than the transepts) and the great dome which crowns it allow the church to be seen and appreciated as a whole.

Interior

The following features are worth particular note in going round the church.

A few yards from the main doorway is a red porphyry disc in the floor marking the spot on which Charlemagne was crowned in Old St Peter's by Pope Leo III on Christmas Day in the year 800.

In the Capella della Pietà (on the right of the north aisle) is Michelangelo's famous "Pietà" (1498–1500). It depicts a youthful Virgin holding in her arms the body of Christ, just taken down from the cross. A ribbon on her breast is inscribed with the sculptor's name. The facial expressions and the consummate skill of the carving reveal Michelangelo as a great artist even at the early age (25) at which he created this work. On the adjoining pier is a monument commemorating Queen Christina of Sweden, who abdicated as queen and became a Roman Catholic.

Right-hand aisle

Just beyond this is St Sebastian's Chapel, with a fine mosaic above the altar (after a painting by Domenichino) depicting the saint's martyrdom. (Most of the paintings in the church have been replaced by mosaics: the originals are in the Musei Vaticani – see entry.)

By the next pier is the mausoleum (designed by Bernini) of Countess Matilda of Tuscany, who played a prominent part in the conflict between the Emperor and the Pope in the 11th c. Next comes the richly decorated Chapel of the Sacrament, to which both Bernini (the tabernacle) and Borromini (the bronze grille) contributed. The chapel was built for Pope Urban VIII, of the Barberini family: hence the bees from the Barberini coat of arms which feature in the decoration. Just beyond this chapel is the tomb of Pope Gregory XIII, reformer of the calendar (1572–85), with the heraldic dragon of the Buoncompagni family to which he belonged.

The right transept was the meeting-place of the First Vatican Council (1869–70), in which 650 bishops took part. The Second Vatican Council (1962–5), when the number of bishops had risen to over 3000, was held in the nave. In the passage beyond the transept is the monument of Clement XIII, a youthful work by Canova (1788–92).

Crossing and dome

Four massive pentagonal piers with a diameter of 24 m (79 ft) and a circumference of 71 m (233 ft) bear the dome, designed by Michelangelo as the culminating point of the church, over the tomb of St Peter. The dome, set over a drum with 16 windows, has a diameter of 42·34 m – 139 ft (slightly less than the dome of the Pantheon, 43·20 m – 142 ft). It consists of an inner dome and an outer protective shell, with enough space between the two for a man to stand upright. Above the dome is the lantern, giving a total interior height of 119 m (390 ft). In niches in the piers are figures of St Veronica with her napkin, St Helen with the True Cross, St Longinus with his lance and St Andrew with his saltire cross, and in the loggias above are displayed, on special festivals, relics of the Passion. Round the dome is a frieze with the Latin text (in letters 2 m (6 ft) high) of the text from St Matthew's Gospel on which the Pope's claim to the headship of the Church is based: "Tu es Petrus . . ." ("Thou are Peter, and upon this rock I will build my church . . . And I will give unto thee the keys of the kingdom of heaven.") Under the dome, immediately above Peter's tomb, is the Papal altar, with a bronze baldacchino (canopy) created by Bernini (1624–33) for Pope Urban VIII, using bronze from the portico of the Pantheon. With its twisted columns and fantastic superstructure this is a masterpiece of Baroque sculpture. In front of the altar, on a lower level, is the Confessio, lit by 95 gilded oil lamps, beyond which is the tomb of St Peter; in it is a marble figure of Pope Pius VI (1775–99), kneeling, by Canova. Against the pier with the figure of Longinus is a bronze statue of St Peter enthroned (13th c.), the right foot of which has been worn smooth by the kisses of the faithful.

Apse

In the apse is Bernini's Cathedra Petri, a bronze throne which shows the same Baroque sense of movement as the baldacchino. It is supported by figures of the four Doctors of the Church (Ambrose, Augustine, Athanasius and John Chrysostom). Above the throne is an alabaster window with the symbolic dove of the Holy Ghost.

Flanking the Cathedra Petri are the tombs of Popes Urban VIII Barberini (on right: by Bernini, 1642–7) and Paul III Farnese (on left: by Giacomo della Porta, 1551–75).

Left-hand aisle

In the left-hand aisle are the tombs of other famous Popes, by leading artists of their day:

In the passage behind the pier, the monument of Alexander VII (carved under the direction of Bernini, 1672–78).

Diagonally across from the huge sacristy built in 1776–84 in the reign of Pius VI the monument of Pius VII (by Thorvaldsen, 1823). This is the only work in the church by a Protestant sculptor, and it gave rise to protests at the time it was commissioned.

In front of the Choir Chapel (opposite the Chapel of the Sacrament), a mosaic copy of Raphael's "Transfiguration".

In front of the Cappella della Presentazione, the tomb of Innocent VIII (by Pollaiolo, 1498), on which the Pope is represented twice (enthroned and recumbent). This is the only monument from Old St Peter's which was transferred to the new church. Opposite it is a statue of Pius X.

In the Cappella della Presentazione are a bronze relief commemorating Pope John XXIII (1958–63: on right) and a statue of Benedict XV (1914–22: on left).

Papal altar

Statue of St Peter

Beyond the Cappella della Presentazione are two monuments commemorating the last of the Stuarts: on right Maria Clementina Sobieska, wife of James the Old Pretender; on left the Old Pretender, "Bonnie Prince Charlie" and Cardinal Henry of York.

Adjoining the Stuart monuments near the Baptistery are the stairs (142 steps) and lift leading to the roof of the church, from which visitors can climb to the lantern by way of a gallery inside the drum and further staircases (sometimes extremely steep). From the roof and the lantern there are magnificent views over St Peter's Square and the city; and from here, too, it is possible to see Michelangelo's dome at close quarters and observe the details of its structure.

Roof

The entrance to the "Vatican Grottoes" (Crypt) is at the pillar with the figure of St Andrew. This spacious undercroft was created when Antonio da Sangallo raised the floor level of the church by 3·20 m (10½ ft) to protect it from damp. The tombs of earlier Popes were transferred here from Old St Peter's, and many later Popes have also been buried here, including the last four (Pius XII, John XXIII, Paul VI and John Paul I). A walk around the tombs of the Popes is one of the most impressive experiences of a visit to Rome.

Sacre Grotte Vaticane

It is also possible, with special permission, to see the excavations (*scavi*) under St Peter's. Here the archaeologists have brought to light the old cemetery on the Vatican hill, including what is believed to be the tomb of St Peter himself, and the foundations of the original Constantinian basilica.

Via Appia Antica (short stretch with old surface)

Via Appia Antica   D4

Buses
4, 88, 90, 93, changing to
118 or 218

Outside the Porta San Sebastiano in the Aurelian Walls (see Mura Aureliane) is the Via Appia Antica, one of the oldest and most important of the Roman consular highways. It was built about 300 B.C. by the censor Appius Claudius Caecus to link Rome with Capua and was extended to Brindisi about 190 B.C. The road is now metalled for almost its entire length. From the port of Brindisi communications were established across the Mediterranean with the eastern territories of the Empire. Just outside Rome, running parallel with the road, can be seen the ruins of some of the aqueducts which supplied the city with water. On either side of the road are the remains of tombs belonging to the aristocratic families of Rome – built outside the city, since burials were not permitted within its walls. The ruins of these tombs and memorial stones combine with the pines and cypresses of the Roman Campagna to give the Via Appia Antica its characteristic and picturesque aspect.

Via dei Fori Imperiali   C3/4

Buses
85, 87, 88

This six-lane highway, built by Mussolini in 1932, runs from the Capitol (see Campidoglio) to the Colosseum (see Colosseo), passing along one side of the Forum (see Foro Romano).

In 1980 the city council, giving priority to archaeology over traffic, decided to remove the road and thus make it possible to excavate the remains of the great days of the Empire which lie concealed under its 64,000 sq. m (76,500 sq. yd) of asphalt.

Via di San Gregorio   C4

This broad tree-lined street, in ancient times the Triumphal Way followed by victorious generals, runs S from the Colosseum (see Colosseo) and Arch of Constantine (see Arco di Costantino) between the Palatine (see Palatino) and Caelian hills, past the church of San Gregorio Magno (see entry), to the SE end of the Circus Maximus.

Underground station
Colosseo (line B)

Buses
11, 15, 27, 81, 85, 87, 88, 90, 118, 673

Via Veneto (officially Via Vittorio Veneto)   B3/4

This handsome and fashionable street, which descends in two sweeping curves from the Porta Pinciana to the Piazza Barberini, has been a Mecca for tourists ever since it was laid out at the beginning of this century. Its elegant fashion shops, lively cafés and exclusive hotels attract those who want both to see and be seen.

Underground station
Barberini (line A)

Buses
52, 53, 56, 58, 90b, 95, 490, 492, 495

* Villa Borghese and Galleria Borghese   B3/4

The great families of Papal Rome had their palaces in the city and their villas in the country, which might be just outside the city or farther afield, sometimes as far away as the Alban Hills. It is always necessary in Rome, therefore, to distinguish between the *palazzo* and the *villa* associated with a particular family name.

The Borghese family, which produced Pope Paul V (1605–21), several cardinals and other prominent figures, had this villa, built in an area of vineyards on the outskirts of Rome for Cardinal Scipione Caffarelli Borghese in 1613–16. The villa is complete with extensive grounds, laid out with artificial lakes and garden pavilions, which now combine with the Pincio Gardens (see entry) to form one of the largest parks in Rome. Prince Marc'Antonio Borghese had considerable alterations carried out by an architect of German origin, Unterberger. Notable features of the gardens are the artificial lake, the Piazza Sena, on which a race meeting is held at the beginning of May, and a number of monuments.

At the E end of the gardens is the Casino Borghese (by Giovanni Vasanzio, 1613–15), which now houses the Museo e Galleria Borghese, with the collection of antiquities assembled by Cardinal Scipione Borghese.

The art-loving Cardinal Scipione Borghese, a great collector of antiquities, also commissioned work from contemporary artists. His collection of antiquities was housed in the Casino and formed the basis of the Borghese Museum – though during

Underground stations
Flaminio and Piazza di Spagna (line A)

Buses
3, 52, 53, 490, 495, 910

Trams
19, 19b, 30, 30b

Opening times
9 a.m.–2 p.m., Sun. 9 a.m.–1 p.m.

Closed
Mon.
(at present temporarily closed)

Villa Borghese

the Napoleonic period Camillo Borghese was compelled to sell some works to the Louvre. At the beginning of the 20th c. the collection of pictures was formed into the Borghese Gallery.

Outstanding works of sculpture in the museum include Canova's figure of Pauline Borghese as Venus (1805); David with his sling (1623–4), commissioned from Bernini by Scipione Borghese; Apollo and Daphne, a masterpiece by Bernini depicting the transformation of Daphne into a laurel-bush to save her from pursuit by Apollo; the Rape of Proserpina, also by Bernini (1621–2); the Sleeping Herma-phrodite (a Roman copy of a Greek original); Aeneas with his father Anchises, by Gian Lorenzo and Pietro Bernini (also son and father); and Bernini's "Truth revealed by Time".

The picture gallery includes works by Raphael (among them an "Entombment"), Botticelli, Pinturicchio, Perugino, Lucas Cranach the Elder, Sodoma, Dürer, Lotto, Domenichino ("Diana the Huntress"), Caravaggio ("Madonna dei Pala-frenieri"), Rubens, Correggio ("Danaë"), Bernini, Bassano, Van Dyck, Titian ("Sacred and Profane Love"), Bellini, Paolo Veronese and Antonello da Messina ("Male Portrait").

---

*Villa Doria Pamphili   C/D1

Buses
31, 42, 144

Adjoining the Janiculum are the extensive grounds of the Villa Doria Pamphili, Rome's largest municipal park, now traversed by the Via Olimpica, a road constructed for the 1960 Olympics.

The villa was built by Alessandro Algardi about 1650 for Prince Camillo Pamphili, a nephew of Pope Innocent X.
On a terrace alongside the Via Aurelia Antica is the Casino dei Quattro Venti (of the Four Winds), which is decorated with statues and reliefs.

**Villa Farnesina   C2

The Villa Farnesina, which now belongs to the State and houses the National Print Cabinet (Gabinetto Nazionale delle Stampe), was built in the 16th c., with all the lavishness and splendour of the period. This Renaissance palace was designed by Baldassare Peruzzi (1508–22) for the banker Agostino Chigi and decorated by famous artists, including Raphael, Giulio Romano, Sebastiano del Piombo, Peruzzi himself and Sodoma. Here Popes, cardinals, princes, diplomats, artists and men of letters were entertained in princely fashion. Illustrious guests were given silver dishes bearing their own coat of arms, which they threw into the nearby Tiber after the banquet (though a net spread in the river enabled them to be recovered afterwards). The palace was acquired by the Farnese family in 1580, and in the 18th c. it passed to the Bourbons of Naples.
On the walls and ceiling of the gallery on the garden side of the villa are scenes from the myth of Cupid and Psyche (after Apuleius) painted by Raphael and his pupils. In a fashion typical of the Renaissance they depict youthful pagan divinities in the setting of Papal Rome, combining Greco-Roman and Christian ideals. In an adjoining room is Raphael's magnificent fresco depicting the triumph of the nymph Galatea (1511).
Other works of particular interest are Sodoma's masterpiece, the "Marriage of Alexander and Roxana" (in Agostino Chigi's bedroom), and the *trompe-l'œil* paintings in the Salone delle Prospettive.

Situation
Lungotevere della Farnesina

Buses
23, 28, 65

Villa Madama

On the slopes of Monte Mario, on the side looking towards the city, is the Villa Madama, now used by the Italian government for receptions and conferences. The villa was designed by Raphael for Cardinal Giulio de' Medici, later Pope Clement VII, and subsequently altered by Antonio da Sangallo the Younger. It passed into the hands of "Madama" Margareta, daughter of the Emperor Charles V, who married Alessandro de' Medici as her first husband and Ottavio Farnese as her second, and thereafter, in 1735, to the Bourbons of Naples. The villa fits harmoniously into its natural setting, and offers a magnificent view of the city.

Situation
Via di Villa Madama

Buses
28, 32, 90, 391

Villa Medici   B3

To the N of the Trinità dei Monti church, a few paces from the Piazza di Spagna (see entry), is the Villa Medici, a late Renaissance mansion with a severe main front and a richly

Situation
Viale Trinità dei Monti

Villa Torlonia

Underground station
Piazza di Spagna (line A)

Bus
115

articulated garden front to the rear, facing the Pincio (see entry). The villa was built by Annibale Lippi in 1544 for Cardinal Ricci da Montepulciano. It later passed to the Medici and the Grand Dukes of Tuscany, and was finally occupied in Napoleonic times by the French Academy, a foundation (still existing) for French artists.

From 1630 to 1633 Galileo was imprisoned in the villa on the order of the Inquisition.

Villa Torlonia   B5

Situation
Via Nomentana

Buses
36, 37, 60, 62, 63, 136, 137

The Villa Torlonia park (area 13 hectares – $32\frac{1}{2}$ acres), with the neo-classical Palazzo Torlonia (early 19th c.), formerly the property of the Torlonia family, was during the Fascist period the private residence of Mussolini. It now belongs to the city of Rome, and the park (though not the villa itself) is open to the public.

Practical Information

Airlines

Via Bissolati 13; tel. 46 88.
Reservations tel. 54 54.

Alitalia

Via Bissolati 48; tel. 47 99 91.

British Airways

Via Bissolati 46; tel. 47 73.

Pan Am

Via Barberini 59–67; tel. 47 21.

TWA

Via Barberini 63; tel. 46 35 14.

Canadian Pacific Air

Antiques

In the narrow streets behind the Piazza Navona are the workshops of craftsmen skilled in the restoration of antique furniture and pictures, however badly damaged they may be. In this area visitors will find numerous little shops, fiercely competitive with one another, selling antique furniture, silver, jewellery, dolls, pictures, lamps, lace mats and much else besides.

Piazza Navona

In Via Coronari, the best known of these streets where the antique dealers are to be found, an exhibition of Italian, French and English furniture is held annually in May.

Via Coronari

Items of particular value and rarity can be found in Via del Babuino (which runs between the Piazza del Popolo and the Piazza di Spagna) and Via Giulia – at prices to match.

Via del Babuino/Via Giulia

There are numbers of secondhand dealers in the streets known as the "Banchi vecchi" between Piazza di Campo dei Fiori and the Tiber.

"Banchi vecchi"

A flea-market is held on Sunday mornings at the Porta Portese in Trastevere.

Porta Portese

Banks

Opening times Mon.–Fri. 8.30 a.m.–1.30 p.m.

Most banks in the city centre will cash Eurocheques. Since each bank may quote a different rate it is worth while comparing rates.

Eurocheques

Caution is necessary in dealing with small street exchange offices: beware of counterfeit currency.

Bureaux de change

Practical Information

Changing money on
Saturdays
(Eurocheques not accepted) On Saturdays and public holidays money can be changed at
the main station (Stazione Termini) and at the Leonardo da
Vinci airport, Fiumicino.

Boat trips

On the Tiber
Amici del Tevere,
Lungotevere Dante 273; tel. 6 37 02 68.
Dep. Sat. and Sun. at 9 a.m. (weather permitting); return about
4.30 p.m.

Ostia
Sightseeing trips to the excavations of Ostia Antica (see A to Z,
Ostia Antica).

Camping sites

Roma Camping,
km 8·2 on Via Aurelia; tel. 6 22 30 18.
250 places.

Flaminio,
km 8 on Via Flaminia Nuova; tel. 3 27 90 06.

Seven Hills,
Via Cassia 1216 (km 18); tel. 3 76 55 71, 3 76 51 00.

Capitol,
Ostia Antica, Via Castelfusano 45; tel. 5 66 27 20.

Camping Tiber,
km 1·4 on Via Tiberina; tel. 6 91 23 14.
In the north of the city.
On the bank of the Tiber.

Car hire

Avis,
Piazza Esquilina 1; tel. 47 01.
Via Sardegna 38A; tel. 4 75 07 28.

Hertz,
Via Sallustiana 28; tel. 46 33 34.

Maggiore,
Via Po 8; tel. 85 86 98, 86 01 37.
Piazza Repubblica 57–58; tel. 46 37 15.

These firms also have desks at the Termini station and the
airport.

Hire of scooters
Scoot-a-long, Via Cavour 302; tel. 6 78 02 08.

Chemists (farmacie)

9 a.m.–1 p.m. and 3.30–7.30 p.m.	Opening times
There is a chemist's shop open 24 hours a day in every district of the city.	Farmacia notturna
Piazza Barberini 49; tel. 46 29 96. Open day and night.	International pharmacy
Chemist open day and night, also selling veterinary preparations: Via Appia Nuova 51–55; tel. 7 55 06 22.	Veterinary medicine

Currency

The unit of currency is the *lira* (plural *lire*).
There are banknotes for 500, 1000, 2000, 5000, 10,000, 20,000, 50,000 and 100,000 lire and coins in denominations of 5, 10, 20, 50, 100, 200 and 500 lire. There is often a shortage of small change, and telephone tokens (*gettoni*) or postage stamps may be used to make up the deficiency. — Currency

There are no restrictions on the import of foreign currency into Italy, but in view of the strict controls on the export of currency it is advisable to declare any currency brought in on the appropriate form (*modulo V2*) at the frontier. There is a limit of 400,000 lire per head on the import of Italian currency. — Import of currency

The export of foreign currency is permitted only up to a value of 400,000 lire per person except where a larger sum has been declared on entry. No more than 400,000 lire of Italian currency can be taken out. — Export of currency

It is advisable to take money in the form of travellers' cheques, which are not subject to any restrictions, or to use a Euro bank card. The principal credit cards are widely accepted. — Travellers' cheques, etc.

See p. 159. — Changing money

Customs regulations

Visitors to Italy can take in, without liability to duty, clothing, toilet articles, jewellery and other personal effects (including two cameras and a small ciné camera with 10 films each, a portable radio and television set, a portable typewriter, a pair of binoculars, a tape-recorder, a record-player with up to 10 records, musical instruments, camping equipment and sports gear), together with reasonable quantities of food for the journey. In addition visitors can take in the usual duty-free allowances of alcohol, tobacco and perfume (varying for EEC nationals, US visitors, other European citizens and overseas residents).
Visitors can take out, without liability to duty, articles they have bought in Italy up to a value of 500 US dollars. For the export of objets d'art and antiques a permit must be obtained from the Chamber of Art.

Embassies

United Kingdom	Via XX Settembre 80A; tel. 4 75 54 41 and 4 75 55 51.
United States of America	Via Veneto 119A; tel. 46 74.
Canada	Via Zara 30; tel. 8 44 18 41 – 45.

Events

January	Mid December to 6 January: Christmas Market in Piazza Navona. 6 January: Epiphany (children receive presents; fair in Piazza Navona). Alta Moda Italiana (fashion show – spring and summer fashions). Roma Ufficio (Office Equipment Trade Fair, continuing into February).
February	Martedi Grasso (Shrove Tuesday), with street processions in costumes and masks (beginning some weeks previously).
March	9 March: Santa Francesca Romana. Consecration of motor vehicles at Colosseum. 19 March: San Giuseppe (St Joseph). *Zeppole* (cream choux) are sold and consumed in large numbers. Spring Festival in Piazza di Spagna (continuing into April)
March/April	Maundy Thursday: Washing of the Feet in St John Lateran (Papal mass). Holy Week: Services conducted by the Pope on Palm Sunday, Maundy Thursday, Good Friday and Easter Saturday. Good Friday: Stations of the Cross in the Colosseum, with the Pope. Easter Day: Papal blessing "Urbi et Orbi" (to the City and the World) from the balcony of St Peter's. Second half of April: azaleas in Piazza di Spagna.
May	Second half: Exhibition of antiques in Via dei Coronari. Rose Show on the Aventine.
June	23–24 June: Midsummer Night (fireworks). Estate Romana ("Roman Summer"): concerts, dramatic performances and exhibitions (mostly in the open air) throughout the summer, continuing to October.
July	15 July: Festa dei Noiantri, a popular festival in Trastevere (fireworks, eating of roasted sucking pigs in the street). Opera season in the Baths of Caracalla. Concert season in Academy of Santa Cecilia. Roma Musica (until September). Season of drama at Ostia Antica. Alta Moda Italiana (fashion show – autumn and winter fashions). Tevere Expo on the banks of the Tiber: an exhibition of products from all parts of Italy.

5 August: Festa della Madonna della Neve (Festival of Our Lady of the Snows), with ceremonies in the church of Santa Maria Maggiore.
Opera in the Baths of Caracalla.
Concerts in Academy of Santa Cecilia.
Drama at Ostia Antica.
Pop concerts and song recitals in the open air.

August

Children's Fashion Show.
Tevere Expo Internazionale on the banks of the Tiber, displaying products from all over the world.
Antiques Fair (continuing into October).

September

Furniture and Interior Decoration Show (MOA).

October

8 December: Immacolata Concezione (Immaculate Conception), with ceremony in Piazza Navona.
15 December: Christmas Market in Piazza Navona (until 6 January).
24 December: Solemn mass in St Peter's.
25 December: Solemn Christmas mass in St Peter's, followed by the Pope's annual Christmas address from the balcony of St Peter's.
Christmas cribs (Nativity groups) in churches and in the Piazza di Spagna.
Natale Oggi ("Christmas Today") exhibition.

December

First Aid (Pronto soccorso)

First aid, ambulance; tel. 51 00.

Red Cross

See p. 190.

Hospitals

Food and drink

Roman cuisine is notable for its use of high-quality ingredients and the careful preparation of dishes according to simple traditional recipes. It prefers natural to camouflaged tastes and has little interest in over-elaborate refinements.

The following are some typical Roman dishes (". . . *alla romana*").

Roast sucking lamb in white wine, seasoned with rosemary.

Abbachio

Eel steamed in white wine.

Anguilla

Stuffed duck with calves' feet.

Anitra

Broccoli in white wine.

Broccoli romani

A kind of pizza, with ham, mozzarella cheese and salami, covered with pastry.

Calzone

Pasta squares stuffed with meat, calf's brain, spinach, egg and cheese.

Cannelloni

Practical Information

Cappone	Capon with bread stuffing, seasoned with cheese.
Carciofi alla giudia	Artichokes fried in oil.
Carciofi alla romana	Artichokes seasoned with peppermint and stuffed with anchovies.
Fettuccine	Ribbon pasta with a sauce of butter, eggs, anchovies and cheese.
Gnocchi di polenta	Maize flour pasta, either grilled or breaded and fried in fat.
Gnocchi alla romana	Semolina dumplings.
Lumache	Snails in tomato sauce, seasoned with ginger.
Panzarottini	Small packets of pasta with cheese and butter, grilled with eggs, anchovies, etc.
Polenta alla romana	Polenta with mutton stew.
Pollo	Chicken in tomato sauce, with white wine.
Salsa romana	A brown sweet-sour sauce with raisins and chestnut and lentil purée (served with game).
Saltimbocca	Slices of veal and ham seasoned with sage, steamed in butter and soaked in marsala.
Suppli di riso	Rice and cheese croquettes.
Testarelle di abbacchio	Lambs' heads fried in oil, with rosemary.
Trippa	Tripe in tomato sauce, with white wine.
Zuppa	Chicken soup with vegetables, meat dumplings, rice or pasta.
Wine	Italians usually drink wine with their meals, almost always accompanied by mineral water.

Galleries

Borghese Gallery	Galleria Borghese, Villa Borghese. Open 9 a.m.–2 p.m., public holidays 9 a.m.–1 p.m. Closed Mon. Collection of Cardinal Scipione Borghese: sculpture by Bernini and Canova (Pauline Bonaparte), pictures by Raphael, Caravaggio, etc.
National Gallery of Ancient Art	Galleria Nazionale d'Arte Antica, Palazzo Barberini. Via Quattro Fontane 13. Open 9 a.m.–2 p.m., public holidays 9 a.m.–1 p.m.; closed Mon.
National Gallery of Modern Art	Galleria Nazionale d'Arte Moderna, Viale delle Belle Arti 131, Open 2–7 p.m., Sat. and Sun. 9 a.m.–1.30 p.m.; closed Mon.

Galleria Nazionale d'Arte Moderna (National Gallery of Modern Art)

The largest collection in Italy of art from the 19th c. to the present day.

Galleria Doria Pamphili,   Doria Pamphili Gallery
Piazza del Collegio Romano 1a.
Open: Tues., Fri., Sat., Sun. 10 a.m.–1 p.m.;
Pictures of 15th–17th c.

Galleria Colonna,   Colonna Gallery
Via della Pilotta 17.
Open Sat. 9 a.m.–1 p.m.; closed Aug.
Works by Tintoretto, Bronzino, Salvator Rosa, etc.

Galleria Spada,   Spada Gallery
Piazza Capo di Ferro 3.
Open: 9 a.m.–2 p.m., Sun. 9 a.m.–1 p.m., closed Mon.
17th c. works.

Galleria Comunale d'Arte Moderna,   Municipal Gallery of Modern
Palazzo dell'Esposizione (2nd floor: entrance in Via Milano).   Art
Open Thurs. and Sat. 9 a.m.–2 p.m.
Pictures by Tenerani, Pinelli, Franz Roesler, etc.

Getting to Rome

It is a long way from Britain or northern Europe to Rome.   By car
Motorists will be well advised, therefore, to use motorways and
main trunk roads as far as possible.

Practical Information

Motorways

Tolls are payable on the Italian motorways (*autostrade*). The tickets for each section should be preserved, since they must be given up when leaving the motorway.

Documents, etc.

Motorists should carry their driving licence and car registration document. An international insurance certificate ("green card") is not obligatory but is strongly recommended. The car should have a nationality plate, and a warning triangle must be carried.

Roads to Rome

There is a wide choice of routes from the English Channel to Rome, depending on individual preferences and time available – through France and over one of the Alpine passes into Italy; down to the S coast of France and then on the coastal motorway into Italy; by France or Germany, Switzerland and one of the Alpine passes or tunnels. The journey can be shortened by using one of the motorail services from stations in NW Europe.

By bus

There are numerous package tours by coach, either going direct to Rome or including Rome in a longer circuit. For information apply to any travel agent.
There are also various coach services between Britain or northern Europe and Rome. Euroways run a regular service from London via Milan to Rome: information from Euroways Express Coaches Ltd, 52 Grosvenor Gardens, London W1; tel. (01) 837 6543, or from a travel agent.

By air

There are daily scheduled flights from London to Rome and weekly flights from Manchester to Rome.
The Leonardo da Vinci (Fiumicino) Airport is 36 km (22 miles) from Rome by the Via del Mare or 26 km (16 miles) by motorway.
There are bus services between the airport and the Air Terminal at Via Giolitti 36 (beside the Termini station).
There is also Ciampino Airport, mainly used by charter flights. Bus services between the airport and the terminal at Via Sicilia 52.

Airlines

See p. 159.

By rail

The fastest route from London to Rome takes just over 25 hours, leaving London (Charing Cross) at 9 a.m., crossing the Channel by hovercraft and changing in Paris. The alternative route, with a through carriage from Hook of Holland to Rome, leaves London (Victoria) at 10 a.m. and takes just over 28 hours.

Hotels (alberghi)

There is a wide choice of hotels and pensions (guest-houses) in Rome, including some run by nuns – so wide that visitors will be well advised to consult a travel agent or a hotel guide.

Categories

Hotels are officially classified into five categories (luxury, I, II, III and IV) and pensions into three.

Tariffs vary considerably according to season. The rates given in the following table (in lire) are based on information given in the Italian State Tourist Office's list ˋof hotels, "Alberghi d'Italia". Increases are to be expected. Hotel bills should be kept in case of enquiry by government inspectors into possible tax evasion.

Tariffs

Category	Single room Rate for 1 person	Double room Rate for 2 persons
Hotels		
L	75,000–320,000	175,000–460,000
I	28,000–135,000	45,000–200,000
II	22,000– 65,000	37,000– 90,000
III	18,000– 45,000	28,000– 60,000
IV	12,000– 35,000	20,000– 45,000
Pensions		
PI	21,000– 48,000	32,000– 65,000
PII	14,000– 36,000	21,000– 48,000
PIII	12,000– 30,000	18,000– 40,000

*Le Grand Hôtel et de Rome, Via V. Emanuele Orlando 3, L. 328 b.

Near Stazione Termini

Mediterraneo, Via Cavour 15, I, 452 b.
Metropole, Via Principe Amedeo 3, I, 440 b.
Universo, Via Principe Amadeo 5b, I, 381 b.
Palatino, Via Cavour 213, I, 380 b.
San Giorgio, Via G. Amendola 61, I, 340 b.
Quiriinale, Via Nazionale 7, I, 339 b.
Massimo d'Azeglio, Via Cavour 18, I, 302 b.
President, Via E. Filiberto 173, I, 249 b.
Royal Santina, Via Marsala 22, I, 208 b.
Londra & Cargill, Piazza Sallustio 18, I, 193 b.
Genova, Via Cavour 33, I, 175 b.
Anglo-Americano, Via 4 Fontane 12, I, 165 b.
Napoleon, Piazzo Vittorio Emanuele 105, I, 141 b.
Mondial, Via Torino 127, I, 138 b.
Atlantico, Via Cavour 23, I, 129 b.
Commodore, Via Torino 1, I, 97 b.
Diana, Via Principe Amedeo 4, II, 293 b.
Nord-Nuova Roma, Via G. Amendola 3, II, 250 b.
Madison, Via Marsala 60, II, 184 b.
Siracusa, Via Marsala 50, II, 176 b.
Globus, Viale Ippocrate 119, II, 174 b.
Torino, Via Principe Amedeo 8, II, 172 b.
Esperia, Via Nazionale 22, II, 163 b.
Lux Messe, Via Volturno 32, II, 161 b.
Archimede, Via dei Mille 19, II, 156 b.
Y.M.C.A., Piazza Indipendenza 23c, II, 154 b.
Milani, Via Magenta 12, II, 150 b.
Sorrento & Patrizia, Via Nationale 251, II, 150 b.
La Capitale e Santa Maria Maggiore, Via C. Alberto 3, II, 137 b.
San Remo, Via M. d'Azeglio 36, II, 120 b.
San Marco, Via Villafranca 1, II, 118 b.
Aretusa, Via Gaeta 14, II, 105 b.
Nizza, Via M. d'Azeglio 16, II, 96 b.
Rex, Via Torino 149, II, 95 b.
Medici, Via Flavia 96, II, 93 b.
Impero, Via Viminale 19, II, 79 b.

Practical Information

Tirreno, Via S. Martino ai Monti 18, II, 77 b.
Ariston, Via F. Turati 16, III, 133 b.
Venezia, Via Varese 18, III, 106 b.
Stazione, Via Gioberti 36, III, 102 b.
Marconi, Via G. Amendola 97, III, 94 b.
Igea, Via P. Amedeo 97, III, 63 b.
Del Popolo, Via degli Apuli 41, IV, 181 b.; etc.

Between the Quirinal and
the Villa Borghese

*Excelsior, Via V. Veneto 125, L, 670 b.
*Ambasciatori Palace, Via V. Veneto 70, L, 267 b.
*Bernini Bristol, Piazza Barberini 23, L, 218 b.
*Eden, Via Ludovisi 49, L, 191 b.
*Hassler-Villa Medici, Piazza Trinita dei Monti 6, L, 190 b.
Parco dei Principi, Via G. Frescobaldi 5, I, 366 b., SP.
Jolly, Corso d'Italia 1, I, 346 b.
Flora, Via V. Veneto 191, I, 264 b.
Regina Carlton, Via V. Veneto 72, I, 229 b.
Boston, Via Lombardia 47, I, 221 b.
Savoia, Via Ludovisi 15, I, 212 b.
Majestic, Via V. Veneto 50, I, 172 b.
Victoria, Via Campania 41, I, 160 b.
Imperiale, Via V. Veneto 24, I, 137 b.
Eliseo, Via di Porta Pinciana 30, I, 97 b.
King, Via Sistina 131, II, 122 b.
Alexandra, Via V. Veneto 18, II, 72 b.; etc.

In the old town

De la Ville, Via Sistina 69, I, 357 b.
Plaza, Via del Corso 126, I, 311 b.
Delta, Via Labicana 144, I, 269 b., SP.
Marini Strand, Via del Tritone 17, I, 212 b.
D'Inghilterra, Via Bocca di Leone 14, I, 185 b.
Colonna Palace, Piazza Montecitorio 12, I, 160 b.
Forum, Via Tor de' Conti 25, I, 156 b.
Nazionale, Piazza Montecitorio 131, I, 139 b.
Raphael, Largo Febo 2, I, 135 b.
Delle Nazioni, Via Poli 7, I, 132 b.
Cardinal, Via Giulia 62, I, 114 b.
Valadier, Via della Fontanella 15, I, 62 b.
Bologna, Via Santa Chiara 4a, II, 195 b.
Adriano, Via di Pallacorda 2, II, 116 b.
Santa Chiara, Via Santa Chiara 21, II, 114 b.
Pace-Elvezia, Via IV Novembre 104, II, 110 b.
Genio, Via G. Zanadelli 28, II, 99 b.
Cesari, Via di Pietra 89a, II, 92 b.
Lugano, Via Tritone 132, II, 53 b.
Sole al Pantheon, Via del Pantheon 63, II, 48 b.
Sole, Via del Biscione 76, IV, 88 b.; etc.

Northern districts

Ritz, Via Chellini 41, I, 612 b.
Residence Palace, Via Archimede 69, I, 323 b.
Beverly Hills, Largo B. Marcello 220, I, 315 b.
Aldrovandi, Via U. Aldrovandi 15, I, 212 b.
Claridge, Viale Liegi 62, I, 166 b.
Hermitage, Via E. Vajna 12, I, 154 b.
Borromini, Via Lisbona 7, I, 147 b.
Lord Byron, Via G. De Notaris 5, I, 91 b.
Restaurant 'Le Jardin'
Fleming, Piazza Monteleone di Spoleto 20, II, 489 b.
Rivoli, Via Taramelli, 7, II, 86 b.; etc.

Porta Maggiore, Piazza Porta Maggiore 25, II, 210 b.
San Giustro, Piazza Bologna 58, II, 98 b.; etc.

*Sheraton Roma, Viale del Pattinaggio (EUR), L, 1174 b., SP.
American Palace (EUR), Via Laurentina 554, II, 160 b., SP.
Dei Congressi, Viale Shakespeare 29 (EUR), II, 152 b.
Autostello ACI, km 13 on Via C. Colombo, II, 142 b., SP.
Piccadilly, Via Magna Grecia 122, (at Porta San Giovanni), II, 92 b.
EUR Motel, Via Pontina 416, II, 43 b.; etc.

*Cavalieri Hilton, Via Cadiolo 101, (at foot of Monte Mario), L,
750 b., SP.; Restaurant 'Pergola'.
Ergife Palace, Via Aurelia 619, I, 1316 b., SP.
Midas Palace, Via Aurelia 800, I, 700 b., SP.
Holiday Inn EUR, V. le Castello della Magliana 65, (to SW of city), I, 648 b., SP.
Holiday Inn, Via Aurelia Antica 415, I, 620 b., SP.
Villa Pamphili, Via della Nocetta 105, I, 513 b., SP.
Visconti Palace, Via F. Cesi 37, I, 489 b.
Cicerone, Via Cicerone 55c, I, 445 b.
Jolly Leonardo da Vinci, Via dei Gracchi 324, I, 415 b.
Princess, Via Aurelia 619, I, 412 b.
Michelangelo, Via Stazione di S. Pietro 14, I, 264 b.
Giulio Cesare, Via degli Scipione 287, I, 139 b.
Motel Agip, km 8 on Via Aurelia, II, 440 b.
Marc'Aurelio, Via Gregorio XI 135, II, 220 b., SP.
Clodio, Via S. Lucia 10, II, 209 b.
Columbus, Via della Conciliazione 33, II, 190 b.
Nova Domus, Via G. Savonarola 38, II, 149 b.
Cristoforo Colombo, Via C. Colombo 710, II, 141 b.
Rest, Via Aurelia 325, II, 135 b.
Fiamma, Via Gaeta 61, II, 127 b.
Pacific, Viale Medaglie d'Oro 51, II, 120 b.
Olympic, Via Properzio 2a, II, 91 b.
Imperator, Via Aurelia 619, II, 79 b.
Nordland, Via A. Alciato 14, III, 198 b.
Beethoven, Via Forte Braschi 2, III, 96 b.
Alicorni, Via Scossacavalli 11, III, 78 b.
Motel Boomerang, km 10·5 on Via Aurelia, III, 76 b.; etc.

Airport, Viale dei Romagnoli 165, I, 453 b., SP.

SP=Swimming Pool

Insurance

It is very desirable to have an international insurance certificate
("green card"), although this is not a legal requirement for
citizens of EEC countries. It is important to have fully
comprehensive cover, and it is desirable to take out short-term
insurance against legal costs if these are not already covered.
Italian insurance companies tend to be slow in settling claims.

British visitors to Italy, like other EEC citizens, are entitled to
receive health care on the same basis as Italians (including free

medical treatment, etc.); they should apply to their local social security office, well before their date of departure, for a certificate of entitlement (form E111). Fuller cover can be obtained by taking out insurance against medical expenses; and non-EEC citizens will of course be well advised to take out appropriate insurance cover.

Baggage insurance

In view of the risk of theft it is desirable to have adequate insurance against loss of, or damage to, baggage.

Libraries

Rome has a large number of libraries containing valuable old manuscripts and books as well as modern books and periodicals. The following is a brief selection of the more important.

Archivo di Stato di Roma

Corso Rinascimento 40; tel. 6 54 38 23.
Open 9 a.m.–2 p.m.

Archivo Storico Capitolino

Piazza della Chiesa Nuova 18; tel. 6 54 26 62.
Open 9 a.m.–1 p.m.

Biblioteca Angelica

Piazza S. Agostino 8; tel. 65 58 74.
Open 8.30 a.m.–1.30 p.m.; also Mon., Wed. and Fri. (except in summer) 4.30–7.30 p.m.

Biblioteca Hertziana

Via Gregoriana 28; tel. 6 79 73 52.
Open 9 a.m.–1 p.m., 4–7 p.m.; closed Sat.
Admission by special permit only.

Istituto di Archeologia e Storia d'Arte

Piazza Venezia 3; tel. 6 78 11 67.
Open 9 a.m.–1 p.m. and 4–8 p.m.; closed Sat. afternoon.

Municipal libraries

Palazzo Borromini, Piazza del Orologio; tel. 6 54 10 40.
Open 9 a.m.–1 p.m. and 5–7 p.m.; closed Sat. and Mon. afternoon.

Via Marmorata 169; tel. 57 64 80.
Open 4–8 p.m.; closed Sat. and Mon.

Via Ottaviano Assarotti 9B; tel. 33 62 42.
Open 4–8 p.m.; closed Sat. and Mon.

Via Gela 8; tel. 7 85 66 45.
Open 4–8 p.m.; closed Sat. and Mon.

Lost property offices (Servizi oggetti rinvenuti)

Airports and railway stations

There are lost property offices at airports and railway stations, usually open continuously.

Via Volturno 65 (near Stazione Termini). Open weekdays 10 a.m.–noon.	Municipal transport (ATAC)
Via Bettoni 1. Open weekdays 9 a.m.–noon.	Municipal lost property office
Telephone enquiries to the lost property offices usually produce no result.	Telephone enquiries

Markets (Mercati)

Porta Portese (inside streets off Viale Trastevere). Sunday mornings only.	Flea-market
Maps and prints are sold in the little market in Piazza Fontanella Borghese. Weekday mornings.	Maps and prints
Market in Via Sannio (near St John Lateran).	Clothes
There are fruit and vegetable markets in every *rione* (ward, district). One of the most characteristic is the market in the Campo dei Fiori in the old town; the largest are those in Piazza Vittorio and the Trionfale district. Held every morning except Sunday.	Fruit and vegetables

Motoring

The main types of road are:
Motorways (*autostrade*), numbered A . . . Tolls are payable.
State highways (*strade statali*), numbered SS . . . Many of them have names (Via Aurelia, Via Emilia, etc.), which are often better known than their numbers.
Provincial highways (*strade di grande comunicazione*), which have no numbers.
Secondary roads (*strade secondarie*), for local traffic.

The road system

Within built-up areas the speed limit is 50 km p.h. (31 m.p.h.). Outside built-up areas the limits vary according to cylinder capacity:

Speed limits

Capacity	Ordinary roads	Motorways
up to 600 cc	80 km p.h. (50 m.p.h.)	90 km p.h. (56 m.p.h.)
up to 900 cc	90 km p.h. (56 m.p.h.)	110 km p.h. (68 m.p.h.)
up to 1300 cc	100 km p.h. (62 m.p.h.)	130 km p.h. (81 m.p.h.)
over 1300 cc	110 km p.h. (68 m.p.h.)	140 km p.h. (87 m.p.h.)

The wearing of seat belts is compulsory.

Seat belts

Traffic on main roads has priority where the road is marked with the priority sign (a square with a corner pointing downwards, coloured white with a red border or yellow with a black and white bordor).
At roundabouts traffic on the right has priority.

Priority

Practical Information

Mountain roads	On mountain roads traffic going up has priority.
Change of lane	Any change of lane (for overtaking or any other purpose) must be signalled with the direction indicator, as must an intention to stop by the roadside.
Overtaking	Outside built-up areas the horn must be sounded before overtaking. It must also be sounded before intersections, side roads, blind bends and other hazards. After dark flashing headlights should be used for the same purpose.
Prohibition on use of horn	In towns the use of the horn is frequently prohibited, either by an appropriate road sign (a horn with a stroke through it) or by the legend "Zona di silenzio".
Lights	**Dipped headlights are compulsory when passing through tunnels and galleries.**
Zebra crossings	Pedestrians have absolute priority on zebra crossings.
Traffic police	The directions of the traffic police (*polizia stradale*) should be exactly complied with. Fines for traffic offences are high.
Drink and driving	There are heavy penalties for driving under the influence of drink.
Accidents	In case of accident make sure that you have all the necessary particulars and supporting evidence (statements by witnesses, sketches, photographs, etc.). If the accident involves personal injury it must be reported to the police. You should notify your own insurance company as soon as possible, and if you are responsible or partly responsible for the accident you should also inform the Italian insurance company or bureau whose address is given on your green card. This agency will give advice and supply the name of a lawyer should the foreign driver be subject to penal proceedings. – If your car is a total write-off the Italian customs authorities must be informed at once, since otherwise you might be required to pay the full import duty on the vehicle.
Petrol coupons	Information about petrol coupons and coupons for motorway tolls can be obtained from the automobile clubs, large banks or the ENIT.
Automobile clubs	Automobile Club d'Italia (ACI), Via Marsala 8; tel. 49 98. Automobile Club di Roma (ACR), Via Cristoforo Colombo 261; tel. 51 06. For information about weather, road conditions, etc., tel. 42 12. Touring Club Italiano (TCI), Via Ovidio 7A; tel. 38 86 58.
Breakdown assistance	Tel. 1 16. Breakdown service: Via Solferino 32; tel. 4 74 24 82/83.
Puncture repair	Look for the sign "Riparazione gomme".

Look for "Officina".

Anywhere in Italy, dial 1 13.

Museums

Museo Archeologico Sacro e Profano, Via Appia Antica 136.
Open Mon.–Wed. and Fri.–Sun. 9 a.m.–noon and 2–5 p.m.

Archaeological Museum

Museo Astronomico e Copernicano, Via Trionfale 204.
Open Tues., Fri., Sat. 9.30 a.m.–noon.

Astronomical Museum

Museo Barracco, Corso Vittorio Emanuele 168.
Assyrian, Egyptian, Greek and Roman sculpture.
Open 9 a.m.–2 p.m., public holidays 9 a.m.–1 p.m.
Tues. and Thurs. also 3.30–8 p.m., closed Mon.

Barracco Museum

Museo Burcardo, Via del Sudario 44.
Theatrical collection.
Open Mon.–Sat. 9 a.m.–1.30 p.m., closed August.

Burcardo Museum

Museo Capitolino, Piazza del Campidoglio.
A collection of major importance, and the oldest in the world.
Open 9 a.m.–2 p.m., Tues. and Thurs. also 5–8 p.m., Sun.
9 a.m.–1 p.m., closed Mon.

Capitoline Museum

Castel Sant'Angelo, Lungotevere Castello.
History of the Roman mausoleum and of Castle Sant'Angelo.
Open 9 a.m.–1 p.m., public holidays 9 a.m.–noon, closed Mon.

Castel Sant'Angelo Museum

Museo delle Celebrità, Piazza della Repubblica.
Open 9 a.m.–2 p.m.

Museum of Celebrities

Museo dell'Alto Medievo, Viale Lincoln 1 (EUR).
Open 9 a.m.–2 p.m., Sun. 9 a.m.–1 p.m.

Museum of Early Medieval Period

Museo di Etruscologia, Facoltà di Lettere, University City.
Open weekdays only by special appointment.

Museum of Etruscology

Museo Nazionale delle Arti e Tradizioni, Piazza Marconi 10.
At present closed; normally 9 a.m.–2 p.m., Sun. 9 a.m.–1 p.m.;
closed Mon.

Museum of Folk Arts and Traditions

Museo Antiquarium Forense e Palatino, Piazza Santa Maria
Nuova 53.
Open Mon. and Wed.– Sun. 9 a.m.–1 p.m.

Forum and Palatine Museum

Museo Francescano dei Cappuccini, Via Veneto 27.
Open daily 9 a.m.–noon, 3–6 p.m.

Franciscan Museum

Museo di Goethe, Via del Corso 17.
At present closed.

Goethe Museum

Sinagoga, Lungotevere Cenci; tel. 6 56 46 48.
Open Mon.–Fri. 10 a.m.–2 p.m., Sun. 10 a.m.–noon.

Jewish Museum

Practical Information

Keats and Shelley House	Casa di Keats e Shelley, Piazza di Spagna 26. Open Mon.–Fri. 9 a.m.–12.30 p.m. and 3 or 4–5 or 6 p.m., closed Sat. and Sun.
Museum of Liberation	Museo Storico della Lotta di Liberazione, Via Tasso 145. Open Sat. 5–8 p.m., Sun. 10 a.m.–1 p.m.
Museum of Musical Instruments	Museo degli Strumenti Musicali, Piazza Santa Croce in Gerusalemme 9A. Open Wed., Fri., Sat. 9 a.m.–1.30 p.m., Tues. and Thurs. 9 a.m.–7 p.m., Sun. 9 a.m.–1 p.m., closed Mon.
Napoleonic Museum	Museo Napoleonico, Via Zanardelli 1. Relics of Napoleon. Open 9 a.m.–2 p.m., Tues. and Thurs. also 5–8 p.m.; Sun. 9 a.m.–1 p.m., closed Mon. and in August.
National Museum (Museo delle Terme)	Museo Nazionale Romano, Viale delle Terme. Open 8.30 a.m.–2 p.m., public holidays 9 a.m.–1 p.m., closed Mon.
Numismatic Museum	Museo Numismatico della Zecca, Via XX Settembre 97. Open Mon.–Fri. 9 a.m.–1 p.m., Sat. 9 a.m.–noon.
Museum of Oriental Art	Museo Nazionale dell'Arte Orientale, Via Merulana 248. Open 9 a.m.–2 p.m., Sun. 9 a.m.–1 p.m.; closed Mon.
Palazzo Venezia Museum	Museo di Palazzo Venezia, Piazza Venezia. Arts and crafts of Roman Latium. Open 9 a.m.–2 p.m., Sun. 9 a.m.–1 p.m.; closed Mon.
Museum of Plaster Casts	Museo dei Gessi dell'Arte Classica, Facolta di Lettere, University City. Plaster casts of archaic and Roman sculpture. Open weekdays only by special appointment.
Museum of Postal Services and Telecommunications	Museo Storico della Poste e Telecomunicazioni, Viale Europa 147 (EUR). Open Mon.–Sat. 9 a.m.–1 p.m.
Prehistoric and Ethnographic Museum (Pigorini Museum)	Museo Preistorico ed Etnografico Luigi Pigorini, Istituto di Paleontologia, University City. One of the most important ethnographic collections in Europe. Open Tues.–Sat. 9 a.m.–2 p.m., Sun. 9 a.m.–1 p.m.; closed Mon.
Museum of Prehistory and Protohistory of Latium	Museo della Preistoria e Protostoria del Lazio; Viale Lincoln 1 (EUR). Open Tues.–Sat. 9 a.m.–2 p.m., Sun. 9 a.m.–1 p.m., closed Mon.
Museum of Risorgimento	Museo Centrale del Risorgimento, Via di San Pietro in Carcere (in Vittorio Emanuele Monument). Open Wed., Fri. and Sun. 10 a.m.–1 p.m.; at present closed.
Museum of Roman culture	Museo della Civiltà Romana, EUR. Reproductions of monuments and sculpture; model of Rome in 4th c. A.D. Open Tues.–Sat. 9 a.m.–2 p.m., Tues. and Thurs. also 3.30–6.30 p.m., Sun. 9 a.m.–1 p.m., closed Mon.

Museo del Folklore e dei Poeti Romaneschi, Piazza San Egidio 16.
Open Tues.–Sat. 9 a.m.–1.30 p.m., Sun. and public holidays 9 a.m.–1 p.m., Tues. and Thurs. also 5–7.30 p.m.

Museum of Roman Folklore and Poetry

Museo delle Mura Romane: entrance at Porta San Sebastiano 18 (Appia Antica).
Displays illustrating the different building phases of the walls.
Open 9.30 a.m.–noon; at present closed.

Museum of Roman City Walls

Museo di Roma, Piazza San Pantaleo 10.
The history and life of Rome in medieval and modern times.
Open 9 a.m.–2 p.m., Tues. and Thurs. also 5–8 p.m.
Sun. 9 a.m.–1 p.m., closed Mon.

Museum of Rome

Museo Tassiano, Salita di Sant'Onofrio 5C.
For admission apply to the priest in Sant'Onofrio.

Tasso Museum

Musei Vaticani, Viale del Vaticano.
World-famous collections of ancient and later art.
Open Eastertide 9 a.m.–5 p.m.; July–Sept. Mon.–Fri. 9 a.m.–5 p.m.; other months 9 a.m.–1 p.m.; Sat. and last Sun. in month 9 a.m.–1 p.m.; closed on all other Sundays and on public holidays.

Vatican Museums (Sistine Chapel)

Museo Nazionale di Villa Giulia, Piazzale di Villa Giulia.
Etruscan material.
Open 9 a.m.–2 p.m., public holidays 9 a.m.–1 p.m., closed Mon.

Villa Giulia Museum

Museo delle Cere, Piazza SS. Apostoli 67.
Open 9 a.m.–8 p.m.

Wax Museum

See p. 164.

Galleries

Music

In addition to performances in the Opera House there are open-air presentations in summer in the Baths of Caracalla.

Opera and ballet

Teatro dell'Opera,
Piazza Beniamino Gigli; tel. 46 36 41.
Season from Dec. to June.

Terme di Caracalla,
Via delle Terme di Caracalla; tel. 5 75 83 00.
Performances from July to mid Aug.

Tickets for the Opera and the Baths of Caracalla can be bought at the Opera box office, Piazza Beniamino Gigli (open 10 a.m.–1 p.m. and 5–7 p.m.).

Box office

Basilica of Maxentius, Via dei Fori Imperiali.
Season: July–mid Aug.

Concerts

Accademia Nazionale di Santa Cecilia; tel. 6 78 39 96.
Concerts in Auditorium, Via della Conciliazione 4, and in Sala Accademica, Via dei Greci 18.

Accademia Filarmonica Romana; tel. 3 60 17 02.

Opening times

Banks	See p. 159.
Churches	The larger churches are usually open until 12 noon and for the most part also from 4 or 5 p.m. until dusk; some of the major churches are open all day. It is possible to see the interior of a church during a service if care is taken to avoid disturbing the worshippers. Visitors should always be suitably dressed, avoiding sleeveless dresses or blouses, miniskirts, shorts, short-sleeved shirts, etc. If inappropriately dressed they may be refused admittance; cover-up garments can be hired at the entrance to St Peter's. During Lent almost all altarpieces are covered over and not shown to visitors.
Clothing shops	Summer 9 a.m.–1 p.m. and 4–8 p.m.; closed Sat. afternoon. Winter 9 a.m.–1 p.m. and 3.30–7.30 p.m.; closed Mon. morning.
Foodshops	Summer 8 a.m.–1.30 p.m. and 5.30–7.30 p.m.; closed Sat. afternoon. Winter 8 a.m.–1.30 p.m. and 5–7.30 p.m.; closed Thurs. afternoon.
Museums	The public museums are generally open from 9 or 10 a.m. to 1 or 2 p.m. and from 2 or 3 to 5 or 6, rarely to 7 p.m.; a few remain open throughout the day, without a lunch break. In winter (when the museums are for the most part inadequately heated) the opening hours are usually shorter, but during the more restricted hours they often remain open without a break at lunchtime. All museums are closed on Sunday afternoons and statutory public holidays; most of them are also closed on Mondays, or sometimes on Fridays. On various other days in the year the state museums are open only in the mornings and other museums are closed all day. In addition there are often closures as a result of staff shortages, strikes, renovation, etc. It is advisable, therefore, before visiting a museum, to check that it will be open: opening times are regularly published in the weekly "La Settimana a Roma" (English edition, "This Week in Rome"), which can be bought at any newspaper kiosk.
Petrol stations	Petrol stations are usually closed between 12.30 and 3.30 p.m. and from 8 p.m. (in winter usually 7 p.m.).
Post offices	See p. 177–8.

Pets

A certificate of health, recording inoculations (particularly against rabies) must be presented when bringing in a dog or cat and when taking it out of the country.

Dogs must wear muzzles and be kept on a leash.

In view of their own quarantine regulations, however, English-speaking visitors are unlikely to want to take their pets to Rome with them.

Carabinieri

Traffic police

Police (Polizia)

Questura (with Aliens Bureau), Via San Vitale 15; tel. 46 86.
Polizia Stradale (Traffic Police); tel. 5 57 79 05.
Vigili Urbani (Municipal Police); tel. 67 69.
Carabinieri; tel. HQ 8 52 91, Emergency 12.

Postal services

Letters within Italy and to EEC countries 400 lire; postcards 300 lire.

Postal rates (1986)

Stamps can be bought· at post offices, at tobacconists' (indicated by a large T above the door) and from stamp machines.

Stamps

The Vatican·state has its own stamps and postmarks. There are Vatican City post offices in the colonnades in St Peter's Square, as well as a travelling post office, at which stamps can be bought, in the centre of the square.

Vatican City

Piazza San Silvestro;.tel. 67 71.
Open 8.30 a.m.–9 p.m. for Giro transactions and telegraphic money orders.

Head post office

8.30 a.m.–2.30 p.m. for money orders, etc.
Sat. 8.15 a.m.–noon.
Open day and night for telegrams.

Post offices   Other post offices are open 8.15 a.m.–2 p.m., Sat. 8.30 a.m.–noon.

Public holidays

1 January (New Year's Day); 6 January (Epiphany); 25 April (Liberation Day, 1945).

Easter Monday; 1 May (Labour Day); Ascension; Corpus Christi.

2 June (proclamation of the Republic: celebrations on following Saturday).

15 August (Assumption: a family celebration, the high point of the Italian summer holiday migration).

1 November (All Saints); 4 November (Day of National Unity: celebrations on following Saturday); 8 December (Immaculate Conception).

25 and 26 December (Christmas).

Rail services

Ferrovie dello Stato (FS)

The Italian railway system has a total length of 16,000 km (10,000 miles). Most of it is run by the Italian State Railways (Ferrovie dello Stato, FS).

Information about rail services can be obtained from the Italian State Tourist Office or from Italian State Railways offices abroad:

United Kingdom

50 Conduit Street, London W1; tel. (01) 434 3844.

United States of America

765 Route 83, Suite 105, Chicago, Ill.
5670 Wilshire Boulevard, Los Angeles, Cal.
668 Fifth Avenue, New York, NY.

Canada

2055 Peel Street, Suite 102, Montreal.
111 Richmond Street West, Suite 419, Toronto.

In Italy

In Rome, Stazione Termini; tel. 47 75; and in towns throughout the country.

Viaggi circolari

Circular tickets are available covering travel on the entire State Railways system for a period of 30 days when issued in Italy or 60 days when issued outside Italy.

Tourist tickets, which can be obtained only outside Italy or at frontier railway stations, cover travel on the entire State Railways system for a period of 8, 15, 21 or 30 days.

Tourist tickets

Children accompanied by an adult travel free up to the age of 4; between 4 and 14 they pay half fare.

Children

Railway stations

Rome has nine major railway stations:

The main station: international services and services to all parts of Italy.
Information: tel. 47 75.
Lost property office: 47 30. – 66 82.

Stazione Termini

Trains to N and S Italy, motorail.
Tel. 4 95 66 26.

Stazione Tiburtina

Trains to Genoa and Pisa.

Stazione Trastevere

Trains to Ostia and to Anzio/Nettuno al Mare.

Stazione Ostiense

Trains to Viterbo.

Stazione Roma-Nord

Trains to Pescara.

Stazione Prenestina

Trains to Grosseto and Viterbo.

Stazione Tuscolana

Local services.

Stazione San Pietro

Restaurants (selection, not including those in hotels)

Hostaria dell'Orso, Via Monte Brianzo 93 (on the Tiber).
El Toulà, Via della Lupa 29.
Al Vicario, Via degli Uffici del Vicario 31.
Alfredo L'Originale, Piazza Augusto Imperatore 30.
Alfredo alla Scrofa, Via della Scrofa 104.
Papa Giovanni, at the Piazza Navona.
Passetto, Via Zanardelli 14.
La Capricciosa, Largo dei Lombardi 8 (at San Carlo al Corso).
Valle-Biblioteca, Largo del Teatro Valle 7–9.
Fontanelle, Largo Fontanella Borghese 86.
La Maiella, Piazza S. Apollinare 45.
Tre Scalini, Piazza Navona 30.
And many others (including snack bars).

Between Piazza Navona, Piazza Colonna and Mausoleo di Augusto

Da Pancrazio, Piazza del Biscione 92.
Piperno, Via Monte dei Cenci 9.
Da Gigetto al Portico d'Ottavia, Via Portico d'Ottavia 21.
Angelino a Tor Margana, Piazza Margana 37; etc.

W of Piazza Venezia

Tullio, Via S. Nicola da Tolentino 26.
Sergio e Ada, Via del Boccaccio 1; etc.

Near Fontana di Trevi

Street restaurants

Between Piazza di Spagna and Piazza del Popolo	Ranieri, Via Mario de' Fiori 26. Dal Bolognese, Piazza del Popolo 1–2. Nino a Via Borgognona, Via Borgognona 11; etc.
Near Via Veneto	Cesarina, Via Piemonte 109. Capriccio, Via Liguria 38. Il Caminetto, Via Parioli 89; etc.
N of Stazione Termini	Coriolano, Via Ancona 14. Taverna Flavia, Via Flavia 9. Berardino, Via Quintino Sella 1; etc.
In Trastevere	Sabatini, Via Arco de San Callisto 45 (near Santa Maria). Vincenzo alla Lungaretta (fish a specialty), Via della Lungaretta 173. Galeassi, Piazza S. Maria in Trastevere 3. Gino in Trastevere (seafood a specialty), Via della Lungaretta 85. Corsetti, Piazza S. Cosimato 27. La Cisterna, Via della Cisterna 13; etc.
Cafés	Greco, Via Condotti 86 (artists' rendezvous). De Paris, Via V. Veneto 90. Harri's, Via V. Veneto 150; etc.

N.B. Keep your restaurant bill, in case of enquiry by inspectors investigating tax evasion.

Shopping

La Rinascente,
Piazza Colonna and Piazza Fiume.
Clothing, perfumes, household requisites.

Coin,
Piazzale Appio (near St John Lateran).
Clothing, textiles.

Upim,
In almost all the major shopping streets.
Clothing, household requisites, stationery; food departments
in many branches.

Standa,
Numerous throughout the city.
Clothing, household requisites, etc.

Croff,
Via del Corso 316, Via XX Settembre 52, Via Cola di Rienzo
197–209, Via Tomacelli 137.
Perfumes, attractive and unusual gifts, china, as well as bed,
kitchen and table linen.

Department stores

The famous Roman fashion houses are to be found around the
Piazza di Spagna, from the Piazza del Popolo to the Piazza
Colonna.

Fashion houses

Valentino, Via Gregoriana 24.

Balestra, Via Gregoriana 36.

Capucci, Via Gregoriana 56.

Sorelle Fontana, Via San Sebastianello 6.

Lancetti, Via Condotti 61.

Mila Schön, Via Condotti 64.

André Laug, Piazza di Spagna 61.

Emanuel Ungaro, Via Bocca di Leone 24.

Roberta di Camerino, Piazza di Spagna 30.

Hermes, Via Condotti 60.

Saint-Laurent, Via Borgognona 40.

Filippo, Via Borgognona 7 bis.

Gucci, Via Condotti 67 (leather goods).

Italian leather articles (particularly handbags and shoes) and
furs are world-famous. The following is a selection of some of
the best shoe salons.

Shoe salons

Salvatore Ferragamo, Via Condotti 66.

Raphael Salato, Piazza di Spagna 34.

Tanino Crisci, Via Borgognona 4.

Barrila', Via Condotti 29.

Rachele Arbib, Via Francesco Crispi 105.

Magli, Varese, Zabato.
These and other shoe shops have branches in the principal shopping streets.

In addition to the well-known shoe salons there are numerous shoe shops all over the city selling attractive models at reasonable prices.

Furs and leather garments   Roland's, Piazza di Spagna 74.

Gucci, Via Condotti 8.

Annabella, Via del Tritone 47–48.

Fendi, Via Borgognona 39.

Francesco Casini, Via dei Prefetti 32.

Watches and jewellery   Bulgari, Via Condotti 10.

Bedetti & Co., Piazza San Silvestro 11.

Buzzetti Attilio, Via Frattina 81.

Angeletti, Via Condotti 11A.

Sightseeing tours

Agencies operating city sightseeing tours (including Rome by night, with visits to two or three night spots) and excursions in the surrounding area, with multilingual guides:

Appian Line,
Via Vittorio Veneto 84; tel. 4 74 48 91.

Carrani Tours,
Via Vittorio Emanuele Orlando 95; tel. 4 74 25 01.

CIT,
Piazza della Repubblica 64, and at Stazione Termini; tel. 4 75 82 77, 4 79 44 08 and 4 74 09 23.

ATAC,
In front of Stazione Termini; tel. 46 95.
City tours without guides.

Horse-cabs

A ride in one of these old-fashioned vehicles, popularly known in Rome as *botticelle* ("little barrels"), is a pleasant way of seeing Rome, particularly recommended for visiting the city's parks, such as the Villa Borghese and the Janiculum.

Carrozzelle (horse-cabs)

For an individual sightseeing tour a guide can be hired through the Sindacato Nazionale CISL Guide Turistiche, Rampa Mignanelli 12; tel. 6 78 98 42.

Authorised guides

Sports facilities

This large sports complex, built in 1938–9 for the Accademia Fascistica della Farnesina, consists of the following:
Stadio Olimpico (Olympic Stadium), a football stadium with accommodation for 100,000 spectators in which the athletic events of the 17th Olympic Games were held in 1960.
Stadio dei Marmi (Marble Stadium), for athletics (20,000 spectators).
Piscina Coperta (indoor swimming pool).
Buses: 1, 32, 48, 391, 911.

Foro Italico

Palazzo dello Sport.
EUR district.
Basketball, boxing contests.
Buses: 93, 97, 393, 493.

The Marble Stadium (Stadio dei Marmi)

Palazzetto dello Sport.
Boxing, roller-skating, wrestling, tennis tournaments, fencing contests.

Tre Fontane Sports Centre.
Athletics, rugby, hockey, roller-skating.

Stadio Flaminio.
Football stadium, training facilities, gymnasia, indoor swimming pool.
Buses: 1, 2, 2b, 95, 202, 203, 204, 205.

Acqua Acetosa Sports Centre.
Swimming pool, football pitch, polo and rugby pitches.

Capannelle Racecourse.
Flat racing, trotting, steeplechasing.

Tor di Valle Racecourse.
Trotting.

Swimming pools (Piscine)

Foro Italico.
Indoor swimming pool.
Open Nov.–May.

Stadio del Nuoto, Foro Italico.
Open-air swimming pool.
Open June–Sept.

Piscine delle Rose, EUR.
Open-air swimming pool.
Open June–Sept.

The seaside resorts in the neighbourhood of Rome can be reached by the Acotral company's buses.
Lido di Ostia is on line B of the Underground.

Seaside resorts

Taxis

All taxis in Rome are yellow. Beware of private cars masquerading as taxis.

Since with constantly rising petrol prices it is difficult to ensure that all meters on taxis are up to date, drivers whose meters show fares at the old tariff rates are entitled to ask for a prescribed addition to the fare shown.
For journeys outside the city limits, for example to the airports, the fare shown on the meter is doubled.

Fares

There are supplements for luggage and for journeys at night and on public holidays.

Supplements

Radiotaxi; tel. 35 70.
La Capitale; tel. 49 94.
Roma Sud; tel. 38 75.

Radio taxis

A list is given in the preliminary pages of the classified telephone directory ("Pagine gialle").

Taxi ranks

Telephone

To the United Kingdom: 00 44.
(Direct dialling not available to the United States and Canada.)

International dialling code from Rome

From the United Kingdom: 010 39 6.
From the United States: 011 39 6.
From Canada: 011 39 6.

International dialling codes to Rome

In dialling an international call the initial zero of the local dialling code should be omitted.

Most bars have public telephones (indicated by a yellow disc above the entrance to the box), operated by tokens (*gettoni*), from which local calls can be dialled. If the yellow disc bears the legend "teleselezione" or "interurbana" international calls can be dialled – though for this purpose you must provide yourself with an adequate supply of tokens. *Gettoni* can be obtained at newspaper kiosks, tobacconists and bars.

Public telephones

Post offices

There are also public telephones in post offices and in the offices of SIP (the state telephone corporation) in the station and in Via Santa Maria in Via.

Theatres

Rome has numerous theatres, and from time to time new ones are opened and old ones close. The following is a selection:

Teatro Argentina,
Largo Torre Argentina; tel. 65 54 45.

Teatro dei Sartiri,
Via di Grotta Pinta 19; tel. 6 56 13 11 and 6 56 53 52.

Teatro dei Servi,
Via del Mortaro 22; tel. 6 79 51 30.

Teatro Goldoni,
Vicolo de' Soldati 3; tel. 6 56 11 56.

Teatro delle Belle Arti,
Via Sicilia 59; tel. 4 75 85 98.

Teatro Eliseo,
Via Nazionale 183; tel. 46 21 14.

Teatro Sistina,
Via Sistina 129; tel. 4 75 68 41.

Box offices

Since the various box offices usually have different opening times it is advisable to ring up and check the time of opening. The most usual hours are 10 a.m.–1 p.m. and 4–6.30 p.m.

Programmes

The programmes of theatres and the Opera House are published in "La Settimana a Roma" (English edition, "This Week in Rome"), which can be bought at newspaper kiosks.

Time

Italy observes Central European Time (one hour ahead of Greenwich Mean Time; six hours ahead of New York time). From the beginning of April to the end of September summer time (two hours ahead of GMT; seven hours ahead of New York time) is in force.

Tipping

A good general rule is to give a tip when some special service has been given; but everyone is pleased to have his or her services recognised in this way.

Tourist information

The first place to go to for information when you are planning a
trip to Rome is the Italian State Tourist Office. Addresses:

1 Princes Street, London W1A 7RA; tel. (01) 408 1254.   United Kingdom

500 North Michigan Avenue, Chicago, IL 60611; tel. (312)   United States of America
644 0990–1.
630 Fifth Avenue, Suite 1565, New York, NY 10111; tel. (212)
245 4822–4.
360 Post Street, Suite 801, San Francisco, CA 94109; tel.
(415) 392 6206–7.

Store 56, Plaza, 3 Place Ville Marie, Montreal, Quebec; tel.   Canada
(514) 866 7667.

Ente Nazionale per il Turismo (ENIT),   In Rome
Via Marghera 2; tel. 4 97 11.
Information bureau: tel. 4 97 12 22, 4 97 12 82, 49 16 46.

EPT di Roma, via Parigi 5; tel. 46 37 48.   Ente Provinciale di Turismo
                                             (EPT)

In Stazione Termini: tel. 46 54 61 and 4 75 00 78.   Other tourist information
On Rome–Milan motorway (A1): Area di servizio Saleria   offices
Ovest; tel. 6 91 99 58.
On Rome–Naples motorway (A2): Area di servizio Frascati Est.
tel. 9 46 43 41.
Leonardo da Vinci Airport (Arrivals Hall): tel. 6 01 12 55.

Ufficio Informazioni Pellegrini e Turisti, on S side of St Peter's   Vatican Information Bureau
Square; tel. 6 98 48 66 and 6 98 44 66.

Compagnia Italiana Turismo (CIT)   CIT
(the official Italian travel agency),
Piazza della Repubblica 64; tel. 4 79 41.

Transport

The main form of public transport is the network of bus services   Buses
which covers the whole city.
Information: ATAC, Piazza dei Cinquecento; tel. 46 95.
(Plans of Rome showing public transport routes.)

Since most buses have automatic ticket machines it is   Fares
necessary to carry plenty of small change. There are no transfer
tickets. Many buses are now equipped with ticket-cancelling
machines, the tickets being bought in advance, either
individually or in a pack, in tobacconists' shops (indicated by
a large T above the door).
A monthly season ticket *(tessera intera rete)*, allowing
unlimited travel on all municipal buses, can be bought from
tobacconists.
Beware of pickpockets in the overcrowded buses!

Practical Information

Underground (Metropolitana)	Line A: Via Ottaviano (near St Peter's), Flaminio (Piazza del Popolo), Piazza di Spagna, Piazza Barberini, Stazione Termini and from there to Cinecittà and Anagnina. Line B: from Stazione Termini via San Paolo fuori le Mura to the EUR district (Via Laurentina).
Local railway	Roma–Lido (branch of Metropolitana, line B, from Piramide station to Lido di Ostia). Roma–Nord (from Flaminio station, Metropolitana line A, to Prima Porta).
Fares	A ticket for the Metropolitana can be obtained from a tobacconist or from a ticket machine at a Metropolitana station. There is also a monthly season ticket.
Trams	If you have plenty of time at your disposal you can have a very pleasant city tour on a No. 30 tram very cheaply. The line runs from Monte Verde Nuovo to near the Vatican by way of Piazza San Giovanni di Deo, Viale Trastevere, Porta Portese (flea market), Porta San Paolo, Piramide di Cestio, Viale del Parco del Celio, Piazza Colosseo, Porta San Giovanni (St John Lateran), Santa Croce in Gerusalemme, Piazza Ungheria, Viale delle Belle Arti and Piazza Risorgimento. The other tram routes run from Stazione Termini towards the outskirts of the city. There are single and monthly tickets.

Travel documents

Passport	British and US citizens require only a passport (or the simpler British visitor's passport). This applies also to citizens of Canada, Ireland and many other countries. If you lose your passport a substitute document can be issued by the British, US, Canadian, etc. consulate. It is a good idea to photocopy or note down the main particulars (number, date, etc.) of your passport, so that in case of loss you can give the necessary details to the police.
Driving licence, etc.	British, US and other national driving licences are valid in Italy, but must be accompanied by an Italian translation (obtainable free of charge from the AA). Motorists should also take the registration document of their car.
Green card	It is advisable (though not essential for EEC nationals) to have an international insurance certificate (green card) if you are driving your own car.
Nationality plate	Foreign cars must display the oval nationality plate.

Youth hostels

Ostello del Foro Italico, Viale delle Olimpiadi 61; tel. 3 96 47 09. 350 beds.

Domus Mariae,
Via Aurelia 481,
Tel. 62 08 45.
Holiday apartments.

Domus Pacis,
Via Torre Rossa 94; tel. 62 01 63.
Holiday apartments.

YWCA,
Via Cesare Balbo 4; tel. 46 04 60 and 46 39 17.

Useful Telephone Numbers at a Glance

Emergency calls
    First aid (Red Cross)   51 00
    Police in Rome/in the whole of Italy   46 86/113
    City Police (quick response)   6 76 91
    Carabinieri   112
    Medical emergencies   4 75 67 41
    Breakdown assistance   116
    Automobile Club d'Italia   51 06

Information
    Italian State Tourist Office:
    London   (01) 439 2311
    Chicago   (312) 644 0990–1
    New York   (212) 245 4822–4
    San Francisco   (415) 392 6206–7
    Rome   4 97 12 22, 4 97 12 82
    EPT (Ente Provinciale di Turismo) di Roma   46 18 51
    Rail services   47 75
    Railway police   4 75 95 61
    Public transport   46 95
    Road conditions   42 12
    Guides   6 78 98 42
    Latest news   190

Airlines
    British Airways   47 99 91
    Pan Am   47 73
    TWA   47 21
    CP Air   46 35 14

Embassies
    United Kingdom   4 75 54 41,
                                  4 75 55 51
    United States   46 74
    Canada   8 44 18 41–45

Hospitals
    San Giovanni   77 05
    Santo Spirito   65 09 01
    Policlinico Umberto I   49 97

Taxis   35 70, 38 75, 49 94

Telephone
    International calls   15
    Dialling code for the United Kingdom   00 44
    Dialling codes for Rome:
    from the United Kingdom   010 39 6
    from the United States or Canada   011 39 6

The Principal Sights at a Glance

(Continued from page 2 of cover)

Baedeker's Travel Guides

"The maps and illustrations are lavish. The arrangement of information (alphabetically by city) makes it easy to use the book."

—San Francisco Examiner-Chronicle

What's there to do and see in foreign countries? Travelers who rely on Baedeker, one of the oldest names in travel literature, will miss nothing. Baedeker's bright red, internationally recognized covers open up to reveal fascinating A-Z directories of cities, towns, and regions, complete with their sights, museums, monuments, cathedrals, castles, gardens and ancestral homes—an approach that gives the traveler a quick and easy way to plan a vacation itinerary.

And Baedekers are filled with over 200 full-color photos and detailed maps, including a full-size, fold-out roadmap for easy vacation driving. Baedeker—the premier name in travel for over 140 years.

Please send me the books checked below and fill in order form on reverse side.

☐ **Austria** $14.95		☐ **Mediterranean Islands** $14.95	
0-13-056127-4		0-13-056862-7	
☐ **Caribbean** $14.95		☐ **Mexico** $14.95	
0-13-056143-6		0-13-056069-3	
☐ **Egypt** $15.95		☐ **Netherlands, Belgium, and**	
0-13-056358-7		**Luxembourg** $14.95	
☐ **France** $14.95		0-13-056028-6	
0-13-055814-1		☐ **Portugal** $14.95	
☐ **Germany** $14.95		0-13-056135-5	
0-13-055830-3		☐ **Provence/Cote d'Azur** $9.95	
☐ **Great Britain** $14.95		0-13-056938-0	
0-13-055855-9		☐ **Rhine** $9.95	
☐ **Greece** $14.95		0-13-056466-4	
0-13-056002-2		☐ **Scandinavia** $14.95	
☐ **Israel** $14.95		0-13-056085-5	
0-13-056176-2		☐ **Spain** $14.95	
☐ **Italy** $14.95		0-13-055913-X	
0-13-055897-4		☐ **Switzerland** $14.95	
☐ **Japan** $15.95		0-13-056044-8	
0-13-056382-X		☐ **Tuscany** $9.95	
☐ **Loire** $9.95		0-13-056482-6	
0-13-056375-7		☐ **Yugoslavia** $14.95	
		0-13-056184-3	

Please turn the page for an order form and a list of additional Baedeker Guides.

A series of city guides filled with colour photographs and detailed maps and floor plans from one of the oldest names in travel publishing:

Please send me the books checked below:

☐ **Amsterdam** $10.95		☐ **Madrid** $10.95
0-13-057969-6		0-13-058033-3
☐ **Athens**. $10.95		☐ **Moscow** $10.95
0-13-057977-7		0-13-058041-4
☐ **Bangkok** $10.95		☐ **Munich** $10.95
0-13-057985-8		0-13-370370-3
☐ **Berlin** $10.95		☐ **New York** $10.95
0-13-367996-9		0-13-058058-9
☐ **Brussels** $10.95		☐ **Paris** $10.95
0-13-368788-0		0-13-058066-X
☐ **Copenhagen**. $10.95		☐ **Rome** $10.95
0-13-057993-9		0-13-058074-0
☐ **Florence** $10.95		☐ **San Francisco** $10.95
0-13-369505-0		0-13-058082-1
☐ **Frankfurt**. $10.95		☐ **Singapore** $10.95
0-13-369570-0		0-13-058090-2
☐ **Hamburg** $10.95		☐ **Tokyo** $10.95
0-13-369687-1		0-13-058108-9
☐ **Hong Kong** $10.95		☐ **Venice**. $10.95
0-13-058009-0		0-13-058116-X
☐ **Jerusalem** $10.95		☐ **Vienna**. $10.95
0-13-058017-1		0-13-371303-2
☐ **London** $10.95		
0-13-058025-2		

PRENTICE HALL PRESS

Order Department—Travel Books

200 Old Tappan Road

Old Tappan, New Jersey 07675

In U.S. include $1 postage and handling for 1st book, 25¢ each additional book. Outside U.S. $2 and 50¢ respectively.

Enclosed is my check or money order for $_____

NAME_____

ADDRESS_____

CITY_____STATE_____ZIP_____